CONFORM, FAIL, REPEAT

"In *Conform, Fail, Repeat*, Christopher Samuel presents a thought-provoking and timely exposition on the sociology of social movements. Drawing upon the concepts articulated by Pierre Bourdieu, Samuel provides fresh insights and new ways of thinking about power and dominance within collective struggles for justice, the conformity and failure inherent to social movement participation, and the conflict between the competing visions that characterize social movements—radical transformative change or the immediate elimination of suffering. *Conform, Fail, Repeat* concludes by sketching out a new model of "symbolic democracy," which academics and activists alike should find to be challenging and informative."

—Tom Warner, Queer activist and author of *Never Going Back,
A History of Queer Activism in Canada* and *Losing Control,
Canada's Social Conservatives in the Age of Rights*

"What might the next left look like? Putting the theories of Pierre Bourdieu to impressive and challenging work, Christopher Samuel suggests a critical and realist approach to twenty-first-century movements struggling for human emancipation. Looking at specific moments including the G20 protests and Black Lives Matter, Samuel provides refreshingly original and non-polemical insight into some of the most contentious issues those movements face—such as how to reconcile political effectiveness with internal democracy and how to avoid the seemingly perpetual pattern of movements losing sight of the revolutionary visions that inspired them. A must-read for leftists as they seek to understand, and to change the very shape of, a storm-tossed political world."

—Ian McKay, author of *Reasoning Otherwise* and *Rebels, Reds, Radicals*

CONFORM, FAIL, REPEAT

How power distorts collective action

Christopher Samuel

BETWEEN THE LINES
Toronto

Conform, Fail, Repeat

© 2017 Christopher Samuel

First published in 2017 by
Between the Lines
401 Richmond Street West
Studio 281
Toronto, Ontario M5V 3A8
Canada
1-800-718-7201
www.btlbooks.com

All rights reserved. No part of this publication may be photocopied, reproduced, stored in a retrieval system, or transmitted in any form or by any means, electronic, mechanical, recording, or otherwise, without the written permission of Between the Lines, or (for photocopying in Canada only) Access Copyright, 56 Wellesley Street West, Suite 320, Toronto, Ontario, M5S 2S3.

Every reasonable effort has been made to identify copyright holders. Between the Lines would be pleased to have any errors or omissions brought to its attention.

Library and Archives Canada Cataloguing in Publication

    Samuel, Christopher, author
        Conform, fail, repeat : how power distorts collective action / Christopher Samuel.

Includes bibliographical references and index.
Issued in print and electronic formats.
ISBN 978-1-77113-337-1 (softcover).—ISBN 978-1-77113-338-8 (EPUB).—
ISBN 978-1-77113-339-5 (PDF)

        1. Bourdieu, Pierre, 1930-2002. 2. Power (Social sciences). 3. Social movements.
4. Conformity. I. Title.

HN49.P6S26 2017   303.3   C2017-903561-4
                                                                                      C2017-903562-2

Text and cover design by David Vereschagin, Quadrat Communications
Printed in Canada

We acknowledge for their financial support of our publishing activities: the Government of Canada; the Canada Council for the Arts, which last year invested $153 million to bring the arts to Canadians throughout the country; and the Government of Ontario through the Ontario Arts Council, the Ontario Book Publishers Tax Credit program, and the Ontario Media Development Corporation.

Contents

Preface *vii*

1 Power and Struggle *2*

2 Critical Theory and Social Movement Research *18*

3 Conformity and Failure *38*

4 Collective Identity and Symbolic Power *66*

5 Tactic and Antinomy *98*

6 Suffering and Justice *124*

7 New Stakes and New Strategies *152*

8 Resistance and Democracy *172*

Notes *185*

Index *205*

Preface

This book offers a philosophically informed study of power and collective struggles for justice. In *Beyond Good and Evil*, Friedrich Nietzsche tells us, "There is a point in every philosophy when the philosopher's 'conviction' appears on the stage—or to use the language of an ancient Mystery: *Adventavit asinus / Pulcher et fortissimus* (The ass appears, beautiful and most brave)."[1] Since its appearance is inevitable, here is my philosophical conviction: Power is supple, its mechanisms hide as often as they reveal themselves, and for those who lack power, there is no obvious strategy for combatting injustice without replicating it. I am also convinced, however, that for groups that are systematically disempowered, that are exploited, excluded, humiliated, or simply made invisible, acting collectively is the only way to overcome the mechanisms by which the powerful maintain their advantages.

Let me also acknowledge the emotional and biographical roots of that conviction. At bottom, my ideas about social movements are informed by feelings of loss, disappointment, and frustration. When I first came out as a queer man, in Alberta in 1998, I had already been involved in left-wing politics for a number of years and was a committed Marxist. Naively, I expected LGBT politics to fit neatly with my radical economic leanings, but I came out in a time and place where liberationist and queer impulses were already more or less swamped by a rights-based political strategy focused on relationship rights and anti-discrimination legislation.

In particular, I recall an activist meeting in Edmonton where the chair, a lawyer and long-time activist, easily sidelined suggestions she didn't like by asserting that "one good idea per meeting is enough," as though that were a well-established rule. Not coincidentally, the radical and difficult ideas never seemed to meet the "one good idea" quota. Power imbalances are not just about laws and police. They are about cultural skills, social connections, and the ability to present partisan preferences as neutral and objective.

Over the next decade, I became increasingly involved with the New Democratic Party, eventually working as a legislative staffer. I also sat on numerous NDP committees, including election planning committees, and worked on the central campaigns for a number of elections. There's nothing like a paid role to teach you the importance of compromise, making the best use of scarce resources, and the need for concrete, practical assessments of political opportunity. I experienced a personal deradicalization that was directly comparable to the deradicalization I mourned in lesbian and gay politics.

It's a hard thing when your head and your heart are so badly aligned. This book is the result of my effort to think through that misalignment and to reconcile my radical impulses with the immediate demands of political life. I am not sure it actually achieves that reconciliation. Instead, the book creates space for being okay with that lack of alignment. I hope it helps people who care about justice to recognize when sincerely held commitments to radical change and pragmatic effectiveness are mutually exclusive and—as importantly—to learn how to act within those kinds of impossible spaces.

I will use key concepts from sociologist Pierre Bourdieu to pry open that door. Bourdieu's work brings together a number of philosophical and sociological trajectories and commits itself to centring social conflict. It is easy to get lost in some of his technical language (*habitus, allodoxia*, and so on), but ultimately, he gives us a way of thinking about how people navigate social spaces that are fundamentally built on the conflicting goals and resources of people in those spaces. Nonetheless, Marxists may find Bourdieu's use of the term "capital" to be somewhat idiosyncratic. For Marxists, capital has specific function and meaning within political economy; Bourdieu uses the term to describe context-appropriate resources. I will explain capital, habitus, and other technical terms as the argument unfolds.

When you get past the idiosyncratic language, Bourdieu's approach shows how economic privilege, class privilege, political access, cultural skill, and collective action translate into advantages and disadvantages in various settings. Specifically, it lets us understand how those often-unrecognized features of power infiltrate settings dearest to those who fight for economic, sexual, racial, environmental, gender, and other forms of justice. Power infiltrates movement and activist spaces; the framework I develop here helps explain why some voices within movements are heard while others are silenced.

Bourdieu also gives us tools to think about the emotional life of domination and social movement participation. For example, activists gain emotional support from the activists around them. Such mutual support often keeps activists afloat in a world where progress seems painfully incremental and easily reversed. It's easy for activists to forget that the emotional support gained through activism is not a common experience for most people. Particularly for many LGBT/Q people, difference is painful. For them, short-term gains and equality based on sameness aren't about selling out, they're about survival. Within the alterglobalization movement, the same is true about activists who are more interested in reducing poverty in the short-term than building toward an anti-capitalist revolution. In both cases, short-term gains are about demanding that people's immediate quality of life not be sacrificed for distant movement successes.

The argument I develop in this book offers new ways of thinking about conformity and failure. Rather than treat conformity and failure as the mistakes and shortcomings of particular movement groups, I show how conformity and failure operate as inherent to social and political spaces. Movements can't help but reproduce conformity and failure because that is how social spaces work. Conceiving of conformity and failure as intrinsic to social space recognizes the complex ways in which movement strategies are connected to practical assessments of the political landscape and informed by the affective realities that are themselves products of that political landscape. Of course, my argument is also rooted in the utopian pull toward something more radical, more sustaining than incremental compromise. Willingness to fight and fail in the name of a vision is a cornerstone of progressive activism.

In short, our world is contradictory and unjust. Power expands and mobilizes those contradictions, for the benefit of some and at the expense of others. There's no easy escape from power's circuits, but by using Bourdieu's concepts to think about conformity and failure, we can make power a little less hidden and, I hope, a little easier to confront.

Acknowledgements

When critiquing social movements, particularly those that bear a close identification with one's own sense of justice and injustice, it is easy to allow critique to overshadow the hard work, dedication, and willingness to risk physical harm and imprisonment that activists have put into those movements. That is not my intention here. However strongly I disagree with much that has happened in contemporary social movements—LGBT/Q and alterglobalization in particular—I nonetheless consider progressive movements to be my political home. In particular, I want to acknowledge the fact that past struggles of the LGBT/Q community, however fraught with contradictions, have made it infinitely easier and safer for me to write this critique.

I also want to single out Eleanor MacDonald for expanding my thinking, challenging me to go further and in new directions. I want to thank Eleanor for her incredible kindness, support, and friendship. I am also truly grateful for the guidance—intellectual and practical—provided by Zsuzsa Csergo, Abigail Backan, and Cindy Patton. I feel privileged to work with Amanda Crocker and the staff and Editorial Committee at Between the Lines and am deeply appreciative of their support for this project. The careful editing work of Tilman Lewis has made the work considerably more readable. My thanks also to Scott Schaffer for his comments and guidance.

A version of chapter four has previously been published as "Symbolic Violence and Collective Identity: Pierre Bourdieu and the Ethics of Resistance," *Social Movement Studies* 12,4 (2013), 397–413, and is available at www.tandfonline.com. A version of chapter five has previously been published as "Throwing Bricks at a Brick Wall: The G20 and the Antinomies of Protest," *Studies in Political Economy* 90,1 (2012), 7–27, copyright © *Studies in Political Economy*. It is reprinted by permission of Taylor & Francis Ltd, www.tandfonline.com, on behalf of *Studies in Political Economy*.

Finally, this project would not have been completed without support from friends and family. Special thanks to my father, Lawrence Samuel, and sister, Kathleen Samuel. My mother, Judy Samuel, passed away before completion of this project, which I regret very much.

Above all, of course, my thanks go to my partner, Cory Hayden. He has lived with this project longer than anyone should have to, and he has done so with love and good humour.

This work was written on the traditional territory of the Huron-Wendat, the Seneca, Mississaugas of the New Credit First Nation, the Anishinaabe and Haudenosaunee, sites of human activity for fifteen thousand years. Today, the meeting place of Toronto is still the home to many Indigenous people from across Turtle Island.

 Power and Struggle

> ... *everything became natural to me, so present in their words and their actions was the "inert violence" in the order of things, the violence inscribed in the implacable wheels of the job market, the school market, racism (also present within the "police forces" that are, in principle, supposed to repress it), etc.*
> —Bourdieu, *The Weight of the World*[1]

Money and Pride

When the leaders of the world's most powerful economies, the G20, descended on Toronto in June 2010, they were met by a state that had spent nearly a billion dollars to host the event—spending that included an infamous $9.4 million security fence and mobilizing thousands of police officers. Leaders were greeted by a chief of police willing to misrepresent the law in the interest of maintaining peace, thousands of peaceful protesters, a contingent of property-smashing Black Bloc activists, and a population that was largely unaware of the political, economic, and ideological stakes involved in the confrontation.[2] Fallout from this struggle included the arrest of a thousand protesters, lawsuits against the Toronto Police Service, and several investigations into police behaviour during the protests.[3] Despite sizable and highly visible demonstrations and protests, the G20 agreed to introduce aggressive austerity measures in their respective economies, the impact of which continue to be felt most by those who are already the most vulnerable, economically and socially.

That same summer, Pride Toronto, the non-profit organization responsible for organizing Canada's largest LGBT/Q festival, made a series of controversial decisions.[4] These decisions brought to the surface struggles among festival organizers, politically engaged queers, municipal politicians, and the significant numbers of lesbians, gays, bisexuals, and trans people who want pride celebrations to be about partying and apolitical cultural visibility. The organization's close relationship with the City of Toronto—and particularly its reliance on $250,000 in annual municipal funding—contributed to its initial decision to require all signs in the 2010 Pride Parade to be vetted by an ethics committee. Although the vetting process was applicable to all potential participants, it was clearly intended to silence a particular group, Queers Against Israeli Apartheid (QuAIA). In light of strong criticism from those who argue that pride celebrations should include contentious political claims and solidarity movements, Pride Toronto replaced mandatory sign vetting with a narrower restriction that specifically prohibited the phrase "Israeli Apartheid."[5] Still facing backlash, including from long-time activists and prominent members of Toronto's LGBT/Q communities, Pride organizers backed down entirely, eventually committing parade participants only to the city's Non-discrimination Policy. Neither QuAIA's core messages nor the phrase "Israeli Apartheid" were considered in breach of this policy.[6]

Immediately following these efforts to censor certain voices within the celebrations, Pride Toronto provoked further anger by participating in a reception for Toronto police chief Bill Blair less than a week after officers at the G20 summit allegedly segregated and detained LGBT/Q protesters, while using excessive force and homophobic language.[7] In 2016, Black Lives Matter–Toronto (BLM TO) brought similar issues to the fore when they briefly brought that year's Toronto Pride Parade to a stop. In a tactic reminiscent of sit-ins and die-ins from the 1980s and 1990s, BLM TO stopped the parade to call out anti-Black racism and other forms of racism and marginalization that have become embedded in Toronto's official pride festivities. BLM TO's most highly debated demand—that police be excluded from future pride parades—unleashed a year-long debate about racism, inclusion, and how to make Pride Toronto supportive of, and accountable to, Toronto's racialized communities. Needless to say, Pride Toronto's institutional and political orientations remain highly contentious.

The task I set myself for this book is to integrate two distinct kinds of inquiry: normative political theory and social movement studies.[8] Normative political theory is the rigorous philosophical pursuit of principles of justice. In particular, this type of political theory is concerned with how social institutions and interactions either promote or hinder justice. For queer and postmodernist readers, the phrase "normative theory" may raise flags. Queer theory and politics resist "normalization" and the idea of "normalcy" as a life goal. Queers resist the violence—both overt and subtle—by which individuals are forced to "be normal," to embody the pliable and passive vision of the good citizen demanded by heteronormativity and consumer capitalism. I share these concerns and hope to show that normative theory can offer a robust defence against the deadening homogeneity produced by normalization and normalcy.

As the philosophical pursuit of principles of justice, normative political theory can find plenty of meat on the bones of alterglobalization and LGBT/Q politics. Freedom of speech and expression, the relationship of capitalism to egalitarianism, civil disobedience, community, and identity are well-covered topics in political theory and activist circles alike. Some theorists and activists go further to ask about the rules of fair political conflict, what constitutes violence, and whether political violence can be justified. Considerable ink has been spilled and comments pages have been flooded with arguments about the relationship of international politics to local communities and of sexual practice to political identities. Political theory, though, too often abstracts those questions in search of general moral principles or democratic mechanisms capable of accommodating these questions without resolving them. As generations of activists can tell you, increasingly sophisticated abstract reasoning will not balance out conflicts over egalitarianism, the role of civil disobedience, and so on. Theory on its own is insufficient; justice demands philosophically sophisticated, thoughtful, and passionate collective action.

In undertaking to integrate normative political theory with social movement studies, I turn to moments from the LGBT/Q and alterglobalization movements for two reasons. First, my own modest activist history is closely connected to those movements. I entered LGBT/Q politics when the Alberta government was fighting tooth and nail to prevent inclusion of sexuality in its civil rights legislation. Throughout that fight and the ensuing struggles, I saw tensions between fundraising-centred legal strategies and feminist-informed efforts to build social and community networks. I saw professionals run meetings in ways that tolerated and then silenced radical and non-conforming activist energies because they were "impractical." Over the next two decades, I've followed and been caught up in various passionate struggles over sexual difference, the meaning of belonging, and how to prevent a single mainstream identity from swamping LGBT/Q communities' diversity. At the same time, I've participated professionally in political organizations that depend for their existence on rules and structure, first as a researcher for the NDP and now for the labour movement. My professional experience has tempered my radical leanings with an appreciation of how important practical victories are for nurturing a long-run political project.

Second, LGBT/Q and alterglobalization movements elegantly illustrate the tension faced by all social movements.[9] This tension has been described in myriad ways: as conflict between reformism and radicalism, pragmatism and idealism, capture and independence, representation and affinity. The tension recurs in philosophic and activist literature because it is maddeningly difficult to overcome. In fact, as I hope to make clear, normative theory will advance only if:

- it develops the tools necessary to perceive and appreciate the poles in these dyads in concrete relations to each other;
- it exposes these relations as symptoms of extensive and often subtle forms of domination; and
- it can find ways of breaking open these relations to uncover novel, more just ways of resisting that domination.

Indeed, the tensions between radical and reformist versions of alterglobalization and LGBT/Q movements represent more than mere alternative strategies. The antagonism between radical and reformist political projects is a feature of domination itself.

Carefully integrating normative political theory and social movement theory will move us toward new ways of resisting domination without falling back into interminable debates over goals and strategies. The goals-and-strategies debates are serious and sincere: activists engage in contentious political activity because they want to change things, and even when large changes seem impossible in the short run, activists still feel compelled to *do* something. Scholars of social movements and normative theory often neglect how viscerally felt activist commitments are—fear of police violence, fear of gay-bashing, witnessing loved ones succumbing to AIDS, or struggling to put food on the table are not merely intellectual commitments. Moreover, activists' desire to do something cannot help but force them into a messy choice between idealism and practicality, and it does so repeatedly across movements and within each activist's own protest career. Because the stakes are so visceral, so lived, it is vital, without abstracting from lived suffering, to recast these debates within a broader framework of justice. Such a framework might shift energy away from accusations and counter-accusations of utopianism or selling out, and toward productive forms of conflict capable of reducing injustice.

Understandably, many activists have an impulse to immediately alleviate suffering. The emphasis on equal rights in LGBT politics, the demand by some elements of the alterglobalization movement for peaceful protests, safe from police violence: these are laudable efforts to reduce suffering in the short term. Nonetheless, the more radical versions of these politics—the queer refusal to be "normal," the Black Bloc willingness to put activist bodies on the line to tear down capitalist modes of property—are similarly interested in reducing suffering. They are simply willing to take bigger risks now in the hope of attaining greater human flourishing and freedom from suffering in the future. Ultimately, it is a question of strategy whether one ought to pursue immediate, practically feasible reductions in suffering or risk short-term suffering for radical long-term transformations.

Still, movement strategies demand both practical and normative evaluation. I will argue that structures of domination distort strategic thinking in normatively important ways and that we need to understand those distortions before evaluating particular strategies and tactics. This understanding depends on our willingness to think about suffering as a social and political phenomenon and on an insistence that the starting point of normative theory should be attention to suffering.

Suffering and Critical Theory

Broadly speaking, this book is an exercise in a specific type of normative theory, namely critical theory. Although critical theory has fairly concrete foundations, thinkers have taken it up in diverse ways, so it is best described as an orientation or philosophical disposition rather than a definite set of tools. The roots of critical theory extend back at least to Karl Marx, but it took on its characteristic combination of methods and strategies through a group of thinkers—Theodor Adorno, Herbert Marcuse, Walter Benjamin, and Max Horkheimer pre-eminent among them—associated with the Frankfurt School (more accurately called the Institute of Social Research) in Germany prior to World War Two. The timing of the Frankfurt School's emergence is important: the rise of the Nazi party meant that the school had to be relocated, forcing the school's leading intellectuals to flee their home while bearing witness to the horrors of the Holocaust.

First-generation critical theorists associated with the Frankfurt School combined Marx, Nietzsche, Max Weber, G.W.F. Hegel, and psychoanalytic thought to challenge dominant philosophical approaches and social and political institutions. This formal philosophical project was, however, motivated by a deeply felt awareness of suffering and a commitment to exposing the oft-hidden and misrecognized relations of power that perpetuate that suffering. Adorno's oeuvre is particularly important in this regard. He worked ceaselessly to expose the Enlightenment roots of fascism, its inevitability given the growing instrumentalization of life and culture within capitalism, and the authoritarian features of that instrumentalization present even in non-fascist states such as the United States. Much of Adorno's postwar writing is a palpable effort to work through his grief in the face of the Holocaust's destruction of life, culture, and philosophy. It is in that spirit that, in taking on the challenge of knitting together social movement and normative political theory, I have tried to maintain the centrality of suffering and its relationship to justice.

Naturally, normative theory is not concerned with every instance of suffering. It is not our task to evaluate the moral import of suffering that happens naturally or by happenstance. Indeed, some pain and suffering is necessary for us to develop a capacity to act in the world. Theory should, however, attend to how suffering is distributed (which groups tend systematically to suffer more than others, and what the form or quality of their suffering is) and how evenly distributed the resources needed to redress or overcome that suffering are. I will argue for a fairly broad conception of both suffering and resources, to make explicit the connection between durable relations of power, durable conditions of suffering, and the diverse skills, dispositions, and social networks that serve as resources relevant to considerations of justice.

This approach exposes the distorting effects of power in two significant areas. First, the power relations that create strategic and tactical impasses also infiltrate and distort the very goals that movements set for themselves. Second, radically unequal relations of power create impasses wherein there is no strategy or tactic that perfectly—or even adequately—balances utopian vision with political practicality. These distortions take many forms, but they are most recognizable where movements reduce their transformative aspirations, often making compromises that benefit some segments of the movement at the expense of others. Conceptually reconceiving justice as a response to suffering in the face of complex and shifting distortions allows us to rethink how movements engage in political conflict.

This kind of conceptual work is not without precedent. Adorno captured one facet of power's disrupting and distorting nature in his insistence that features of the world ought to be described as both true and false. He argued, for example, that separating psychological and sociological explanations for human activity is true because there is an actual split between the psychological and sociological: we cannot understand individuals by explaining their actions only through reference to social structures any more than we can understand society as simply an aggregation of actors. Nonetheless, biographically individual agents are socially constituted in normatively important ways, so analytically separating the sociological and the psychological appears false.[10] Recognizing the simultaneous truth and falsity of social phenomena is the first step in identifying the mechanisms of power that allow social paradoxes to persist. Next we need to understand what damage these paradoxes create and who benefits from this damage.

Paradox need not be conceptualized in abstract, formal terms—in fact, it shouldn't be. For example, same-sex marriage and popular pro-LGBT YouTube campaigns (which we will look at more closely in chapter four) are likely to bear truth, in that they mitigate some forms and instances of suffering, but also falsity, insofar as they reproduce and conceal others. In certain political contexts (as we will see in chapter five), collective action is bound to be self-defeating, forcing activists to turn to one of two equally ineffective protest tactics. Here, paradox turns activist energies back on themselves, rendering protest both true and false.

Using critical theory to evaluate social movements should not, therefore, mean trying to establish the truth or falsity of one set of movement goals over another, or of one set of tactics over another. We should interpret the tension between truth and falsity in these instances in order to catch a glimpse of new possibilities. Critical theory starts with the premise that not only do unnecessary suffering, harm, exploitation, environmental destruction, and myriad forms of oppression structure existing social relations, but harm, exploitation, and destruction also systematically benefit some groups at the expense of others.[11] The practical work of using critical theory to critique harm and exploitation proceeds by understanding the mechanisms of suffering and destruction that currently exist, and mining existing social relations for glimpses into a world that would be less harmful and destructive. Suffering, destruction, and exploitation make social relations false, but resistance to those relations provide a hint of possible truth. Critical theorists and activists alike use existing injustices as a sort of inverse roadmap to more just relations. As Loïc Wacquant argued, critical theory "trains the weapons of reason at socio-historical reality and sets itself the task of bringing to light the hidden forms of domination and exploitation which shape it so as to reveal by contrast the alternatives they thwart and exclude."[12]

Negating the Negation

Critical theorists often describe exposing hidden forms of domination as "negating the negation." The phrase has Hegelian roots, but for now, let's think of "negation" as the social and political institutions that prevent—or negate—full human experience and expression. Negating that negation entails challenging confining and dehumanizing institutions to open spaces outside or beyond them, without necessarily articulating a complete vision of what a just, negation-free society would be. Critical theorists defer articulating such a vision, largely because the existing negation—oppression, violence, unequal power relations—obscures our vision of how truly just social arrangements might appear. Instead, critical theorists help articulate and expose existing negations to support political efforts to alter or cancel them out.

The strength of social movement theory, in contrast to critical theory, is that it treats collective action as a puzzle to be explored and not simply a force to be unleashed by a set of critical insights. The *collective* aspect of collective action cannot simply be assumed. The tensions between the biographically individuated bodies of activists—their individually experienced emotions, sensations, and visceral reactions to suffering on the one hand, and sociologically distributed commonalities, political opportunities, and the social and cultural production of meaning on the other—are politically and morally significant. Social movement theory offers a wide range of conceptual tools and empirical evidence to help understand the dynamics through which movements resolve these tensions in order to challenge domination.

Individuals join together to engage in political action, but their transformation from individual agents to a collective actor traverses a contradictory and uneven terrain of possibilities and obstacles. Therefore, the distortions and impasses facing social movements are as relevant to normative theory as the injustices that provoke collective action in the first place. Both parts of the phrase "collective action" merit critical analysis, and although power's intransigence demands that we move beyond critique and into confrontation—that is, action—domination's complexity requires dialogue, debate, and plural strategies to figure out how to act collectively. Collective action brings no guarantees, and *how* we negate the negation matters a great deal. Integrating normative theory with social movement research will allow us to identify false or distorted efforts to negate the negation. That is, it allows us to identify modes of resistance that do not free us from the harm and destruction of existing social relations because they in fact replicate, without negating, those relations.

Bourdieu: Structure and Agency

Pierre Bourdieu, the French sociologist and activist intellectual on whose framework I draw, fits squarely within the critical theoretical camp, relying on a constellation of Marx, Weber, and phenomenology. Bourdieu's central contribution was what he called a "general science of the economy of practice" capable of overcoming "the most fundamental, and the most ruinous" division in social science: the opposition between objectivism and subjectivism.[13] The technical language of objectivism and subjectivism represents a fairly familiar debate for Marxists and other left-wing thinkers: Can we best understand human activity through reference to broad structures (class, the economy, gender, ideology, and so on), or should we focus on individual people's ideas, preferences, biases, and desires? Bourdieu's genius was in developing a way of understanding structure and individual as intricately linked. He recognized that, although there are rules and practices that are relatively stable, people make choices within those rules and practices. That is, people do not simply act out the demands imposed on them by class and gender, they engage in practical strategies to navigate within those structures. In short, he restored a sense of *agency* to how we understand individuals in relation to social structures.

To explain how people can act as agents—that is, how they exercise agency within social structures—he developed a novel form of social phenomenology.[14] Where traditional phenomenologists make claims about agents and their ability to act in the world through close analysis of experience, Bourdieu's critical appropriation of phenomenology insists on interpreting experience dually: both as an agent's effort to act in the world and as the product of sociologically structured and durable relations of power. Bourdieu's social phenomenology includes a motivational structure (interest or *illusio*), a set of dispositions through which agents act (habitus), and an agonistic social space (field) in which agents struggle to accumulate the resources (capital) necessary to improve and/or defend their position in that space. We'll look at these features in some detail in chapter three, focusing on habitus in particular. Over the course of the book, I'll link each component to social movement research.

It is something of a puzzle that North American scholars (particularly political scientists) have been slow to attend to Bourdieu's novel sociological approach. His work is well known in European contexts, and his contemporaries—particularly Michel Foucault and Jacques Derrida—are staples in North American social, cultural, and political thought. Bourdieu's absence may be partially explained by the fact that his work is not intelligible within North American disciplinary boundaries.[15] Bourdieu gave little attention to political science's traditional areas of concern such as demonstrations, strikes, state policy, war, legislatures, constitutions, decision-making, and coalition building.[16] Nor did he focus on social movement theory specifically.[17] Moreover, although sociologists and political scientists have taken up Bourdieu in areas of concern to political science such as the study of nationalism, state theory, and international political economy, there is little social movement research using Bourdieuian insights.[18] The absence is not total; there have been a few attempts to integrate Bourdieu's thinking tools with social movement categories. Nick Crossley, for example, has argued that Bourdieu's most important conceptual innovation, the habitus, needs to be rethought both for its potential to become a "radical habitus" disposed toward further participation in contentious politics and in terms of the more general question of how habitus can be transformed, more or less intentionally.[19] Others have sought to make use of Bourdieuian analysis to understand political violence, collective identity, ethnic conflict, institutions and opportunities, and cultural change.[20]

Although this list may appear comprehensive on first blush, compared to the voluminous debates over the complexities of social movements, it is surprisingly small. Worse, it includes a somewhat glaring omission: there have been almost no attempts to integrate Bourdieu's sociology simultaneously into social movement research and normative political philosophy.[21] In part this may result from Bourdieu's own scholarly bias. Notwithstanding his belief that intellectuals ought to be part of a collective effort to identify and critique hidden hierarchies and sites of domination, Bourdieu was wary of social and political theory generally.[22] Nonetheless, Bourdieu's sociological framework provides precisely the conceptual tools needed to critically move from empirical observation of institutions and patterns of domination into normative evaluations of efforts to resist domination. Again, in the language of critical theory, Bourdieu's conceptual tools allow us to analyze how existing social relations negate human experience and to make normative judgments about how collective actors resist that domination—how they negate the negations created by existing social relations.

Bourdieu argued that any analysis of social practice must begin with empirical observation of the practice itself, and he limited his own theoretical innovation to developing and refining what he called "thinking tools" based on empirical observations.[23] He insisted that these tools be deployed in context-sensitive ways to avoid reifying them. That is, he cautioned against turning his tools into dead concepts, applied without attending to concrete conditions and experiences. Moreover, each tool is fundamentally incomplete and incoherent without its relational integration into the others. Thus, Bourdieu's central thinking tools—habitus, field, and capital—represent inseparable components of a theory of practice intended to link the production, meaning, and experience of subjectivity and action to the demands and opportunities of objective structures.

Bourdieu's tools provide a novel account of behaviour, namely that agents are only able to act because of the inextricable link between the social context (field) in which they act and the practical reason they use to select strategies within that context. He called the set of dispositions that produce practical reason "habitus," and he used the concept to overcome the division between objectivist and subjectivist approaches to social science. Further, Bourdieu developed a specific critique of how relations of power foster a logical consensus capable of concealing the domination this consensus supports. He called this effect "symbolic power," and he used it to explain the complicity of dominated actors in their own domination. I will argue that Bourdieu's understanding of the relationship between individual practical reasoning and the structure of the social space within which that reasoning occurs permits a more nuanced understanding of the relationship between key social movement concepts: "collective identity" and "repertoires of contention." A Bourdieuian critique of the particular social relations that concretize domination-concealing consensuses about meaning will help social movement researchers understand how movements in contemporary capitalist societies are pushed into strategic impasses and sapped of their transformative potential.

As valuable as Bourdieu's framework is, it does not tell the whole story. Here again, political theory as a distinct project sits somewhat uncomfortably with Bourdieu's own methodology. The difference is fairly simple: Bourdieu insisted on close empirical observation in order to understand action, whereas political theory makes general claims about justice and injustice. The version of political theory that I offer here relies on conceptual critique to understand power's relationship to justice. My arguments sit in a middle space between close empirical observation and detached, abstract reason. My reliance on LGBT/Q and alterglobalization movements is, therefore, illustrative rather than empirical. Bourdieu dismissed normative political theory as "merely metaphysical."[24] His dismissal devalues the role that critical inquiry plays and, despite his own normative commitments, unhelpfully distances scholarly inquiry from movements.

What constitutes "metaphysical thinking" deserves some attention, because Bourdieu is wrong to treat normative theory and metaphysical thought as the same. I agree that metaphysical thinking can be damaging. Students of political philosophy will be familiar with metaphysical thinking from Plato and Aristotle, who were interested in trying to understand how particular and transient phenomena relate to absolute and universal phenomena. They saw deviations from the absolute and the universal as aberrations to be remedied. This is the root of the kind of thinking that Bourdieu rightly rejected. Metaphysical thinking in this sense is a deep-seated and often-unrecognized belief that the world is fundamentally morally well ordered and that injustice is a symptom of departure from that order. With Hegel and Marx, the supposedly well-ordered nature of the world took on a more dynamic character, but for them, suffering and injustice remain aberrations to be worked out through historically developed ideas and action. In its contemporary mode, metaphysical thinking often takes the form of a relentless ideology of positive thinking or, worse, the often-heard consolation that when something bad happens it is because "the universe is trying to tell you something" or "has plans for you."[25]

In whatever form it appears, metaphysical thinking serves two functions. First, metaphysical thinking holds the promise of a roadmap. It promises that if we understand the order of the universe, we can work out pathways in keeping with the universe's moral order and toward a more just set of social relations. Second, it provides comfort. However bad things are, metaphysical thinking tells us, they are only temporary. Eventually the justice intrinsic to the universe will manifest through some gravitational mechanism—rational thought, religion, class conflict, political theory—that will pull us inexorably toward a state of things in accordance with the universe's well-ordered nature. Metaphysical thinking therefore provides an account of how to act and the psychological energy to keep fighting. Unfortunately, the hope provided by metaphysical thinking is false, or at least misplaced. Imagining that the universe is well ordered fosters unhelpful dispositions toward suffering and action, and adds to the ties binding us to futile debates about strategy and tactics. My goal is to escape metaphysical thinking in order to act more directly on the world before us as it actually is.

While I agree with Bourdieu regarding the importance of rejecting metaphysics, he was nonetheless wrong to equate normative political theory with "merely metaphysical" thought. On the contrary, Bourdieu's sociology offers philosophical and sociological resources to disentangle movement debates from their metaphysical distortions while nonetheless making positive claims about how to act collectively. LGBT/Q history is rife with the erroneous belief that reducing suffering in the quickest way possible will bring us inherently closer to a state of justice. By treating reductions in suffering as intrinsically justice-promoting, the movement forgets that it matters how the negation is negated. Worse, mainstream LGBT strategies risk ossifying distorted social relations by validating rules of social space that hierarchically distribute rewards, authorize some groups at the expense of others, and promote pro-conformist dispositions. Similarly, although the alterglobalization movement shows symptoms of mistaking action as such with agency, it also provides an opportunity for careful reconsideration of core concerns of political theory such as autonomy and representation. Erasing the distinction between acting and acting successfully, as some proponents of the alterglobalization movement do, inserts a metaphysical sort of optimism where none is warranted and, I suspect, where most activists would be surprised to find it. I challenge these metaphysical errors by insisting that action be understood as the product of hierarchically distributed opportunities, misrecognized rules that benefit some at the expense of others, and ultimately, preconscious calculations of chances and resources.

In what follows, I articulate LGBT/Q and alterglobalization dilemmas as primarily constructed through the tension between conformity and failure. Careful readers will recognize conformity and failure as a variation on reformist/radical, pragmatic/idealist oppositions. The version of this tension I develop is rooted in the claim that although failure to conform to the rules of specific social spaces provides a measure of freedom, success requires conforming to that space's demands and replicating its rules and hierarchies. Therefore, I suggest that within social movement politics there is a fundamental tension between freedom and success. However, by conceiving of the tension between conformity and failure as a background condition, I hope to empty conformity and failure of their value-laden affective content and their tendency to unduly focus attention on outcome. On its own, action as such is unrelated to justice and, where people act in conditions of domination, the outcomes of action can be true only at the cost of also being false. Action therefore bears on justice only when it is pulled out of the hierarchies of opportunities and rules for action that appear to make the action possible. Normative value does not come from the quality of action or the quality of outcomes, but from the relationship we cultivate toward the background conditions of suffering, conformity, and failure.

Moving from sociological theory and social movement research to a mode of acting collectively and without metaphysics is no simple task. The next two chapters establish conceptual foundations through a critical overview of social movement theory and my adaptation-centred use of Bourdieu's key thinking tools. I then move on to two illustrations of how social movement theory can be mobilized for normative analysis: North American LGBT/Q movements and the G20 protests in Toronto, 2010 (chapters four and five, respectively). Both illustrate the tension between conformity and failure. In the case of LGBT/Q communities, the choice appears to be between reducing short-term suffering while enforcing sameness and inequality on the one hand, and producing new forms of difference without political impact on the other. At the G20 protests there appears to have been no strategy that could be simultaneously ethical and effective. In both cases, movement participants rely on unjust sources of power derived from broader patterns of domination to move forward their political vision, generally at the expense of either freedom or success.

In bringing together moments from LGBT/Q identity struggles and alter-globalization tactical debates, I hope to follow Nietzsche's advice and approach the separate elements of my argument "like cold baths: quickly into them and quickly out again."[26] This allows me to bring several concerns into a single constellation: the relationship of suffering to justice; suffering, violence, and political vision; and strategic impossibilities. Following my brief illustrations of how power operates within movements, I return in the later chapters to theoretical questions more generally. I specify the connection between suffering and justice, which is an underappreciated aspect of normative theory. Indeed, how theorists understand suffering (or whether they even acknowledge it as a theoretical concern) orients their thinking about what constitutes justice, what its background conditions are, and what is needed to bring it about. Responding to current debates about deliberative and radical democracy, I then propose procedural strategies to promote justice through and within collective action.

 Critical Theory and Social Movement Research

> *Critical thought must, with zeal and rigor, take apart the false commonplaces, reveal the subterfuges, unmask the lies, and point out the logical and practical contradictions of the discourse of King Market and triumphant capitalism.*
> —Wacquant, "Critical Thought as a Solvent of *Doxa*"[1]

A Troubled Relation

Critical theorists concern themselves with searching existing institutions and relations of domination for glimpses of better ways to organize social, economic, and political arrangements. Adorno's insistence that things can be both true and false is essential to this project. Adorno largely intended this distinction to be applied epistemologically as, for example, in how we understand an individual both as a biographically discrete entity and as a product of de-individualizing sociological and economic processes. We don't need to stop there: the same tension can be found in how we think about social movements and political protest.

Starting from the idea that categories of thinking as well as institutions can be both true and false makes possible a sort of double critique. Most obviously, critiquing social movements themselves can demonstrate how these movements are true—they reduce some kinds of suffering and achieve some progressive political goals—and false—they also produce distortions that move us away from justice. Implicitly, however, normative critiques of social movements must also challenge dominant approaches to the *study* of movements precisely because those approaches are unable to capture the dual reality of movements as both true and false.

Naturally, the dual critique I envision does not dismiss mainstream approaches entirely. Contemporary social movement theory is relatively sophisticated, and it has developed valuable conceptual tools. Movement research's methodological sophistication allows it to parse, compare, and explain specific elements of a broad range of movement phenomena. However, as Adorno suggests in the dedication to *Minima Moralia*, critique must resist the transformation of the wide-ranging projects of philosophy into a limited and short-sighted method: philosophy must remain oriented toward "the teaching of the good life."[2] My goal, therefore, is to wed research methods to teaching the good life. I do not want to simply understand the when and why of social movements, which is generally the focus of mainstream research. I want to understand whether movements move us toward or away from the good life. Nonetheless, before moving to specific arguments about suffering, justice, conformity, and failure, it is worth contextualizing these arguments by tracing the evolution of research on social movements and its most promising elements.

Typically, social movement researchers, whether working empirically or theoretically, start by sorting out a definition of what exactly constitutes the object of their study. What counts as a social movement is not as obvious as it might initially seem. Yet, concise definitions and definite boundaries matter. The strength of explanatory claims often depends on how well they capture all the phenomena the researchers are studying and also only the phenomena they are studying. Observers struggle, therefore, to decide what criteria need to be met in order to legitimately call a group or a set of actions a social movement. To complicate matters, criteria exist in a number of dimensions: the number of people involved; whether groups make political, economic, or cultural claims; how groups articulate and broadcast their demands; whether groups target the state and/or other social actors; and how extensive or radical the group's ambitions are. Generally, definitions of what counts as a social movement are functional rather than absolute; what we label a social movement depends on what we hope to learn.[3]

For my purposes, I rely on Alberto Melucci's definition:

> A movement is the mobilization of a collective actor (i) defined by specific solidarity, (ii) engaged in a conflict with an adversary for the appropriation and control of resources valued by both of them, (iii) and whose action entails a breach of the limits of compatibility of the system within which the action takes place.[4]

Although Melucci focused on empirical research, the three analytic dimensions this definition captures—solidarity, conflict, and breach of limits—are particularly useful because they provide us with considerable leverage for normative and empirical arguments. Building solidarity, engaging in conflict, and breaching limits are not just aspects of resistance to domination; the processes they represent also reproduce domination in complex and nuanced ways. Movements, like the patterns of domination they resist, are complex processes rather than singular, fixed objects. Moreover, prior to collective action there are always processes of collectivization, and these processes—including production of collective identity, production of solidarity, and orientation toward goals and strategies—are themselves made up of myriad smaller processes and bound to the social logics of the spaces in which they operate.

Melucci's definition of social movements allows me to narrow my critique to these processes of solidarity-building, strategic decisions, and tactical choices, but it also lets me focus my critique in another way. Movements respond to diverse kinds of problems. Some of these problems are produced by various kinds of crisis, such as severe economic downturns, famines, or wars. Other movements express and challenge antagonisms that are inherent to a given arrangement of social, economic, and political institutions. Although the line between these two categories can be blurred and porous, my interest is in those movements that express socially embedded conflicts.

All movements mobilize within systems of semi-autonomous but interconnected social fields, as will be understood here through a Bourdieuian conception of social action. Each of these fields has some flexibility in the range of new relationships or patterns of relationships it can tolerate without causing a radical transformation. For example, recognizing unions and allowing them some influence over workplace health and safety practices, employment benefits, and so on might alter dynamics in the economic field, but giving workers direct control over factories, taxation policy, and production decisions would radically alter the field. Social movements have the potential to introduce new relationships or patterns of relationships that could radically transform the fields in which they operate and, through a ripple effect, the broader ways in which various fields are connected. Of course, key to my argument is that patterns of domination, as they are reproduced within movements, mitigate such radical, transformative potential. Given the Bourdieuian unification of the material and cultural foundations of power that I advocate, defining social movements according to the processes through which they mobilize and by assessing their limit-breaching potential will be essential for showing how the logic of power underpinning complex systems binds movements to dynamics of conformity and failure, truth and falsity.

With a general conception of what constitutes a social movement in hand, we can turn to a brief overview of social movement research. In the decades leading up to the 1960s, researchers understood protesters as disoriented and somewhat neurotically unable to cope with social change, and they therefore treated protesters as bordering on pathological. Researchers focused on psychological and cultural explanations, often equating protests to mobs running wild during periods where normal social rules and taboos are suspended.[5] In the 1960s, analysts began to turn away from the assumption that protest expresses a breakdown in an otherwise well-functioning social system. Partly because many social movement researchers in the 1960s were activists themselves and therefore had both an interest in treating protesters as rational and some experience with the injustices that lead to protest, researchers began to argue that disorientation and discontent are endemic features of society.[6] That is, even when society appears to be functioning "normally," it nonetheless contains conflicts between those who benefit from that functioning and those who do not. Seen in this light, protest is a rational response to injustice and domination rather than an irrational, emotional response to temporary social breakdown.

When you assume that conflict is constant and that protest is a rational response to conflict, then the scholarly challenge becomes one of explaining when and how movements emerge to express this discontent.[7] Over the next decades, researchers began to develop approaches based on rational choice theory, political structures, and culture.[8] During the 1960s and 1970s, what Doug McAdam, Sidney Tarrow, and Charles Tilly (McAdam et al. hereafter) refer to as the "classic social movement agenda" emerged. That agenda focused on four key concepts derived from these rationalist, structuralist, and culturalist approaches: political opportunities, mobilizing structures, collective action frames, and repertoires of contention.[9] Unfortunately, most researchers during this time worked within ideological and methodological silos. Analysts tended to adopt a single framework—rationalism, structuralism, or culturalism—and sought to demonstrate why that framework best explained movement outcomes. By the 1980s this practice began to shift; researchers started to pay attention to all four of the key concepts just mentioned, but differed in how they emphasized particular parts. The resulting research produced a more balanced, but still not fully integrated, approach known as political process theory. Observers of social movements took the position that any model based solely on rationalism, structuralism, or culturalism would be incomplete at best and untenable at worst, insofar as it failed to incorporate explanatory insights from the other approaches.[10]

The political process approach is useful because it provides detailed social scientific accounts of specific mechanisms and the concatenation between identity, state structures, and cultural shifts.[11] That is, political process approaches look for the specific ways that identity, state structure, and culture affect one another reciprocally and repeatedly. Social movement research's key areas of focus—political opportunities, mobilizing structures, collective action frames, and repertoires of contention—have demonstrable explanatory power and allow for sophisticated, concrete causal analyses. These approaches nonetheless have serious limitations. Methodologically, debates about the relative causal weight of explanatory factors continue to plague social movement research. Researchers have not come to terms with how exactly culture interacts with rational assessments about changes in political opportunities, which indicates incomplete understandings of how social structures relate to individual agents. As such, political process research provides snapshots of movements, but has minimal capacity to situate those snapshots within broader historical contexts and patterns of domination.

For example, research on mainstream LGBT politics has come to focus on such things as the relationship between local political cultures and political outcomes or the impact of social movement successes on further mobilization (that is, how successful outcomes create new political opportunities).[12] In these studies, researchers rely on statistical analyses to measure the impact of causal factors on movement outcomes. This is important, but normatively limited. Statistical research cannot tell us whether a successful outcome—or the range of new opportunities that that outcome creates—is a good thing. Observers still need additional conceptual resources to normatively interrogate those outcomes.

Even the historical institutionalist approach, a sophisticated method with important similarities to political process frameworks, does not extend empirical analysis onto normative terrain. Historical institutionalism carefully examines the relationship between opportunity structures and policy outcomes, as in Miriam Smith's work on the relationship of the Canadian Charter of Rights and Freedoms to the overall direction of LGBT activism in Canada. Smith shows that the Charter encourages movements seeking political success to modify their goals in conformity with structures of rewards and punishments the Charter introduced. This analysis gives important insights into movement changes, but it still provides few tools for questioning whether shifting from a protest frame to a rights-talk frame is a good thing. It allows us to understand how rights talk became dominant and what successes rights talk facilitated, but not whether those successes are in line with justice.

Proponents of rights-based approaches argue that whatever new social and cultural space same-sex marriage (a key goal of rights-based mobilization) creates will foster broader social and political critiques.[13] However, there has been little empirical research to provide evidence of whether legal recognition of same-sex marriage subsequently promotes broader critiques of monogamy, the relationship between marriage status and social benefits (including employer-paid health care, tax breaks, cultural esteem, and so on), or the potential cultural value of sex-positive attitudes.[14] These movement goals were central to groups that mobilized under the protest frame, and while historical institutionalism helps us understand what happened, it does not help us to normatively critique that history.

McAdam et al. have developed a method for social movement research that integrates rationality, culture, and structure, an early expression of which they published in *Dynamics of Contention*. In that work, the authors recommend an ad hoc theory that eschews general covering laws in favour of concatenating causal mechanisms linked together into causal processes. Put another way, instead of trying to find rules or principles that can explain every movement everywhere, they began to understand movements as emerging from small mechanisms that interact with each other depending on concrete contexts. McAdam et al. were particularly interested in mechanisms that occur across numerous cases but that produce varying outcomes depending on the dynamics of the context. They identified a number of mechanisms—including repression, brokerage, identity shift, and opportunity spirals—that are intended both to capture a dynamic, relational interaction among state and civil society actors, and to integrate rational, structural, and cultural causality.[15]

Despite the dominant position that McAdam et al.'s approach has achieved in social movement studies, the project has serious flaws. Critics note that the authors have been frustratingly unclear in their definition of what a causal mechanism is or why some practices constitute a causal mechanism while others do not. Moreover, the method appears overly structuralist at times (ignoring rationalist and culturalist insights) and can only demonstrate weak connections between macroeconomic conditions and political opportunity.[16] Most relevant to my argument, just like statistical and historical institutionalist approaches, the dynamics of contention approach is also fundamentally amoral: it provides no guidance for normative evaluation.

In large part, the failure of the dynamics of contention approach to provide normative resources comes from its founders' interest in replacing universal covering laws with concatenating mechanisms bearing no intrinsic relationship to one another beyond historical context. Rather than claiming, for example, that shifts in elite alliances combined with a politicized identity will always lead to social movements, McAdam et al. focus on specific mechanisms (repression, brokerage, identity shift, opportunity spirals, and so on) and how those mechanisms amplify each other to iteratively shape the emergence, characteristics, and outcomes of contentious episodes. This move is part of a larger refusal to connect macro-level patterns of domination to suffering and the movement strategies available to alleviate that suffering. This refusal fragments and conceals the logics of power that precede these mechanisms.

Keeping with this strategy, McAdam et al. focus on "contentious politics," which, according to their definition, necessarily involve the state as an actor or target of action.[17] This simultaneously reduces the relevant relations of power to those directly in the state's orbit and sets up a false equivalence between challengers seeking reform, challengers seeking transformation, and challengers seeking radical, utopian transformation. McAdam et al.'s approach provides insight into movement dynamics, but it does not give us a way to differentiate between types of success. It cannot, for example, normatively distinguish between the successes of Canadian LGBT activism that resulted in same-sex marriage rights and its failure to achieve the earlier and more radical goals of gay/queer liberation.

Taken together, McAdam et al.'s focus on unconnected mechanisms and state-oriented struggle cannot, broadly speaking, connect social movement processes to power and domination. If you value conceptual tools that allow normative judgments about movements and resources to question the relationship of social and political struggle to justice, then you will find merely describing discrete phenomena to be insufficient. Just as Adorno committed philosophy to teaching the good life, critical social movement theory needs to teach the good struggle, resisting the reduction of deep-rooted and normatively laden social conflicts to discrete, disconnected mechanisms. Such critique requires social theory that is capable of mobilizing empirical conceptual tools within a power-sensitive understanding of complex systems of domination.

Bourdieu's notion of symbolic power, in conjunction with his other thinking tools (which we will explore more in chapter three), offers a way of reversing the fragmentation that results from analyzing disparate, loosely connected mechanisms in isolation. Formations of symbolic power are historically contingent, though they have a structured logic of development, so Bourdieu's analysis does not reintroduce universal covering laws. It does, however, account for how some actors, on the whole, seem to systematically benefit from the various logics contained in different social spheres, and how those spheres can be semi-autonomous while operating according to similar logics. That is, the distribution of rewards, successes, and exclusions in various areas of social interaction—economic, cultural, and political, for example— may operate autonomously, but the logic that underpins each area is similar. I will elaborate on this notion further, but for the present it is worth noting that Bourdieu's framework explains how existing sets of relations shape and constrain the mechanisms of contention that McAdam et al. identify. Further, Bourdieu's conceptual tools allow us to examine whether goal modification generally trends toward compatibility with liberal capitalist and neoliberal social, economic, and political forms. In other words, Bourdieu's work shares historical institutionalism's emphasis on attending to specific contexts in understanding the relationships between opportunities, goals, and strategies. By multiplying the sites in which these relationships play out for individual and collective actors, he developed conceptual tools that could provide greater nuance and power-sensitivity for understanding how context impacts social movements. Further, by integrating these multiple sites of struggle conceptually, he was also able to conceptualize domination—symbolic violence in his language—as an emergent property of these semi-autonomous contentious contexts.

Bourdieu's insistence on tightly integrating his various conceptual tools and applying them to specific questions nonetheless poses a particular challenge. On the one hand, integrating his conceptual tools allows us to bring together disparate features and expressions of domination to capture the trends and tensions that movements offer. On the other hand, if we treat his integrated conceptual tools as a single overarching law, we may fail to attend to the empirical and normative specificity of diverse movements and concrete moments within those movements. My strategy for navigating this dilemma is to attend to the general philosophical reorientation that Bourdieu sought, provide a brief overview of his tools to give a sense of how they work together philosophically, and then illustrate in a preliminary way how the normative critique I envision might work by pairing Bourdieuian conceptual tools to key concepts from social movement theory. In particular, I will use the relationship between symbolic power and collective identity to critique North American LGBT/Q politics, and the sociological concept of repertoires of contention to suggest that protest fields create divisive impasses for alterglobalization activists.

To set the stage for these illustrations, let us first focus on the conceptual development of collective identity and repertoires of contention within

Collective Identity

Social movement research has not always been sensitive to the aspects of collective action based on cultural and identity. By the 1960s, social movement research moved decisively away from the pathologizing assumptions of earlier collective behaviour approaches to emphasize resource mobilization and political process. However, research from the 1960s and 1970s was heavily influenced by rational choice theory. The core logic behind rationalist approaches suggests that actors will pursue the most efficient strategy available in pursuit of a desired end or goal.[18] Heavily influenced by economic theory, rational choice approaches assume that individuals enter political fields with preformed preferences and seek to satisfy those preferences by expending the least possible resources. While rationalist approaches take agency more seriously than earlier approaches, they do not actually conceive of movement participants as independent agents: once an agent forms a preference, rationality commits them to a single trajectory, the most efficient one. To paraphrase Bourdieu, rational choice replaces mechanical determinism with a sort of "teleological finalism."[19] If actors are bound to the most efficient path to satisfy their preferences, it means they make no real choices about strategy or tactic; they merely play out the logic of the range of options in front of them. For rational choice theory to work, it must assume that any two agents occupying the same space would take identical actions, given basic assumptions about rational connections between location, interest, and strategy.

To address this shortcoming, a number of approaches and analyses that are sensitive to culture began to emerge in the 1980s. The most important of these emerging perspectives focused on questions of identity and sought to reintroduce social-psychological conceptual tools to the study of social movements. The argument about power that I make in this book relies heavily on Melucci's conception of collective identity, which set the stage for much of the theoretical work on solidarity-building and identity that followed. Melucci described collective identity as follows:

> An interactive and shared definition produced by a number of individuals (or groups at a more complex level) concerning the *orientations* of their action and the *field* of opportunities and constraints in which such action is to take place. By "interactive and shared" I mean that

these elements are constructed and negotiated through a recurrent process of activation of the relations that bind actors together.[20]

Collective identity construction requires participants to negotiate how to integrate tensions produced by conflicting definitions of the ends (goals), means (strategies; possibilities and limits), and the field of opportunity (environment) in which action takes place. These processes involve

- cognitive calculations about ends and means (however contradictory and internally conflicting these calculations may be);
- communication within networks of active relationships; and
- emotional content that always gives the cognitive processes a non-rational, though not irrational, texture.[21]

Taking collective identity seriously as a process of negotiation and integration allows us to make a distinction between collective actors and the work that those actors do to construct a schema of grievances, goals, and tactics with which potential movement participants can identify.

For example, LGBT/Q processes of collective identity formation involve understanding the differences embodied in queer sexual desires and practices, queer gender identities, and queer communities, and constructing an account of dominant society's devaluation of those differences. LGBT/Q collective identity processes then articulate that assessment of difference into an orientation toward specific goals and strategies to redress the suffering those devalued differences accrue. Tensions between queer and mainstream lesbian and gay political movements can therefore be understood as expressions of divergent conceptions of collective identity and of how identity orients collective actors toward goals and strategies. With few exceptions, most queer critics of mainstream politics argue that mainstream movement goals miss out on or actively marginalize alternative political projects, particularly around physical and mental health, community building, and sex-positivity.[22] This critique is rooted in competing assessments of the value of difference and the relationship difference has to suffering.

Most traditional collective actors devote significant resources to giving an appearance of unity to the complex processes by which these differentiated elements are articulated.[23] Collective actors such as LGBT lobbying organizations—Egale in Canada or the Human Rights Campaign in the United States—are therefore instances of complex processes coalescing into an institutional form within a specific system of opportunities. They function as amplifiers for the vision of collective identity that they embody, allowing them to make claims and—more importantly—to encourage LGBT people to take up and internalize a specific understanding of homophobia and a general political orientation to combat it.

Researchers working from social-psychological perspectives have articulated a number of psychological processes to understand how individuals come to take up, internalize, and/or challenge collective identities. Examples include identity amplification (embellishing and strengthening an existing identity); identity extension (increasing the number of situations in which an identity is relevant, for example, constructing sexual identity as more than a bedroom issue and also an employment issue, a recreational issue, and a taxation issue); identity transformation (encouraging individuals to adopt identities that are new to them); as well as diagnostic, prognostic, and motivational framing (ascribing characteristics to political and social actors in order to establish the source of, and potential remedy for, harms and to motivate resistance). In essence, social-psychological researchers specify mechanisms by which groups accomplish the orienting task of collective identity production.[24]

Ultimately, to assess the value and use of collective identity we must adopt a dual vision. On the one hand, collective identity is an analytic tool. It is a descriptor that analysts and researchers impose on complex social processes.[25] Awareness of collective identity as an analytic tool and process description can help prevent researchers from reifying collective identities and mistaking a momentary crystallization of these processes in the form of a collective actor for an independently existing object with stable and uncontested characteristics. On the other hand, collective identities are nothing if not subjectively experienced phenomena that are bound up with political projects. The processes that collective identity captures as an analytic tool are lived and practical processes through which movement participants actively struggle to understand their past and current experiences and transform the conditions of future ones. Collective identity's experiential level is closely connected to its instrumental value as a strategic tool for making political claims.[26]

Collective identity is both a task and an outcome of social movements. More accurately, collective identity constitutes a number of diverse outcomes:
- cultural support for previously stigmatized identities;
- a location from which to challenge cultural stigmatization;
- a predisposition toward further social movement action; and
- a symbolic resource available to participants even after the movement disbands or demobilizes.

Identities can also produce symbols and strategies that resonate with and become available for appropriation by subsequent movements, and may permanently alter the political landscape. For example, there is now a widespread expectation that decision-makers will at least pay lip-service to considering the putative interests of people of colour, women, environmentalists, and LGBT/Q people.[27] Some research has even suggested that, in the wake of failed contentious events, access to a collective activist identity may help participants overcome feelings of disempowerment, which can lead to demobilization. The collective identity provides narratives that can frame failures as successes, as when a failure to change policy is claimed to be offset by experiences of community, tactical innovations, and so on. A key finding, however, is that these anti-disempowerment resources are unavailable to movement participants who do not already have an "activist identity." That is, those who do not have the social networks and sense of community, solidarity, and shared objectives of those networks are not exposed to, and therefore do not receive the benefits of, sustained and persuasive alternative narratives.[28]

This latter finding points to a major shortcoming of existing approaches to collective identity: they fail to treat identity as an unequally distributed and unequally contested play of resources. Most social-psychological accounts rely implicitly on some version of symbolic interactionism. Symbolic interactionism shares rationalist assumptions that humans are actors with agency but departs from rationalist perspectives by arguing that action and interaction are shaped by shared meanings (definitions of situations) developed through interaction.[29] While many push beyond traditional interactionism by recognizing that social structures constrain definitions—meaning that not all possible definitions of a given situation are equally possible within specific structured contexts, and identity is therefore not free-floating, ephemeral, or purely subjective—they nonetheless treat participants in symbolic interactions as antecedentless, as free from durable dispositions, in short, as free from the embodied and differentially constructed constraints of habitus.[30]

Moreover, descriptions of collective identities as negotiated processes tend to conceal the unequal resources that various participants bring to bear on these negotiations. Negotiation, as it appears in collective identity literature, depends on unmarked and uninterrogated assumptions about reflexivity and debate. Reflexivity requires an object of reflection—in this case the collective identity under construction—but also a reflecting subject and a medium of reflection (such as language or consciousness).[31] As we will see in the discussion of habitus in the next chapter, the reflecting subject—the person or people reflecting on collective identity—has dispositions that are shaped by durable social conditions. Those dispositions and their associated distributions of cultural capital have implications for how ideas and claims about the object under reflection circulate. Finally, the reflecting medium is not neutral terrain. It is a structured field in which various actors experience differential access to linguistic, cultural, and symbolic capital. Given the nature of the differential distribution of various forms of capital and its genesis in broad patterns of domination, collective identities as the objects of reflection and conflict are not neutrally constructed reflections of objective grievances and opportunities. Instead, they reflect broader patterns of domination. If we can find mechanisms for tracing how distortions enter into the reflection and negotiation processes, then we can use those distortions to better understand—indeed to reflect back upon—the power relations that produce them.

This shift has important ethical and political implications. Visions of social movement politics that rely upon conceptions of collective identity as the product of engaged but neutral reflection and negotiation suggest that activists should focus on creating open, "unconstrained" arenas for debating and evaluating the differences and complexities that contemporary society produces.[32] By contrast, a Bourdieuian interpretation of the ethics of collective identity formation requires highly constrained arenas of debate and political conflict within movements themselves. Collective identities can only minimize the distortions produced by unequal distributions of various forms of capital if the circulation of that capital is constrained by equalizing and universalizing mechanisms. I will illustrate this argument in chapter four, when we look at the production of collective identity in North American LGBT/Q politics.

Repertoires of Contention

The concept of repertoires of contention, which Charles Tilly introduced through his 1977 study of how forms of protest evolved over three centuries in France, remains essential for understanding social movements.[33] Over the next decades Tilly refined the idea and in 1995 he gave the following definition:

> The word *repertoire* identifies a limited set of routines that are learned, shared, and acted out through a relatively deliberate process of choice. Repertoires are learned cultural creations, but they do not descend from abstract philosophy or take shape as a result of political

propaganda; they emerge from struggle. People learn to break windows in protest, attack pilloried prisoners, tear down dishonoured houses, stage public marches, petition, hold formal meetings, organize special-interest associations. At any particular point in history, however, they learn only a rather small number of alternative ways to act collectively.[34]

Nick Crossley has cogently drawn out the central themes that structure Tilly's descriptions of repertoires as well as how the idea has been taken up in social movement research. Repertoires constrain behaviour and choice. This implicitly requires that repertoires involve know-how or acquired skill in specific protest forms. Repertoires are practically constituted, out of struggle and everyday life activities, as opposed to being derived from abstract thinking. Repertoires involve deliberate choice, though choice is constrained by the stock of tactics available within a given repertoire. Finally, repertoires are identified with specific historical periods.[35]

For my purposes, though, I want to emphasize four key features:
- the dynamics of collectivization;
- repertoires' communicative underpinnings;
- their evolutionary logic; and
- their embeddedness within practical reason.

The importance of collectivization—as both strategy and process—in social movements cannot be overstated. At its most basic, collectivization is the key mechanism by which members of dominated groups combine their dispersed and often meagre power to compete with the highly concentrated and effective power of dominant agents. Repertoires of contention depend on collectivizing forms of capital that are relevant to the field in which contention takes place. This is not an inherently straightforward process. Although economic capital can be easily aggregated—through donations and fundraisers—other forms of capital (cultural, social, political) cannot be combined in as straightforward a way. Unequal distributions of cultural capital and symbolic power within a movement tend to distort that movement's collective identity and goals. Some organizational forms appear to be more conducive than others for aggregating, accumulating, and organizing resources in support of various tactics. "Collectivization" is therefore an umbrella term for the complex logics by which movements bring together participants' dispersed resources (including the participants themselves—their bodies, their voices, their actions) for concrete contentious activities.

Attention to collectivization as both process and strategy diminishes the risk of individualizing the notion of repertoire, which is intended to capture a collective and, more specifically, interactive and communicative phenomenon. Repertoires of contention always refer to collective, not individual, performances because they always involve more than one collective actor or individual agent. The smallest unit of contentious political action involves two participants—a contending actor (for example, a group of workers) and a target of demands (their bosses). These sets aggregate and collectivize up to the level of national politics. Collective claims may or may not involve conflict—there is no conflict in affirmations of shared identity, for example—but when claims do conflict, Tilly suggests that we are able to speak of contention. Thus, "repertoires of contention are the established ways in which pairs of actors make and receive claims bearing on each other's interests," and these claims are made within culturally and symbolically structured sets of shared meanings.[36]

In this light, repertoires are communicative structures, in two senses. First, contentious action, in the restricted sense of sets of actors making claims that impinge upon each other's interests, is homologous to linguistic practice. In both cases, the success or failure of actions is determined in part by a preexisting consensus about which actions are legitimate and which are illegitimate. Within the general realm of language and speech acts, this consensus is both codified, in dictionaries and official grammar texts, and informal, with accepted slang, colloquialisms, and so on. Contentious action is similarly bound by official, codified rules of legitimacy as established through laws, criminal codes, and so on. Like slang, contentious actions may also technically break rules but be considered legitimate within certain contexts. Spontaneous demonstrations, for example, may be seen as legitimate political expressions even when they are in contravention of bylaws or even of the criminal code.

Also like slang and official grammar, legitimacy in actions can be hotly contested and often context-specific. For this reason, analyses of repertoires of contention must distinguish between technical competence and social competence. Agents demonstrate technical competence when they follow the official or informal rules. Their social competence is determined by the symbolic space in which they act and—as importantly—by the position in the symbolic space that they occupy. As with speech acts more generally, the success of contentious actions depends upon the cultural, economic, and other relevant forms of capital a collective actor brings to bear within a field, as well as the actor's overall disposition, comprised, at the collective level, by collective identity, organizational orientations, and ideological commitments.

Unequal distributions of capital and conflicting dispositions expose some actors disproportionately to the same negative outcomes experienced by speakers with minimal linguistic capital: they are more likely to be misunderstood, less likely to be given the benefit of the doubt when their intentions or their intended meanings are unclear, and more likely to face disproportionately harsh sanctions for failing technically (via grammatical mistakes or lawbreaking) or stepping beyond their social competence (speaking too informally to an authority figure or making unwelcome claims on public resources). Unlike linguistic acts, however, contentious actions are underpinned by the aggregated individual habitus and cultural capital of participants, as well as the outcome of the collectivization processes described above. As such, competence is determined not only by the person or people speaking on behalf of a group—the spokesperson's eloquence, logic, and persuasiveness—but the symbolic value of the group on whose behalf they speak. Ultimately, contentious actions are always situated within the history of their movement, of other movements, of perhaps generations of cultural and economic struggles and the entire history of contentious action, and that space is constituted by unequal distributions of various forms of capital and by a symbolic schema of meaning, classification, and intelligibility. The communicative potential of any given tactic cannot, therefore, be reduced to the tactic itself.

Repertoires of contention are also communicative in the sense in which critical theorists have been trying to bring protest into the realm of deliberative democracy. Iris Marion Young, most prominently, has shown that even though protest does not meet the criteria for the calm exchange of reasons traditionally demanded by deliberative democrats, it nonetheless provides a much-needed counterbalance to the rationalistic tendencies of deliberation.[37] Indeed, contentious action performs a communicative function that is outside language as such: protesters expose and make explicit the reality of otherwise muted conflict, not by describing it verbally or by making arguments, but by stimulating tensions that pre-exist collective action and that, indeed, motivate it in the first place. Most obvious among these conflicts are the tensions between police agencies who have a clear image of the order they wish to maintain and protesters who neither share that vision of order nor are willing to abide by it. Similarly, protesters bring to light conflict between classes, between political and economic insiders and outsiders, between ideological commitments, and—in the G20 protests that we will look at—between the G20 participants shielded by a massive barricade and the protesters forced away from that site of power and exposed to searches, violence, and arrest.

As I will explore more carefully in my discussion of the G20 protests in chapter five, the notion of repertoires as a shared language is integral to anarchists' efforts to develop a "new language" of civil disobedience that falls between Gandhian non-violence and outright (armed) insurrection.[38] Politically motivated property destruction, in this view, is both a communicative tactic and an effort to transform the meaning of property destruction and its value as a communicative act. As with any object or action, the meaning of property destruction could never stand on its own as a discrete phenomenon. Therefore, transforming the meaning of vandalism would require changing the meaning of property and authority as such, which are core anarchist goals.

This brings us to repertoires of contention's conceptual dependence on a logic of repertoire evolution. Tilly's initial articulation of the idea of repertoires was intended to account for changes and continuities in the modes of protest that groups relied upon across historical periods, which already implies that no particular tactic exists transhistorically.[39] For Tilly, repertoires evolve according to a basic logic of interaction and innovation.[40] In fact, the core of Tilly's argument is that, as institutions changed, groups built on and modified familiar tactics in order to respond to new institutional conditions. The emergence of political parties, trade unions, and centralized national governments forced protesters to develop new ways of making claims. Protesters replicate successful tactics and leave unsuccessful tactics to fall by the wayside, with some periods of contention fostering high levels of experimentation and innovation. Over time, movements refine and routinize once-novel tactics and, when these tactics cease to be successful, abandon them.[41]

As claimants gain experience with new forms of collective action and as those forms gain legitimacy, they become easier to use and to diffuse across groups and movements. However, repertoire evolution can never be fully separated from collectivization. It would be wrong to hive off the process of experimentation from the hierarchical distributions of capital within movements themselves. As strike tactics evolve, unions assert or reassert organizational control over their deployment. Movement participants with higher stores of cultural and other forms of capital struggle with whether a tactic fits with their overall vision for the movement and seek to dissuade or prevent the use of tactics that fall outside that vision. Further, because repertoires always involve sets of actors, the targets of protest engage in counter-innovations to reduce the efficacy of novel forms of protest.[42] Innovation and counter-innovation always take place within fields that are already characterized by uneven distributions of resources and opportunities, including uneven distributions of symbolic capital and so-called common sense understandings of what counts as legitimate. Such terrain, not only uneven but misrecognized as natural and therefore not even available for open contest, allows the strategies of the already-powerful—the wealthy, parliamentary insiders, and so on—to stay consistently ahead of opposition strategies. Opposition strategies inevitably come too late, because they are bound up in a repertoire dynamic that undercuts efforts to resist the unspoken justifications for that unequal distribution.

Ultimately, this means that there is no "correct" strategy waiting to be discovered. Insofar as every action alters the social field in which it takes place without fundamentally altering the basic principles by which the field evolves, there may be no principles of action that are capable of achieving a revolutionary redistribution within a field. This is particularly the case if action is limited to strategies that are already culturally legitimate but also predictable and therefore capable of being countered. Lack of correct strategy (as I will argue in chapter five) reflects unrecognized features of domination and raises specific normative challenges for movement participants and allied critics alike. In turn, these normative challenges open new conceptual terrain for thinking about suffering and justice more broadly, while stimulating demand for novel strategies for overcoming suffering and the absence of current ways to protest "correctly."

The tools provided to us by mainstream social movement research are, indeed, both true and false. They are true insofar as they offer explanatory insights into a spectacularly diverse and complicated field of study. It is no easy feat to capture the continuities and variations among historically, geographically, and socially wide-ranging movements. Collective identity and repertoires of contention are particularly central because they allow us to understand how collective actors orient themselves toward grievances and opportunities.

Nonetheless, the tools currently offered are also false. They fail to capture continuities in domination in ways that allow for normative critique of movement goals and strategies. This disjuncture between conceptual tools and patterns of domination requires a theoretical framework that is capable of unifying material and cultural conditions to the logic of collective action.

Bourdieu's sociology provides such a framework. Therefore, I turn, in the next chapter, to an overview of Bourdieu's key epistemological and philosophical reorientations, the logic of practice that these reorientations allowed, and an argument for how to connect Bourdieu's sociology to normative theory.

Conformity and Failure

Habit is as essential to the movement of history as innovation and creation, since history, even a history of rapid change, presupposes the sedimentation of actions that allows them to build upon one another. History is not the succession of discrete events, past and present, but their cumulative penetration in an unfolding process.
 —Crossley, "The Phenomenological Habitus and Its Construction"[1]

A Productive Tension

Social change is kind of amazing. It can be beautiful, inspiring, devastating—or all of these things at once. But what is particularly amazing about social change, in some respects, is that it happens at all. Social systems tend to reproduce themselves, for all the reasons rendered visible by the LGBT/Q and alterglobalization movements, but that hamper movements and plague social spaces more generally. Technology, economic crises, and other factors may push change in the content of social fields, but the hierarchical and unjust form of these fields remains distressingly consistent.

Nonetheless, it is fair to say that most people who commit themselves to the study of social movements are themselves fairly progressively minded. As a result, we bear a slightly misleading relation to the objects of our study. We tend to see xenophobia, oppression, and privilege as aberrations caused by power relations rooted in some distant past; they are moral accidents that social movements seek to remedy. A tendril of this kind of metaphysical thinking, faith in an intrinsically well-ordered world, binds us to the hope that if we can understand when and how people mobilize against moral aberrations, then we can help ensure that mobilization happens more often and more successfully. In this chapter, I want both to amplify our sense of wonder at social change—because the roots of change reflect something of the greatness of human potential—and to dampen our optimism about the possibilities of merely working past the myriad forms of domination that stall and distort progressive change.

I do not, however, intend to erase that optimism entirely. This chapter outlines the key elements of Bourdieu's sociology and the epistemological and philosophical innovations that made his sociology possible. In turn, his sociology can inspire new modes of democratic practice and resistance. At the core of Bourdieu's sociology lie three primary thinking tools: habitus, field, and capital. Each tool is fundamentally rooted in an embodied and structured encounter with the social, as opposed to voluntarist and consciousness-based conceptions of how individuals act. My recounting of field, capital, and especially habitus has a concrete critical goal: to pull from Bourdieu's work a sense of the incompleteness of domination, and to develop a foundation for making the tension between conformity and failure a productive one. Properly constituted conflicts among movement participants can (as I will argue in chapter seven) help social movements overcome the kinds of obstacles exemplified by collective identity formation and tactical selection. I don't offer hope for a way to permanently and finally overcome these problems, only a method for collectively making visible hidden patterns of domination and for collectively glimpsing fragments of justice.

Bourdieu set himself the unenviable task of breaking with and recombining two dominant philosophic and sociological trajectories, which he identified as subjectivism and objectivism. Subjectivist approaches, including existentialism, phenomenology, and rational choice, explain behaviour as the result of conscious, cognitive deliberation. Among the subjectivist approaches, Bourdieu was particularly critical of intellectualist and idealist philosophical traditions, treating Cartesian and Kantian dualisms as especially pernicious. Subjectivist modes overemphasize the importance of consciousness in agency; they erroneously consider action to be oriented by reference to ends, and consider these ends to be defined through acts of disembodied free choice. Bourdieu broke from this vision of individuals as monologically constituted, atomistic, rational selves. Instead, he argued that individuals are dialogically constituted agents who rely occasionally on rational deliberation, but more generally on bodily forms of knowledge.[2] Embodied judgment means action is rarely the product of consciously evaluated options and preferences; it is a practical response to the imminent demands of the actor's environment. In short, action is produced by embodied dispositions and habits rather than by conscious deliberation and willing.

To get to a conception of action as embodied, Bourdieu also broke from what he called objectivist modes of thinking. His primary target here was structuralism. Objectivism rejects the subjectivist reliance on primary, conscious knowledge in favour of regularities, norms, rules, and social patterns that exist independently of individual experience, consciousness, or will. That is, objectivists explain action through reference to regularities, norms, and rules while excluding subjective experiences from explanatory consideration and reducing consciousness and will to the status of epiphenomenal rationalizations or ideologies.³ Because durable relations exist between and among objects in the form of official rules, class dynamics, and norms, objectivists argue that the causal strength of these relations cannot be reduced to individual consciousness. Therefore, structuralism must on methodological grounds exclude any active participation, decision-making, or production of meaning on the part of social actors that is not produced by objective relations between structural elements.

Against objectivism, Bourdieu first argued that the subordination of practical knowledge and action to structural rules, norms, and so on was tantamount to constructing a map representing all possible routes for all possible travellers without paying attention to the routes that are actually maintained and used, the "beaten tracks." Objectivist observers, attending to official rules rather than to the actions actually taken, mistake their own formal model for the actual determinant of action.⁴ In short, the distance between the official map and the routes actually taken by agents exposes the inadequacy of objectivist approaches.

Second, Bourdieu argued that, in their search for formal models that can account for social practice, objectivists telescope actions by artificially collapsing temporally distant actions into a single logic or rule. This ignores the fact that the time an action takes, the unfolding of action in social space, matters as much as the ultimate intention of the action itself. Bourdieu's analysis of gift exchange, for example, shows that the time between receiving a gift and offering a counter-gift is integral to understanding the practice. A counter-gift offered too soon would appear crass and expose the interested economic value lying beneath an apparently generous and selfless act. Even more, the time between gift and counter-gift is laden with tension insofar as, until the counter-gift is given, there is uncertainty about whether the original gift will be reciprocated, met with a snub (a refusal to offer a counter-gift), or if the recipient cannot afford or achieve a suitable response, condemn them to an unfulfilled obligation. By reducing gift exchange to formal norms of reciprocity, objectivists collapse action, response, preresponse tension, and the practical agency required to resolve that tension into a single moment structured by a formal rule. This rule excludes the nuanced practical and temporal strategies and constraints involved in gift exchange.⁵ Objectivists' adherence to formal rules and official logics ignores the practical and constructive aspects of agency.

Against subjectivism and objectivism, Bourdieu proposed a third path: his theory of practice. He retained structuralism's relational thinking, as well as the agentic and strategic elements of subjectivism, and integrated elements of objectivism and subjectivism through an integrated conception of fields, capital, and habitus.

Bourdieu relied on his conception of fields to overcome the objectivist claim that agents act according to a static set of rules and norms. Instead, agents construct social space according to dynamic and generative logics that connect differences and spatial relations from one moment to the next: a logic of practice, and moreover, a shared logic of practice. According to such shared logics, any agent's claim to a new position in social space is either recognized or challenged by other actors. Field, then, refers to groups of actions and position-taking within social space, clustered around a particular type of activity and mobilized according to a specific logic relevant to that type of activity. Bourdieu uses the term "field" to locate action within bounded sets of practices, bearing the history of social interactions that led to those practices and an uneven distribution of resources (including authority and competence) that gives some agents within a field advantage over others.[6]

In keeping with structural linguistic methods, Bourdieu argued that the meaning of any object within a field can only be determined in relation to all of the other objects within that field. Such a system of meaning would be free-floating entirely were it not anchored by convention.[7] Therefore, Bourdieu's social fields are spaces bounded by unrecognized or preconscious agreement on what elements (objects, actors, capital, and practices) belong within that space, the meaning of the various forms of those elements, and the value ascribed them. Bourdieu uses topographical metaphors to treat social space as analogous to physical space: just as the reciprocal externality of a bounded set of objects constitutes a physical space, social space is constituted through mutual exclusion or distinctions. The value of any agent or action comes from its not being other, less valued, agents or actions within the bounded set of possible objects, agents, and actions that constitute the outer limits of a given social space.[8]

Within the artistic field, for example, consumption of so-called high-brow art expresses an aesthetic disposition—which is the product of specifically classed familial and educational experiences—oriented toward certain "legitimate" aesthetic objects and capable of experiencing them in legitimate ways, and not an aesthetic disposition oriented toward base or unrefined tastes.[9] The value of Chopin is that it isn't monster truck rallies, or—as I argue in relation to the political field below—the value of peaceful mass demonstrations is that they aren't riots. Benefiting from such distinctions depends on symbolic power, the ability—by virtue of social location and possession of relevant forms of capital—to assert the distinction and have it recognized by other participants in a social field.

The relative durability of fields comes from two features of the social world. First, every field's rules are doubly inscribed in the social world: subjectively in the structured dispositions of the habitus-bearing agents, and objectively in the social space itself. Second, the fact that resources are objectively distributed across social space means that observers can map out resources from an external perspective. Authorizing titles and qualifications, geography, and physical structures are key examples of objectively observable distributions of resources. For example, the concentration of corporate and political power on Wall Street is not a simple coincidence of real estate; it reflects complex processes by which objective distributions of economic resources have become geographically sedimented. In turn, having a corporate location on Wall Street conveys a certain economic and political authority to those dispositions (habitus) attuned to recognizing it.[10]

One can say that there are as many fields as there are clusters of practices bound together by a relatively autonomous logic. Bourdieu envisioned a broad social field made up of multiple bounded and relatively autonomous subfields, each with its own system of meaning and rules for ranking and distributing objects, agents, and practices within its parameters. Generally speaking, key fields include the educational, artistic, scientific, linguistic, and, of course, political. Although each field is anchored by its own morally arbitrary assumptions, they are all homologously organized, which is to say that they share structural similarities. What is valuable in the domestic field—submission to parental authority, respect for elders, participation in the collective efforts of the family—has similar value in the educational field in the form of submission to teachers' authority and willingness to participate in learning as a collective process replete with behavioural norms, benchmarks for success, and so on. Similarly, whether in a church or a classroom, authority is located at the front (not the back) and is often elevated (on a dais or by standing in front of seated students). These parallel divisions make the value of objects intuitively recognizable across contexts. We rarely need to learn the rules of a new space entirely from scratch, because we unconsciously recognize key rules and values across contexts. The structural similarity of the relational logic underpinning all subfields within the broader social field enables habitus to act intelligibly and consistently across social contexts, which reinforces the naturalized sense of the system of classification in any particular field.

Because social actors always exist in more than one field simultaneously, and because they bring the same habitus to each field, it makes sense that agents must also transport resources from one field to another, though this transport requires appropriate acts of conversion. Bourdieu calls assemblages of more than one field "a field of power." The homologous and ultimately porous operation of fields explains why actors who are dominant in one area—the economy, for example—are able to dominate in others, such as the political field. Of course, there is no simple, one-to-one transfer of domination from one field to another, because within a field of power, subfields are structurally comparable but not identical. To move from a dominant position in one field to a dominant position in another, agents must undertake "labours of conversion." Fully understanding how power operates across particular fields requires working out the specific labours required to transform a strong position in one field into a strong position in another, as well as the mechanisms and restrictions by which agents achieve this transition.[11]

Insofar as a field has its own rules of practice and its own rewards, it also has its own kinds of resources that actors can use to support their actions. Generically speaking, Bourdieu calls these resources various forms of capital, his second thinking tool. Bourdieu identifies three main forms of capital:

- Economic capital is what we generally think of in terms of money; it is institutionalized primarily as property rights.
- Cultural capital is the ability to distinguish between different symbolic goods, such as cubist and abstract expressionist art or correct and incorrect language usage. This ability to distinguish between symbolic goods also includes the ability to behave "appropriately" in various social spaces. Cultural capital is accumulated through long processes of classed socialization, and it is institutionalized through educational qualifications, among other ways.
- Social capital is the network of relations that an actor can mobilize in pursuit of new position-taking within various fields.[12]

Agents accumulate any type of capital through strategic position-taking within social space and by performing lengthy labours of acquisition. For example, one doesn't acquire the skills and dispositions—the cultural capital—to behave "properly" at a fancy restaurant overnight. The process requires long-term and consistent investments in labours of correction from parents and social networks that are already invested in those skills and in passing them on.

All forms of capital are unevenly distributed, which is what gives various agents their varying ability to successfully lay claim to positions within social space. To fully understand how uneven distributions of capital create durable conditions of domination, cultural capital is key. This is because one form of cultural capital is the habitus, Bourdieu's third thinking tool. Habitus primarily performs an explanatory function in his work. However, the most direct route from Bourdieu's sociology to normative theory depends on teasing out an underappreciated aspect of habitus: adaptation.

Habitus is a nuanced, though contested, concept and it provides the cornerstone of Bourdieu's work. Let's start with Bourdieu's most-cited definition:

> The conditionings associated with a particular class of conditions of existence produce *habitus*, systems of durable, transposable dispositions, structured structures predisposed to function as structuring structures, that is, as principles which generate and organize practices without presupposing a conscious aiming at ends or an express mastery of the operations necessary in order to attain them.[13]

The habitus emerges from an individual's structured encounter with other individuals, through the minutiae of everyday life and through micro-rewards, but more powerfully through "reproachful looks" or "tones" and "disapproving glances." We incorporate the powerful, often silent injunctions by which parents, teachers, peers, and other authorities police our posture and our behaviour directly into our bodily comportment. What's more, we do so without thinking about that incorporation, reflecting on it, or articulating it through language. This embodied sense organizes how we perceive our social and physical environments and how we distinguish the various components of these environments.[14] These inscriptions are not haphazard or individualistic. They are the products of particular "classes of conditions," which is to say that people occupying particular regions of social space will be systematically reproached and sanctioned by the rules and standards specific to that region of social space. In this way, we can speak of a working-class habitus and a bourgeois habitus, as well as habitus that are inflected with differences based on region, ethnic background, gender, and sexuality.

The central elements of the habitus then, are the following:
- it is structured through encounters with other habitus-bearing actors;
- it is an embodied "feel for the game," a set of rules by which we interpret the social world from our particular, and therefore always partial, perspective within that world;

- it is a system of "perception and appreciation" that can function consciously and reflexively, but that fundamentally works on a preconscious and embodied level; and
- it generates dispositions that are consistent across various social fields and contexts, without predetermining specific actions.

The habitus's embodied nature is centrally important for Bourdieu, as this embodiment is the result of the inculcation of the rules, divisions, and hierarchies of social space. Since agents embody rules and divisions rather than consciously obeying them, the rules, divisions, and hierarchies of social space are forgotten, or at least, not consciously recognized as such. Because they are so fundamentally inscribed in our body, in how we are disposed to view the world, these divisions appear natural to us; we misrecognize their social and power-laden nature.

Habitus identifies differences of various kinds: up/down, hot/cold, good/bad, male/female, authorized/unauthorized, likely to succeed / likely to fail, and so on. None of these differences expresses an intrinsic property of an object: habitus constructs differences between two objects as relevant differences, as differences that are important in some way, based on the system of classification the habitus has adopted.[15] Therefore, habitus allows us to differentiate among objects, to relate them spatially to one another, and to give those relations a value-laden, moral character. When habitus cognitively maps out spatial relations, it does so according to a schema of rules inscribed on it by structured encounters with other habitus. Therefore, habitus replicates, with varying degrees of success, a field that pre-exists and that structures the habitus itself. This replication includes both a schema of perception—how to organize objects in space—and a schema of appreciation—how to value those objects.

Think of the raft of makeover shows that have appeared in the last decades: *What Not to Wear*, *Queer Eye for the Straight Guy*, *Love at First Swipe*, or any of their many variations. In each, upper-class experts react with revulsion and disgust at the dress and mannerisms of the show's working-class victims. What makes these shows work is their ability to identify fashion rules, make them appear obvious and non-arbitrary (when they are neither), and then give those rules a physical, affective, power through revulsion and disgust. The victims undergo both a fashion transformation and a moral one. They move from hapless objects of ridicule to upstanding, economically and romantically viable citizens of popular culture.[16]

Habitus here performs a number of functions. It makes the experts visible as experts while concealing the class-based foundations of their supposedly objective advice. These shows admonish viewers to adopt the manners and dispositions of upper classes, even when the resources (including the cost of high-quality clothing and accessories, the comportment to wear them with confidence, and the time it takes to gain expertise in current trends) may not be available to them. Finally, habitus, by misrecognizing arbitrary rules as natural ones, predisposes itself to naturalize other similarly arbitrary rules.

The dynamic of regularity and adaptation that habitus captures permits new ways to consider questions of regularized distributions, institutionalized practices, and embodied dispositions as questions of justice. Although traces of adaptive dynamics can be found in fields, capital, and symbolic power, it is most clearly identifiable in habitus. Treating habitus as primarily an adaptive phenomenon can help correct the common mischaracterization of habitus as something passively acquired, often referred to as socialization or enculturation, in a one-directional way.[17]

Habitus Conforms: Exposure, Strategy, Adaptation

Two of Bourdieu's central claims point toward habitus-as-adaptation while also providing foundations for habitus's conceptual apparatus. First, he claims that we acquire the dispositions comprising habitus because we are exposed to the necessities and regularities of the world. Second, that subjectivity emerges through a primary, binary distinction between self and other, a distinction that engenders our attachment to, and investment in, the social world. In Bourdieu's consideration of how the social comes to be individualized within biological bodies, he reworks phenomenology, thematically attending to the fact of our exposure to the world:

> With a Heideggerian play on words, one might say that we are *disposed* because we are *exposed*. It is because the body is (to unequal degrees) exposed and endangered in the world, faced with the risk of emotion, lesion, suffering, sometimes death, and therefore obliged to take the world seriously (and nothing is more serious than emotion, which touches the depths of our organic being) that it is able to acquire dispositions that are themselves an openness to the world, that is, to the very structures of the social world of which they are the incorporated form.[18]

Key phenomenological claims operate in this passage. In particular, Bourdieu relies on a three-part claim about the biological nature of the human animal: human bodies have a conditionability about them; conditionability is not only a survival mechanism, it fundamentally orients us toward the world outside us; and conditionability expresses itself through regulated but evolving habituated dispositions. Bourdieu was clearly relying on phenomenologist Maurice Merleau-Ponty's notion of "corporeal schema" as the site of knowledge acquisition. Corporeal schema is incorporated practical sense and bodily "know-how," which Merleau-Ponty distinguished from propositional knowledge ("knowledge-that").[19]

Knowledge-that consists of facts about the world that we might call to mind. It connotes a sense that what is known is entirely independent from the person doing the knowing. The knower may or may not hold a proposition in mind, but whether they do has little influence on the knowledge itself. By contrast, know-how is deeply connected to the knower. Fundamentally, the kind of knowledge that Merleau-Ponty intended corporeal schema to capture is a functional, but not necessarily conscious, sense of the knower's body and the space around them. This schema allows the knower to constitute the space around them, to bring it into relation to their body, and to subordinate it to their interests. We rely on corporeal schema, as opposed to propositional knowledge, all the time. When you reach for a cup of coffee you are unlikely to calculate its distance, its weight, and your strength and to hold these propositions in your mind as you stretch out your hand and lift up the cup. Rather, your body, having a functional sense of the distance between you and the cup and a good prediction about its weight, readies itself to alter the distribution of things in space, and then reaches out to move the cup to your lips. Dancing, fighting, sports, typing, walking, and indeed most of what we do rely on know-how rather than knowledge-that; we act through a non-conscious awareness of the location of our body in relation to external elements, and by putting those external elements to practical use.[20]

Merleau-Ponty was interested in demonstrating that the habituation by which the corporeal schema develops an expanding repertoire of know-how provides a more convincing account of learning than that offered by behaviourism. In particular, Merleau-Ponty was keen to show that habituation is not a mechanical response to fixed situations, the product of repeated accidental triggers, but a general and flexible power to respond to general situations. Habituation requires innovation, hypothesis testing, and the ability to transfer skills from one body part to another through practical analogies. In short, agents actively explore the world to which they are exposed and adapt, through an embodied and practical understanding, to the challenges and opportunities it offers. We recognize those with particularly well-adapted know-how by their appearance of competence and purposive action. They demonstrate outstanding success at adaptation through a seemingly effortless ability to constitute the space around them and subordinate it to their interests. Of course, that effortlessness is helped along if the social space you constitute and subordinate is a good match for your adaptations. If, for example, you are a white male in spaces that privilege whiteness and masculinity over racialized and female adaptations, you enjoy an effortlessness that others likely do not.

Habitus's core dynamics—mimesis and correction—flow from phenomenology's claim that hypothesis testing and innovation are elementary components of learning. To be clear, mimesis does not involve "pretending" to be like the object being imitated; pretending assumes a conscious, imitating subject when it is precisely the emergence of subjectivity that requires explanation. Rather, mimesis works through preconscious observation—the product of our openness and exposure to the world—and identification to generate a "practical reactivation" of the posture, emotion, and orientation of what is mimed.[21] As agents strive to gain practical mastery over their surroundings, through experimentation and miming, they are inevitably and constantly confronted with corrections, rewards, and reprimands. Indeed, Bourdieu says the habitus

> emerges from an individual's structured encounter with other individuals, through the minutiae of everyday life and through "reproachful looks" or "tones" and "disapproving glances." The powerful, often silent injunctions that police our posture and our behaviour are inscribed directly into our bodily comportment without necessarily passing through language and consciousness. This embodied sense then organizes how we perceive our social environment and how we distinguish its various components.[22]

The practical mastery that agents gain over their surroundings through these processes is habitus: practical know-how organized into generative and transferable dispositions. These dispositions give our actions consistency across social spaces because they apply structurally similar know-how in relatively diverse contexts. The way we "know" how to walk is related to the way we "know" how to dance. By extension, all of the silent and explicit injunctions that organize appropriate behaviour in family, educational, and similar contexts provide the foundation for how we perceive and interact with any subsequent context that we might encounter.

The environment over which agents seek practical mastery is both natural and social, but the objects of mimesis and sources of correction are almost exclusively social. Therefore, the structured incorporation of those worlds through practical mastery of them, organized into habitus, entails incorporation of social space.[23] The habitus replicates the social world's regularities, rules, distinctions, opportunities, and foreclosures at a preconscious level. It is therefore intrinsically social and historical, in direct contrast to Cartesian, existentialist, and other philosophies of subjectivity that emphasize *causa sui*, individualized and ahistorical consciousness. In short, the intellectualist tradition is wrong to conceive of individuals as monologically constituted, atomistic selves who have representations of the outer world in their mind and who use these representations to make decisions and judgments.[24] Instead, action is at times based on conscious calculation, but it is generally based on deeply rooted, embodied, habituated but active and structured adaptations to the world, achieved through mimesis, experimentation, and correction.[25]

Because the world to which the habitus adapts is social, Bourdieu's dialogical model recognizes the deep penetration of the social into the individual, or more accurately, the constitution of the individual subject through deeply social processes. Again, while phenomenologists and other intellectualists refuse to account for the construction of the principles by which agents act upon the world, habitus permits a rich and nuanced account of how agents develop a schema through which they interpret and act upon their reality.

Habitus allowed Bourdieu to wed his critical use of phenomenology to structuralism via the structured social environment into which subjects are always inserted and from which their subjectivity emerges. However, subjectivity is surely something more complex than an aggregation of learned dispositions and know-how, and habitus alone may not get beyond the deterministic objectivist sociology that Bourdieu sought to overcome. Critics have pointed out that Bourdieu himself seemed unsettled about the nature of "the subject" and whether a sociological analysis, even one that develops a nuanced theoretical link between the individual and the collective, can proceed without psychological or psychoanalytic categories.[26] Nonetheless, in his last major work, *Pascalian Meditations,* Bourdieu offered glimpses into the connections between habitus, social structure, and psychic processes, though the connections remain underspecified. This relationship between habitus, social structure, and psychic processes turns on what Bourdieu takes to be a founding pedagogical prerequisite, on the basis of which mimetic identification and correction become possible, namely "the transition, described by Freud" wherein the child moves from a narcissistically organized libido

> in which the child takes himself (or his own body) as an object of desire, to another state in which he orients himself towards another person, thus entering the world of "object relations," in the form of the original social microcosm and the protagonists of the drama that is played out there.[27]

At stake in this transition is the question of how a child's general openness to the world comes to be organized into a specific openness to the social world and the structures (rules, constraints, opportunities, dangers) that make the social world a context to which habitus can adapt. The emergence of a cognitive mechanism upon which psychological operations (projection, identification, transference, sublimation) ultimately depend is fundamental to this process.[28] That cognitive mechanism is the ability to construct a binary distinction between self and other:

> Absorbed in the love of others, the child can only discover others as such on condition that he discovers himself as a "subject" for whom there are "objects" whose particularity is that they can take him as their "object."[29]

The context of this cognitive achievement and of subsequent psychic organization is already social. Therefore Bourdieu locates, in this founding cognitive accomplishment, a search for recognition. Bourdieu continues:

> In fact, he is continuously led to take the point of view of others on himself, to adopt their point of view so as to discover and evaluate in advance how he will be seen and defined by them. His being is a being-perceived, condemned to be defined as it "really" is by the perception of others.[30]

Although Bourdieu does slide between sociological and psychoanalytic language here, his reliance on phenomenology orients habitus in a decidedly different direction from psychoanalysis. Psychoanalytic thought generally relies on trauma as the foundation of subjectivity.[31] When an infant discovers that all the nurturing and comfort that make up their early physical experience is not an extension of themself, the resulting primary trauma establishes a lifelong, and hopeless, drive to reproduce not just an original state of plenitude, but the original relation to the now separate source of that plenitude: the mother, her breast, and so on. This pursuit is hopeless both because the original condition can never be reproduced and because it was a fiction in the first place; the infant was never continuous with their environment and never had control over the comfort and nurturance that that environment seemed to offer. Nonetheless, the primary trauma becomes a site of intense psychic investment and a location of both attachment and aggression, and subjects repeatedly re-enact this primary scene. For the psychoanalytic narrative, this primary ambivalence is ultimately productive. Our constant pursuit of hopeless attachments, energized by sexual and other drives and shaped by the particular objects and opportunities available in our environment, is what keeps us connected to the social world.

So far, the psychoanalytic story seems to fit well with Bourdieu's pedagogical prerequisite. The traumatic discovery that we are subjects in a world of objects, some of which are subjects themselves that take us as objects, combined with drives that invest us in pursuit of social relations expose the subject to the conditioning produced by a world of rewards and reproachful looks. The ambivalence produced at the site of primary trauma commits psychoanalytic analysis to a world in which that ambivalence is always unresolvable and ultimately drives action. By contrast, phenomenology envisions subjectivity as a gradual cognitive accomplishment rooted in experimentation, exploration, and mastery. Notwithstanding Bourdieu's apparent equivocation on the role of psychodynamics and subjectivity, both explanatory advantages and normative implications can be derived from phenomenological causal descriptions.

Although both psychoanalytic and phenomenological approaches contain elements of adaptation, they lead to different conclusions about the experience of power and powerlessness. In psychoanalytic accounts, because subjectivity is rooted in trauma and unconscious dynamics of internalization and repression, the agent is never fully secured. Even the apparently most privileged are driven to symptomatically surround themselves (literally or figuratively) with the trappings of wholeness in order to compensate for their inability to fully heal their initial trauma.[32] The tension that psychoanalytic perspectives posit is parallel to much of queer theory's commitment to the notion that (hetero)sexuality can never be fully accomplished, that it is doomed to be a site of ambivalence and failure because sexual identity is not rooted in a fixed, achievable state of being. Queer theory suggests that the ostensible power and plenitude of dominant groups and identities are based on fictive senses of identity. They are therefore inherently unstable and, despite the violence and harm perpetrated by the bearers of these identities and the institutions they dominate, apparently not so powerful after all.

By focusing on habitus as phenomenologically grounded and primarily adaptive, however, I want to suggest another possibility: that power has affective manifestations, and that chief among those manifestations is an experience of the world as obvious, natural, without a hitch. The fundamental conceptual contribution of Merleau-Ponty's corporeal schema is that agency develops through a gradual cognitive and embodied perception of the surrounding environment and ability to subordinate that environment to our interests. We gradually learn that our physical environment includes things that are interesting, possibly because they, or similar objects, have previously provided pleasure. We then learn to grab at them or call to them, to bring them closer to us. Further, we sometimes develop such a high level of mastery that mastery itself is an accomplishment. We can give ourselves over to the pleasures of dancing, eating, and other activities without anxiety precisely because we have mastered them.

Two implications flow from the possibility of mastery. First, anxiety is not inevitable. There are pleasures that agents derive from exploring and learning rather than through the murky dynamics of traumatic repetition. Second, and this is fundamental, opportunities for mastery are not evenly distributed and, therefore, neither is the potential to experience the world as subordinate to our interests and desires. Existing physical and social structures foster and/or mitigate an agent's opportunities both to acquire and to express mastery depending on class, gender, (dis)ability, and race. This provides grounds for critiquing the social world in terms of how affect is produced and distributed; it also permits an account of psychic energy as a form of capital requiring investment and providing a valuable resource. Those who enjoy the world as obvious and perfectly fit to their specific adaptations are free to invest and expend their psychic energy in areas that allow them to build upon their existing store of other forms of capital. Activists call this privilege. People who face daily micro-aggressions, who see doors slamming in their faces at every turn, must not only scrape together the social, economic, and cultural capital they need to survive, but must also expend stores of psychic capital in a way that is not required of the privileged.

On its own, observing this disparity is not new; oppressed groups have described these phenomena with nuance and passion. However, linking adaptation to disposition (via habitus), in contrast to psychoanalytic reliance on trauma, provides a direct connection between social structure and the affective dynamics that underpin symbolic power. Even more, it explains the appeal of conformity. Conformity holds out the promise of relief from micro-aggressions; it also promises the pleasure of mastery. For anyone who has never experienced the world as obvious and effortlessly navigated, gaining the capital needed to improve their position in social space can provide a life-saving reduction in suffering.

Aside from untangling its admittedly messy relation to psychic dynamics, fully appreciating habitus requires us to hold together two conceptual links: the cognitive ability to distinguish between self and other, an ability that can then be extended to distinguishing and ordering component parts of physical and social structures; and a psychic investment (interestedness or illusio in Bourdieu's language) in achieving recognition from the social world. Mimesis and correction depend fundamentally on this combination of cognitive ability and social investment. With clear indebtedness to Jean-Jacques Rousseau, Bourdieu calls social investment an "egoistic quest for satisfactions of *amour propre* which is, at the same time, a fascinated pursuit of the approval of others" and the root of symbolic capital.[33]

I will pursue this dynamic in social movement mobilization through a discussion of identity and collective identity in chapter four and diverse tactics in chapter five. Because my conception of justice depends on the relationship between habitus and field, however, it is worth specifying certain aspects of that dynamic. What is the nature of the social world in which we are investing? What is the cost of recognition?

Openness toward the social world and exposure to continuous preconscious bodily correction sensitize subjects to structured differences. More to the point, they incorporate sensitivity to those differences and to the social meaning of those differences at a bodily level and organize them into the habitus. Moreover, those structured differences provide an opportunity to acquire recognition. The family field provides the initial location of a dialectic between constraint and opportunity, wherein infants renounce narcissistic drives and self-love in favour of recognition and amour propre.[34] In fact, the "cost" of recognition first manifests in the family field. In order to obtain parental recognition in the form of affection, reward, and verbal admiration (expressed in phrases such as "how well-behaved he is" and "what a good girl"), the child must first internalize the rules of respect, authority, and deference as they map onto the various locations in social space—to whom good behaviour is owed and what gendered, racialized, and other socially located forms it ought to take—and demonstrate a willingness to submit to those rules. This original investment goes unnoticed by agents adapting to these rules and entails no deliberate commitment. Nonetheless, it profoundly structures how the dynamic between drives—now structured into increasingly specific desires and ambitions—and opportunities for satisfying those drives are reproduced between the habitus and fields outside the family.[35]

Ultimately, the cost of recognition is conformity. People conform to the rules of various fields to gain recognition from other actors who possess the tools to judge and reward rule-obedience and correct action. Even where an officially correct action is impossible—perhaps because it requires greater financial resources than an agent can muster—agents will acknowledge the action's official value. Bourdieu's work on cultural consumption, for example, identified the practice of aesthetic substitution among working classes, wherein affordable products are substituted for "legitimate" expensive ones (for example, sparkling wine for champagne). Such substitutions indicate recognition of the officially authorized style or practice and therefore submission to that cultural authority. Nonetheless, all agents recognize that substitution is at once technically illegitimate and necessary, given working-class financial resources. The recognized and accepted distance created between legitimate practice and available practice is (as I will elaborate in later chapters) the basis for symbolic violence.[36]

Symbolic struggle is ultimately a struggle over the definition and imposition of the officially accepted style; therefore, official styles and sanctioned competencies are expressions of power.[37] This is no neutral struggle. Indeed, because the strategies deployed and the chances of success are structured by unequal distributions of various forms of capital even within social movement contexts, movements ascribe official meanings to goals and strategies, with the effect of marginalizing alternative meanings, goals, and strategies. This is the heart of the conformist face of habitus collectivized into social movements: officialized movement meanings that best conform to the competencies and values established outside the movement are also well positioned to mobilize resources successfully. At the G20, for example, protesters whose definition of legitimate protests best accorded with official democratic values were consistently praised in contrast to those who failed to adhere to official values.

Before moving on to the ways in which habitus fails, conceptually and through refusals to conform, let us consider one final feature of habitus's adaptive nature. That feature is our capacity not simply to adapt but also to anticipate. This capacity makes habitus more than a reactive set of dispositions; it is also the cognitive and dispositional apparatus through which agents orient themselves toward various future possibilities. Attention to agents' active interpretation of contingent opportunities takes us beyond the habitus as simple adaptation to regularities in the physical and social world, through psychically invested habituation and correction, and toward adaptation as an embodied capacity to anticipate imminent demands of the social field and to adjust to those demands.

Bourdieu characterizes the habitus's development as akin to "a train laying its own tracks."[38] The analogy captures the adaptive and adjustment-intensive nature of the relationship between habitus and social space. The incorporated sense of social space, the rules and authorizations that structure it as well as the opportunities for recognition it provides, orient agents toward fields within which their habitus is likely to garner success. Agents bring to fields a combination of various forms of capital, a sense of the game (which is really cultural capital embodied in the habitus), and various kinds of competency. But what agents bring to fields also influences the fields to which agents bring themselves. That is, some fields will be excluded from consideration entirely, while others demand further renunciations, corrections, and specifically constituted investments as a price of entry. The academic field, for example, has appeal primarily for those who share, among other characteristics, an interest in a certain degree of abstraction and distance from the practical world, but it demands of its entrants a willingness to internalize rules of citation, evidence-giving, argumentation, and so on. Therefore, the train laying its own tracks does not do so either randomly or in a predetermined direction, but through a dialectical relationship between the habitus's incorporated sense of the social and the contingent opportunities that various fields offer or forbid.

The train metaphor not only points to the boundedness of habitus and its history, but also to its trajectory. Here, though, trajectory is not deterministic in a structural sense, but the product of habitus's practical comprehension of the world and most importantly of its capacity to anticipate it. This capacity for anticipation, manifested only in concrete situations, relies on practical precategorization, that is, on the cognitive ability, evolved over thousands of years into habitus, to identify and classify—to construct—social and natural regularities and thereby to make predictions about the trajectories of those regularities and elements within them based on previous experience.[39] This anticipatory capacity lies at the core of strategy and is intimately connected to habitus's perception of space and time. Bourdieu's logic in this regard relies heavily on Edmund Husserl, particularly Husserl's vision of interested agents prereflexively adjusting themselves to, and preparing for action in, an imminently forthcoming future. This entails an active construction of that future based on schemes of classification incorporated in the habitus and then preconscious orientation toward it.

> Husserl did indeed clearly establish that the *project* as a conscious aiming at the future in its reality as a contingent future must not be conflated with *protension*, a prereflexive aiming at a forth-coming which offers itself as a quasi-present in the visible, like the hidden faces of a cube, that is, with the same belief status (the same doxic modality) as what is directly perceived....[40]
>
> The imminent forth-coming is present, immediately visible, as a present property of things, to the point of excluding the possibility that it will not come about, a possibility which exists theoretically so long as it has not come about.[41]

It bears emphasizing that this imminent forthcoming is not just one possibility among many, but an already-present future that is necessitated by the arrangement of objects, agents, and dynamics that already exist in a situation. Bourdieu frequently refers to sports metaphors, pointing to the prereflexive way in which a tennis player moves to where the ball will be rather than where it currently is.[42] That is, the certainty of where the ball will be collapses the practical (action-oriented) perception of two points in time into a prereflexive unity. The tennis player moves without thinking because the certainty of the development of the space of the game (the location of the ball) leaves reflexive consideration unnecessary and unprovoked. Moreover, this certainty is not just an objective certainty based on laws of physics; it is also a subjective certainty based on the player's finely honed sense of the game. More experienced players will have more certainty about where the ball will be. The regularities of the space of a tennis game are analogous to the regularities of social space generally, and therefore habitus gives us a more or less well-adapted sense of the game being played in any social context. Again, while there is possibility for conscious deliberation, the bulk of how we engage the social life is through our prereflexive sense of where the social world is moving and what our place is within that trajectory. In particular, this leads us to select social settings—restaurants, schools, careers—that are "for us" and avoid those that are not.[43]

As gay and lesbian politics and certain trajectories of the alterglobalization movement show, when it comes to collective action, the distinction between protension and project is essential. To echo Husserl's phrasing, protension refers to an immediate response to what is already present or happening in contrast to the longer-rage action and planning involved in a project. Acting in response to an immediate set of circumstances—a protest against an emergent issue, for example—and attempts to marshal resources for a long-run struggle against institutions, norms, and practices with considerable durability are very different from each other, and those differences are normatively fraught. Institutionalized collective actors are best able to accumulate social and political capital because those actors exist over time, even if only in the form of a durable collective identity. On the other hand, conforming to the rules of accumulation that allow this to happen requires epistemic exclusions and marginalization of those who refuse to internalize official meanings and values. The politics of representation that offer the best hope for progressive change, then, appear doomed to replicate the fields and capital distributions that generate the need for change in the first place.

Habitus Fails: Gaps, Bad Fits, and Reflexivity

Reading Bourdieu's description of habitus with an eye toward adaptation provides a sociological explanation for conformity as well as for conformity's strategic value. My intention in treating conformity sociologically is to strip it of its value-laden connotations and establish it as both an effect of the durability of social and physical worlds and a viable strategy within those worlds. Nonetheless, adaptation and conformity are only part of the story. As Bourdieu's critics have pointed out, habitus may fail to adapt. Indeed, some take the point further to suggest that habitus must inevitably fail to adapt.

Most objections to the notion of habitus centre on one of several charges levelled against Bourdieu's overall framework:
- the apparent determinism produced by the close relationship between field and habitus;
- the question of whether Bourdieu is sufficiently able to account for the reflexivity that critics take to be integral to agency itself and to be a key component of the empirical fact that structures are sometimes transformed or replaced, not just reproduced; and

- whether habitus is simply too coarse a concept, too reliant on statistical regularity to tell us about the nature of subjectivity—gendered and queer subjectivity, in particular—and therefore about the nature of social practice.

Habitus's failure as a concept and as a phenomenon is worth exploring briefly because, although conformity has sociological foundations and strategic value, movements are also forced to confront—and at times embrace—failure. In short, habitus's conceptual and strategic failures provide glimpses into modes of action that promise transformation rather than reproduction.

Critics who argue that Bourdieu's integration of field and habitus is deterministic tend to point toward what queer theorist Judith Butler calls two levels of "inclination." On the one hand, the habitus is inclined to adapt to the imminent demands of an objectively structured field. On the other hand, objectively structured fields are inclined to present certain opportunities and barriers and not others. That is, fields such as the economy, cultural fields, and so on develop according to—though not completely determined by—their own internal logic. This double inclination might manifest, for example, in children of working-class parents feeling inclined to pursue educational and career strategies (attend technical colleges rather than Ivy League universities) based on dispositions incorporated through exposure to working-class conditions. Prolonged exposure to objective conditions produces a sense of the game and therefore a set of strategies based on the anticipated development of those objective conditions. In essence, Butler argues, Bourdieu's model is deterministic insofar as habitus shapes fields, which in turn shape habitus.[44]

If critics are correct in their assessment of determinism, then Bourdieu's attempt to account for strategic, practical thinking is nothing more than a fancied up, more nuanced version of rational choice. Worse, a deterministic read of Bourdieu would not even permit actors the freedom to select ends that rational choice affords: all actors would, by their habitus, be predisposed to select particular ends and then predisposed to pursue the only strategy the field makes available. Given what I argued about conformity and adaptation in the previous section, it would then follow that change is impossible, as successful strategies would merely conform to, and thereby reproduce, existing conditions.

There are, however, ways out of this determinism. One could point, for example, to the centrality of capital to Bourdieu's theory of practice. Action cannot be understood solely in terms of field and disposition because practical thinking does not merely play out a disposition on an existing context;

it evaluates that context in terms of the strategies made possible by the stock of resources—including skills, insights, financial clout, social status, and any other relevant form of capital—that might be put to use. Capital introduces a significant degree of contingency into fields, precisely because distributions of capital are typically uneven. The fact that capital can be accumulated in various forms means that a strategy might play out not merely in the context of the field as it currently exists, but also the field as it might exist tomorrow or in a generation's time. So, while habitus and field might not incline someone to go to university (because it is not for them, because they can't afford it, because they didn't do well enough in lower levels of education), that does not forbid a strategy wherein, for example, they accumulate the economic resources to allow their offspring to pursue higher education.

Further, the partial nature of an actor's perception of the field and their own resources should not be underestimated. Actors' perceptions are partial in the sense that they are disposed toward appreciating certain goals and strategies, and also in the sense that they can never have a god's-eye view of a field or of the results of the multiple strategies that participants are pursuing at a given time. This means even the best-resourced strategies are prone to failure, which opens up new opportunities for challengers. It is often said in democratic systems that opposition parties do not defeat governments; governments defeat governments. This may be true of dominant actors generally. Any number of factors—conceit, wilful ignorance of external pressures on their domination (through, for example, technology or changing economic practices)—might foster errors that give dominated actors a bit more breathing room or that make dominated forms of capital a bit more valuable. Disposition, resource, and opportunity work together in highly contingent ways to make available a number of strategies, but practical reason does not select from them in the fully autonomous and omniscient manner that would make strategy selection a foregone conclusion. Capital and partiality intervene via practical reason to break the chain of dual inclination to which Butler objects.

Moreover, capital and the partiality of perception are not the only ways that contingency and uncertainty can creep in. In fact, psychoanalytic and discursive critics may be correct in arguing that habitus cannot adequately capture the ambivalence at the core of subject formation, and that therefore Bourdieu's understanding of how subjects adjust to fields and how power operates rests on a shaky foundation.[45] Pointing to the insights of queer theory, Beverley Skeggs notes:

> Bourdieu's terribly well organized habitus cannot encompass all the practices between gender and sexuality, the contradictions, plays, experimentations, swappings, ambiguities and passings both within gender and between gender and sexuality (which, of course, are always informed by class, race and age).[46]

Skeggs's point is well taken. Recall the twofold basis for adaptive learning at the core of the habitus: the ability to distinguish between self and other, and a willingness to renounce narcissistic self-love for amour propre gained through recognition. According to Bourdieu, this renunciation requires a willingness to submit to a "socialization of drives" through "a permanent transaction in which the child makes renunciations and sacrifices in exchange for testimonies of recognition, consideration and admiration."[47] The dispositions acquired through this renunciation and orientation toward authority allow the reproduction of political power, because they foster the fundamental docility incorporated through schooling, habitual submission to legal and other state apparatuses, and misrecognition of the arbitrary bases of authority.[48] However, this model cannot account for drives that refuse to be socialized into forms sanctioned by the family and other fields. Specifically, drives organized into queer desires—desires that are by definition contrary to logics of classification and evaluation that structure society-level sexual economies and that dispose their bearers toward practices that are not only devalued but also historically actively condemned and punished—would have to be treated, in Bourdieu's model, as permanently failed transactions. They are transactions in which renunciations and sacrifices are refused, denied, and perhaps merely pretended for the sake of recognition. This would figure queer desire as somehow intrinsically antisocial and install a heterosexual humanism as the threshold for subjectivity. Surely this is not Bourdieu's intention.

Perhaps, though, Bourdieu is best understood as treating the queer and psychoanalytic subject (constituted through repression, splitting, denial, sublimation, and so on) in the same way as he treats the phenomenological one (material, embodied, adaptive): as a contingent, historical product whose existing forms require historicization. The phenomenological and psychoanalytic subjects' historical character gives them a statistical regularity that is amenable to sociological and political analysis precisely because their potential for variation and irregularity does not detract from the concrete and non-arbitrary conditions that produce regularity and even regular variation. Indeed, Bourdieu explicitly argues that the statistical character of the "accidental" influences and events that shift agents from the social trajectory inscribed in their social origin as a field of possibilities means that a fraction of any class will end up on a higher or lower trajectory than the modal path of agents from similar backgrounds.[49]

The variations and ambiguities that queer theory centres, while Bourdieu's approach elides them, may be methodological remainders that demand attention for the sake of rounding out empirical findings. But treating such variations as mere methodological problems fails at the level of normative political analysis precisely because these regular variations are embodied by living— and often suffering—subjects. In fact, because their remainder status is made up of both statistical anomaly and hierarchical distributions of suffering and the resources needed to overcome suffering, the remainders provide an essential starting point for critiquing domination. In this sense, domination is not a closed, complete system. Reproduction is not a natural inevitability but the product of constant strategic deployment of resources to maintain the status quo on behalf of those who benefit from it. If, in this framework, queerness appears as antisocial, it is not opposed to sociality as such, just to forms of sociality that demand normalization and sameness as the price of admission.

The possibility of habitus's failure also lends a stake in the social world that Bourdieu himself may have underappreciated. The adaptive and anticipatory habitus that we explored in the previous section functions primarily because it is exposed to regularities in the world. However, the partiality of agents' perspectives means that they are also exposed to considerable uncertainty. It is, though, not a neutral uncertainty in the face of which someone might reasonably toss a coin. Particularly for those who are in dominated social positions, experimentation and adaptation are not a rote project for emotionally detached but curious subjects. For them, uncertainty is loaded with emotional dangers warning them that failure could have negative, even violent or traumatic consequences. Bourdieu's vision of attachment seems somewhat sterile in comparison to the punishments to which many groups are exposed.

Illusio, having a stake in the game, seems to be merely a question of habit in Bourdieu's work. Through mimesis and adaptation, a body comes to adopt a certain orientation toward fields and the actors and objects those fields contain. Through habit and unconscious recollection, this orientation produces affective responses manifesting as desire for the objects themselves, as well as gratification for having the object, or recognition and praise from actors in the space. But Bourdieu's casual hand-waving toward "various psychic processes" does more than conceal the mechanisms at work: it conceals the fundamental question of why we experiment, why we explore in the first place.

Without entirely adopting discursive or psychoanalytic frameworks, we might nonetheless accept that agents bear a fundamental incompleteness, an insatiability rooted not in our own overabundance of desires, but in a world incapable of providing individuals with complete psychic fulfillment. Indeed, it might be worth exploring—elsewhere—whether this incompleteness is a reflection of foundational trauma/separation (in keeping with psychoanalysis) or perhaps, in a more Adornian vein, a reflection of contradictions within the social world itself. That is, a subject's insatiability may be a symptom of a broader system of insatiability and unsettledness that the habitus embodies.

What Bourdieu's sociology does offer, however, is attention to the divergent resources that are available to pursue desires that exceed the rules of existing fields. We may all embody gaps and contradictions, as Skeggs suggests, but a central normative question remains. How do fields distribute the resources that are available to soothe these gaps and contradictions or to externalize the distress they produce? Such distributions determine what forms of economic, cultural, or perhaps psychic capital are available and whether cultural capital is available to expand our thinking about how to satisfy desire and how to understand our incompleteness. From another direction, thinking about the distribution of resources allows us to consider the costs that a disposition toward non-normative forms of soothing those gaps might impose, as well as the psychic costs imposed on queer desires and practices by heteronormative social relations. Similarly, we can consider the emotional tolls that poverty—whether externally imposed or as a refusal to conform to capitalist economic demands—exacts from economic dissidents.

In a more Nietzschean vein, however, we might also ask: Why completeness? Why satiability?[50] It is tempting to treat desire as a relationship between goal and satisfaction; desire orients action—exploration, adaptation—toward resolving incompleteness and encourages us to look at the resources available to do so. Conformity, the logic of obeying rules, consciously or not, in order to obtain an object or status, sneaks in when we should possibly be inquiring after failure. What might be the affective experience of a drive to failure rather than to success? Failure may have hidden benefits for community, for politics, and for life. Put another way, failure might avoid some of the costs to life and community that conformity bears.

Even more, because our ability to act on the world (via habitus) depends on our possession of dispositions adapted to the world, and because these adaptations are to a world that is hierarchically organized and its durability is ensured by our misrecognition of the morally arbitrary nature of this organization, failure offers the potential for a kind of Nietzschean evil: the evil that refuses the "good" of internalized and embodied regimes of authority, deference, and maldistribution. If oppression stifles or even destroys some part of what it means to be fully human, then agents find themselves in a double bind: failure offers a path toward recouping what is lost, but conformity provides the means to travel that path. Thus, while Bourdieu may have been on methodologically solid ground to treat the gaps and contradictions as statistical outliers, breaks and failures should not be ruled out as bearing equal moral value to that of conformity. On its own terms, neither conformity nor failure is morally preferable.

Habitus is adaptive and anticipatory. In most cases, habitus conforms to various fields' morally arbitrary schemes of classifications in exchange for recognition and the opportunity to accumulate a field's particular form of capital. Emphasizing the adaptive nature of habitus, its orientation toward recognition, lays the groundwork for understanding how exposed habitus-bearing agents are to the dominating effects of symbolic power.

My interest is in the fact that although the generative nature of habitus makes action theoretically infinite, the practical constraints imposed on agents severely restrict that theoretical horizon. The distance between theoretical possibility and practical opportunity is a measure of power. Power makes the theoretically infinite practically finite. Adaptation, strategy, and practical reason transform social space from a static objective structure into a dynamic object of unequal and often unfair contest over whose preferred meaning adheres to particular objects or practices, and the extent to which specific actions and possibilities are feasible for certain groups and individuals but not for others. Indeed, an agent's willingness to experiment and thereby develop novel strategies and adaptations may itself be contingent on the context of the experimentation (the stakes involved, the resources an agent can mobilize to reduce the impact of possible negative repercussions, and so on) as well as on how well disposed the agent is toward risk-taking and creative imagination. Invested in the pursuit of social recognition, of amour propre, the habitus-bearing agent is not a conditionless subject asserting its will within a social space, but the bearer of a conditioned set of dispositions and orientations struggling to gain recognition and—as we will see in the next two chapters, especially—struggling to reduce myriad forms of suffering. Therefore, both individual and collective capacities to impose limits on theoretically infinite practices and to establish social spaces that are more or less arbitrary, more or less hierarchical, and more or less dominated must be taken seriously as a central consideration of political action.

Bringing habitus, field, and capital to bear on social movement activities allows movement participants and observers to historicize the strategies by which agents transform the pursuit of amour propre and struggles over meaning into collective political struggles. Because broader patterns of domination, unequal distributions of capital, and rules of practice that are skewed in favour of the already-powerful pre-exist collectivization of identity and tactical selection, participants bring to movement processes unequal resources and skills, and conflicting orientations toward the kinds of social recognition that ought to be sought.

The dynamics of group and collective identity formation, as I will illustrate through reference to LGBT/Q movements, are bound up in normatively evaluable struggles over meaning undertaken by actors with vastly unequal distributions of skills and resources. Such struggles over meaning and definition are not neutral efforts to understand the truth of social fields but are value-laden efforts to impose an interpretation of those fields that supports particular strategies to accumulate symbolic power. Similarly, the symbolic terrain on which these struggles take place can be so uneven that oppositional politics become, in a sense, impossible. The capacity to experiment, to risk failure, and to overcome suffering is therefore as much at stake in social movement struggles as the specific claims that these movements make.

Collective Identity and Symbolic Power

> What I want to say can be summed up in a generative formula: every expression is an accommodation between an expressive interest and a censorship constituted by the field in which that expression is offered; and this accommodation is the product of a process of euphemization which may even result in silence, the extreme case of censored discourse. This euphemization leads the potential "author" to produce something which is a compromise formation, a combination of what there was to be said, which "needed" to be said, and what could be said, given the structure of a particular field.
>
> —Bourdieu, *Sociology in Question*[1]

Beyond "Getting Better"

In September 2010, the deaths by suicide of four American teenagers brought popular attention to the risk that queer youth face for self-harm and suicide, particularly, as in these cases, self-harm that is linked to bullying and anti-gay harassment.[2] The most visible response to these suicides was the It Gets Better Project, launched after sex-columnist Dan Savage and his partner Terry Miller uploaded a video to YouTube, with this central message:

> IT GETS BETTER. However bad it is now, it gets better, and it can get great, it can get awesome. Your life can be amazing, but you have to tough this period of it out and you have to live your life so that you can be around for it to get amazing.[3]

Within two years of Savage and Miller posting their video, over fifty thousand more videos had been posted in solidarity with queer youth, and It Gets Better had been branded and incorporated as a not-for-profit organization.[4] Beyond simply assuring young LGBT/Q people that a life exists beyond high school bullying, It Gets Better became an important site for fundraising, networking, supporting the development of Gay-Straight Alliances in high schools, and constructing anti-gay bullying as a social problem and legitimate target for political and cultural action. Certainly, few doubt the heartfelt intentions that underpin the project.

Queer critics—especially racialized and working-class critics—were immediately sceptical of It Gets Better. Most of these critics point out the narrow range of LGBT/Q people for whom life does get better after high school.[5] The assurance that things get better resounds differently for racialized queers, working-class queers and queers living in poverty, queers with disabilities, trans and non-binary queers, and myriad other people experiencing intersecting structures of marginalization. For many, the supposedly inevitable path from homophobic torment to a fabulous urban gay lifestyle is fraught with obstacles, detours, and exorbitant tolls. What's more, fitting into the increasingly homogenized, sanitized, and consumption-driven gay and lesbian spaces that are currently on offer promises to replace bullying and harassment at the hands of homophobic peers with new forms of exclusions, new humiliations, and new forms of domination within racial, gender, and aesthetic hierarchies—often from the very people who tearfully uploaded promises that things get better.[6]

The campaign's founding video, for example, describes homophobic childhoods followed—and ostensibly overcome—by the romantic love, parenthood, and travel of the video's apparently gender-conforming and comfortably middle-class authors. Take this vignette, for example:

> So, I went out at four o'clock in the morning and strolled through the streets of Paris with DJ [Savage and Miller's son] as the sun came up. And we talked ... he was maybe five years old, maybe four and we chatted and strolled around Notre Dame and the Marais and the bakeries opened and we went to the back door of a bakery and ordered some croissants with sugar crystals on them. We got some juice and sat and watched the sun come up, the Eiffel Tower off in the distance, and it's one of my happiest memories.[7]

Savage's literally saccharine recollection of sugar-coated croissants weds the promise of successfully surviving the oppressions of youth and settling into an urban gay lifestyle to a privileged travel experience. In doing so, it reiterates the constructed connection between tourism, mobility, and gay identity noted by queer theorist Hiram Perez.[8] This connection is founded on "coming out" as a founding metaphor for gay transition from secrecy and shame to freedom and self-determination. Gay recreational travel represents a lifestyle-rooted affirmation that visibility and pride guarantee the formerly bullied teen an adulthood featuring liberated, cosmopolitan freedom. This trope of queer mobility, however, masks the matrix of privilege and material resources that mediate the journey from oppressed closet-dweller to liberated traveller. Queers who are prevented from, incapable of, or unwilling to make this journey fall outside the promise that it gets better.

For many, aspirations to leave behind childhood torments, to eclipse them with the Eiffel Tower and Parisian sunrises, conflict sharply with economic reality. A report by the Poverty and Employment Precarity in Southern

Ontario (PEPSO) research group suggests that as many as 50 per cent of people in Toronto—home to Canada's largest LGBT/Q community—are unable to find secure, predictable employment with wages above the poverty line. The likelihood of not finding secure employment is even higher for racialized groups and new Canadians.[9] While economic prospects are getting worse for many middle- and low-income LGBT/Q people, the cost of getting into the world of the "better"—rents, cover charges at bars, iPhones, gym memberships, and fashion—continues to rise.

Regardless of the good intentions motivating the It Gets Better Project, at best, whatever benefits accrue from the campaign have been unevenly distributed. At worst, the campaign reinforced a problematic homonormative and homonationalist reworking of lesbian and gay identities into neoliberal patterns of domination. It Gets Better is a microcosm of the ambiguous promises of the dominant gay and lesbian political strategy of the past two decades. The outrage sparked by the suicides may reflect a sense of indignity on the part of middle-class white men for whom fitting in was supposed to bring an end to homophobic suffering.[10] Moreover, the almost entirely aesthetic, video-based medium of the campaign provided minimal direct political challenge or material changes for bullied youth or racialized and working-class queers. What has been the point of decades of struggle for formal legal equality if not to make gay and lesbian lives bearable, or even celebratory and thriving? For liberationist and queer critics of the pursuit of formal equality at the expense of community building and grassroots organizing, unevenly distributed benefits and a reduction in the critical capacity of queer communities were exactly the dangers posed by the mainstream gay and lesbian movement.

There is no question that in many ways, things are better for many gays and lesbians in North America. At the minimum, decriminalization of the most typical forms of gay sex in Canada and the United States, widespread anti-discrimination legislation in Canada and growth of the same in the United States, and widespread popular culture visibility provide legal and cultural space for many gays and lesbians. Broader questions about the relationship between legal rights, cultural visibility, livability, and justice, though, are certainly more complex than a simple assertion that things are better. If nothing else, the ways in which things are better mask how continued criminalization of the poor, racial discrimination, employment inequities, and normalizing pressures on dissident sexual practices all impact the lives of LGBT and queer people in uneven ways. Indeed, QuAIA and BLM TO's interventions at Toronto's Pride Parades call attention to the ways in which colonization, racist police practices, and other forms of exclusion march on, despite formal legal equality.

Attention to these uneven experiences in relation to mainstream gay and lesbian political efforts takes its conceptual direction from critiques of homonormativity, which are themselves rooted in the queer theory that scholars and activists began articulating in the early 1990s. Queer theory and politics orient themselves toward "regimes of the normal" to identify and resist ways in which society is organized institutionally to support a narrow range of opposite-sex romantic and sexual practices while excluding, othering, and punishing all other practices. Critics of homonormativity point to how a similarly narrow range of "acceptable" same-sex romantic and sexual practices replicate heteronormative exclusions. In short, homonormativity effects its own form of normalization by eradicating, denying, and reducing forms of difference within LGBT communities, largely through self-policing. Homonormative erasure of difference is fundamentally driven by a desire—whether acknowledged or not—to be "normal" and thereby escape the stigma and suffering that come from being different. For example, the current gay and lesbian insistence that "love is love" is exemplary of homonormative fear of difference. For queers, loving in the face of oppression and violence is an accomplishment that is qualitatively different from the love experienced by people whose lives have always been condoned and supported by mainstream society. Many queers—myself included—experience the phrase "love is love" as devaluing a lifetime of resistance to being called sinful, perverted, self-indulgent, and otherwise unworthy of loving or being loved. It is particularly painful because this devaluation of our experience of difference comes from the very community that should be celebrating it.

In short, the political lynchpin of homonormativity is that the rights the LGBT community have fought so hard to achieve have too often been purchased by a willingness to demonstrate a capacity for and commitment to monogamous love that is "just like" heterosexual love, military service in support of nationalist and/or patriotic defences of western imperialism, and a general willingness to act as responsible citizens within neoliberal structures of accumulation, privatization, and governance. At its core, homonormativity unites two traditional elements of liberal inclusion: apolitical consumer lifestyles and juridical protections for gay and lesbian private spheres.[11]

If LGBT and queer communities have collectively journeyed from the era of closets and shame, through a collective coming out and demand for recognition, into an era of homonormativity, then where does that leave us today?

Where have we arrived, and with what kinds of lives? Who has been left to struggle along behind, and whose own reduced livability has paid the fare for the journey of the white, male, gender-conforming, able-bodied gay subject for whom things have gotten better? While many of these questions can be answered empirically, in this chapter I rely on habitus, field, and capital to produce a normative critique capable of tracing distortions in movement goals and outcomes to unequal distributions of skills and resources among movement participants.

As we saw in chapter two, collective identity captures the idea that groups of people can be more than aggregates of individuals who happen to share some characteristic such as gender, geography, or sexuality. Individuals come to see their shared characteristic as important, as somehow setting them apart from people who are not "like them." They also experience collective identity as a sort of lens through which they understand themselves and the world around them. Collective identity links personal experiences to the public realm. It encourages individuals to interpret their private, affective experiences as the product of shared objective conditions, while also, within those conditions, orienting them toward certain goals and away from others. Far from being the natural or objective implication of an individual's sense of self or identity, collective identity—and the lens it applies to identity-holders' emotional and rational interpretation of their surroundings—is the product of complex processes and interactions.

In the previous chapter, I described habitus as an adaptive capacity by which agents are oriented toward the possibilities and constraints offered by social fields. I emphasized how habitus conforms and how it fails in order to draw out some of its conceptual nuances—and problems—while drawing attention to the social and moral stakes borne by conformity and failure. In this chapter, I bring habitus more directly into the constellation of moral theory through the form of capital most closely associated with agents' dispositions: cultural capital. Cultural capital has numerous forms (including formal qualifications such as university degrees and legal recognition such as citizenship), but the species of cultural capital that is central to understanding the processes of collective identity is the set of practical skills and affective dispositions embodied through habitus. Cultural capital is intrinsically linked to the body and to the incorporated practical sense that dispositions provide.

In turn, cultural capital is closely linked to symbolic capital, symbolic power, and what Bourdieu calls *allodoxia*, the tendency of dominated agents to adopt the viewpoint and interests of the dominant and thereby submit to their own domination. Symbolic power is essential for understanding the justice claims I am developing, because it is the mechanism by which the hierarchical and morally arbitrary structures of fields operate directly on embodied agents, limiting and constraining some avenues of action while making others appear more desirable, more feasible, and more practical.[12] In the context of collective identity processes, cultural capital and symbolic power make practical reason something more than mechanical evaluations of resources and opportunities; practical reason is an interest- and power-laden schema of perception by which agents seek recognition for themselves and for their evaluation of a field of power.

Without the affective and historically structured lenses through which habitus orients agents toward fields, strategic thinking would be merely a formal intellectual exercise. Strategic thinking, in the Bourdieuian sense I am using, is fundamentally rooted in the inherent partiality of agents' perspective, a partiality that is derived from affective commitments and biases—hopes and desires, as well as fears and traumas—and the impossibility of achieving a god's-eye view of a field and its possibilities. Partiality in this sense imbues agents with a relative feeling of authority; it gives some agents a sense that one action is "for me," that it is okay to do or try, while for others the same action is not "for them." To an extent that cannot be overstated, partiality in practical reason influences action, and this influence is preconscious and embodied.

Practical reason and collective identity are linked insofar as collective identity collectivizes—or perhaps homogenizes—practical reason. Put another way, the purpose of collective identity is to facilitate mobilization by building consensus about what goals and what strategies are "for us." By making them appear as obvious as possible, by encouraging people to misrecognize socially constituted goals and strategies as objective and natural, movements free up valuable resources that can be put toward collective action. Thus movement participants may experience collective identity negotiations as neutral debates between diverse views and opinions. Since collective identity is rooted in at least a minimal commitment to togetherness, though, collective identity negotiations only masquerade as disinterested, as not relying on strategy and power. Precisely the opposite is true: movement participants mobilize cultural and symbolic power to see their own preferred vision for a collective identity triumph. As in any competition, the playing field is highly uneven. As a result, uneven distribution of the capital needed to succeed in internal struggles over collective identity produces distortions in movement goals, strategies, and outcomes.

For observers of social movements, collective identity's value is conceptual: it provides a language through which we can show that the supposedly obvious and natural connections that movements claim connect social location to political interest are in fact socially constituted goals and desires. Although demands for same-sex marriage, military service, and liberal equality rights have become nearly synonymous with gay and lesbian politics, there is no intrinsic link between access to same-sex marriage and a flourishing, better life. There are good arguments to support the lesbian and gay focus on marriage and equality, and there are good arguments to support queer efforts to destabilize the institutions that reward normalcy while punishing difference. Conceptually, collective identity lets us step back from these debates to evaluate how a movement prioritizes some goals over others and how, as in the case of same-sex marriage, some goals are made to appear to be so obvious, so natural that their desirability becomes nearly beyond debate.

For movements themselves, the conceptual nature of collective identity is overshadowed by its functional role. A collective identity orients its bearers within a field of struggle and motivates participation in specific political projects. It provides those who share the identity with an account of why they experience suffering, what remedies would address that suffering, and what strategies are most feasible for achieving those remedies. By encouraging individuals with shared identities to see their interests as either identical with or closely aligned to group interests, it fosters a sense of solidarity. It can also provide psychic energy and affective desire to participate, to do something; it is therefore key for mobilization. Social movement researchers need to be sensitive to how collective identities select goals (marriage versus cultural subversion, for example), but also to when and to what degree collective identities are used to foster mobilization, and when constructing collective identities is a means of opening new cultural or political space without reference to a specific goal.[13] The It Gets Better campaign, for example, has led to calls for specific measures against bullying, but its prime function was to construct a shared sense of identity among LGBT youth around a shared experience of suffering harassment as youth but then escaping into a liberated, less-harassed adulthood. The campaign gives youth a particular narrative through which to interpret their experience, and it uses the affective intensity of suicide to mobilize movement participants of all ages toward creating a cultural space in which young queers can survive.

I turn to LGBT/Q movements to illustrate the connection between broad patterns of domination, uneven distributions of cultural capital, and collective identity processes for two reasons. First, because as the It Gets Better campaign amply illustrates, LGBT/Q movements have been simultaneously successful and disastrous; they conform *and* they fail. Second, as a form of identity politics, they are representative of many tasks common to other identity-based movements, namely the arduous work of simply carving out some space for LGBT/Q people to feel like life itself is "for me." LGBT/Q personal and political narratives are rife with personal and collective struggles to assert that that someone "like me" could even exist:

> How can I tell you. How can I convince you, brother, sister that your life is in danger: That every day you wake up alive, relatively happy, and a functioning human being, you are committing a rebellious act. You as an alive and functioning queer are a revolutionary. There is nothing on this planet that validates, protects or encourages your existence. It is a miracle you are standing here reading these words. You should by all rights be dead.[14]

The urgent need to defend even the right to live has, obviously, never been unique to LGBT/Q lives. Consider, for example, Audre Lorde's vivid description of the "societal death wish" directed against Black women in America from their moment of birth:

> From that moment on we have been steeped in hatred—for our color, for our sex, for our effrontery in daring to presume we had any right to live.... We are Black women born into a society of entrenched loathing and contempt for whatever is Black and female. We are strong and enduring. We are also deeply scarred.[15]

When a group or individual is beaten down, when we feel like we don't even have the right to exist, strategic thinking takes on a decidedly problematic flavour. If the capacity to act is not merely a question of technical ability but also of social authority, then resistance becomes more than a question of what weapons are available, or what tools can be mobilized to build alternatives. It is, fundamentally, a question of how diverse visions of what is "for us" get structured into concrete movement goals and strategies. The connection between the durable feeling that life is not "for us" and practical reason is not unique to LGBT/Q political history, but it is particularly strong there. What's more, the intersecting forms of hate faced by queers of colour and the backlash from white gays and lesbians against BLM TO show that the question of what is "for us" cannot be divorced from the question of who counts among us.

Naturally, collective identity is only one portion of the complexly layered processes by which LGBT/Q lives and politics have struggled against homophobia, heterosexism, and the myriad other institutional and cultural mechanisms by which sexualities are produced and regulated. Indeed, it is only a part of the broader context within which movement successes—whether it has gotten better—can be measured. Further, the central questions collective identities seek to answer are questions with which all social movements struggle (including the alterglobalization movement, whose repertoire of contention I will consider in more detail in the next chapter). Nonetheless, struggles over LGBT/Q collective identities offer particularly salient illustrations of how processes of collective identity construction replicate broad patterns of domination and injustice and, through the strategies these constructions inform and motivate, transmit those patterns of domination and injustice into the new possibilities for identification and subjectivity that social movements produce in the long run.

The following analysis juxtaposes two ways of understanding and critiquing queer collective identity to show that, because each tells only part of the same story, neither is complete. The critique I offer attends to how movement participants mobilize cultural and other forms of capital in the construction of collective identities; it therefore draws out new connections between processes of collective identity construction and considerations of justice. I argue that mainstream social movement approaches to collective identity are overly mechanistic and lack much-needed normative content. By contrast, queer critiques of the normalizing tendencies of gay and lesbian collective identities are overly discursive and overly reliant on unspecified causal assumptions. By linking struggles over capital to collective identity formation, I focus on the symbolic and epistemic violence that is endemic to collective identity processes.

The chapter ends with an effort to move beyond critique of mainstream gay and lesbian politics to show that understanding collective identity through the lens of symbolic violence also moves us away from queer objections based on normalization. Foucault and Butler, in particular, have provided considerable intellectual inspiration for queer challengers to gay and lesbian dominance and the homogeneity that formal equality promises. However, queer theorists working in this trajectory make the additional claim that because the homogeneity that normalization pursues is impossible, the necessary abjection and inclusion of certain lives is a constitutive feature of both modern power and the rights discourse on which LGBT politics have relied. This wrongly promises a politics of subversion and failure as a mode of resistance.

The Bourdieuian conception of power that I rely on, by contrast, draws attention to the relationships that symbolic fields produce among power, submission, and action. Symbolic fields impose distinctions between various social positions, and those positions permit unequal possibilities for action. This conception points toward the power of success in contrast to queer failures, and permits analysis of the ethical content of collective identities. That is, it permits treating collective identity as a site of justice, which is a separate project from treating collective identities as instrumental either in the sense of traditional movement outcomes (policy change) or the kinds of outcomes associated with new social movement theory and, implicitly, anti-normalization critics (cultural change, affirmation of self—that is, improved subjective sense). Further, collective identities are sites of justice where the conditions of justice—the background conditions within which individuals come together to understand and ameliorate suffering—tend predominantly to reproduce existing inequalities in complex and problematic ways. In turn, collective identities therefore become lenses through which we can critique existing patterns of domination, in part through the extent to which they produce and reproduce themselves in those collective identities.

Epistemic Violence

Fundamentally, collective identity entails constructing a sub-episteme: a way of knowing (episteme) about suffering that diverges from or contradicts dominant ways of knowing, precisely because dominant epistemes explicitly legitimate suffering, render suffering invisible, or construct suffering as a non-problem. For example, in the 1980s homophobic accusations that AIDS is a punishment for queers were based on an episteme that connected AIDS's genesis and transmission to a lifestyle rather than to a virus. This episteme—and the years of delay between the emergence of the virus and official support for researching and treating it—offers a deadly example of how ways of knowing can give suffering official legitimacy. Similarly, neoliberal constructions of poverty and exclusion as the fault of the poor and the excluded, and a reflection of their supposed lack of marketable merits, exclude economic suffering from political contention by rendering it a non-political, fault-based form of suffering.

Collective identities challenge dominant ways of knowing, offering alternative connections between culture, science, and law on the one hand and the experience of suffering and oppression on the other. However, not all oppositional ways of knowing are equally valuable. The mere presence of challenges to dominant epistemes, to dominant ways of recognizing or erasing suffering, tells us little about the correctness or usefulness of that way of knowing. In political terms, the mere existence of a collective identity tells us little about whether the challenges that that identity presents to dominant relations of power will tend to alter those relations in a direction that is more or less just.

In a community that is marked by multiple forms of difference, LGBT/Q political divisions have tended to fall along one side or the other of a central question: whether LGBT/Q people are better served through formal equality (branded "assimilationist" by its detractors) or by challenging normalcy and conformity more generally (a perspective opponents consider radical and alien to mainstream interests). These partisan debates are important, but they have rarely been undertaken as a purely rational exchange of ideas. Rather, these debates—and the success or failure of arguments within them—have been shaped by durable social fields that unevenly distribute cultural capital, dispositions, and opportunities to advocate for one position or another. Therefore, rather than simply evaluating the merits behind the arguments, critical analysis of social movement politics needs to look at aspects of social existence that structure collective identity formation and their associated political projects.

To fully appreciate collective identity as both a site of justice and a device for critiquing patterns of domination, two philosophical shifts are necessary: we must escape liberal humanist assumptions about the equality of participants in collective identity negotiations, and we must insist upon the centrality of epistemic violence within collective identity processes. To escape liberal assumptions about equality, let us first distinguish between moral and practical equality. Liberal political philosophy is particularly invested in equating personhood to viable political participation. Yet, conflating moral equality with an equal distribution of the skills, dispositions, and capacities required to participate effectively in political settings and negotiations ignores the effects on disposition and cultural capital of living under durable conditions of suffering.

For example, the suffering that LGBT/Q people experience because of their sexual or gender "difference" is a durable experience of exclusion. It can be expected to produce a legitimate orientation toward alleviating that suffering in the most expedient means available, even if—to queer and liberationist dismay—the most expedient means is to reduce the appearance of difference rather than to elevate difference's devalued status. In this sense, many LGBT/Q people come to what appear to be negotiations over collective identity with dispositions that are already shaped by the durable experience of embodying a devalued cultural status, and they are therefore prone to colluding with existing relations of symbolic power through difference-reducing strategies. These dispositions fundamentally impinge upon whether a particular sub-episteme will resonate and whether arguments in favour of that episteme will be successful. As Bourdieu argues in his critique of aesthetic universalism:

> One cannot, in fact, without contradiction, describe (or denounce) the inhuman conditions of existence that are imposed on some, and at the same time credit those who suffer them with the real fulfilment of human potentialities such as the capacity to adopt the gratuitous, disinterested posture that we tacitly inscribe—because it is socially inscribed there—in notions of "culture" or "aesthetic."[16]

In terms of collective identity, what is true of the cultural and the aesthetic is also true of political practice. The inhuman conditions against which queers struggle are loathsome precisely because they prevent those who suffer and who resist those conditions from achieving their full potential, whatever it might be. To be clear, I am not suggesting that people who are highly excluded or highly marginalized are not capable of political thought and practice, nor do I intend to erase the active negotiation of social spaces undertaken by any social agent. I am arguing that the durable conditions in which the most dominated groups exist—the conditions faced by those queers for whom things have not gotten better because of their race, class, gender identity, or sexual practices—do little to provide the cultural, material, and affective resources necessary to resist symbolic domination and to impose a queer vision of the world on movement organizations.

One mechanism of racism, for example, is to devalue the modes of speaking and presentation through which racialized groups express themselves. Such symbolic devaluation prevents critiques from registering within officially legitimate discourse. This devaluation allows white people to ignore or reject arguments about racism through a sort of proxy rejection of how people of colour express themselves. In short, it is particularly pernicious to conflate moral and practical equality, because doing so erases the inequalities that mitigate practical outcomes and thereby characterizes practically disadvantaged actors as morally culpable for their own disadvantage. Whether in democratic decision-making processes, collective identity formation, or myriad other realms of supposed practical equality, moral equality provides no shield against the subtle yet brutal strategies available to those better endowed with the skills, dispositions, social authority and other resources needed to navigate hierarchical social and political fields.

If we refuse to equate moral equality with practical equality, we are forced onto the terrain of practical difference. To account for the mechanisms of that difference, I turn to Bourdieu's somewhat idiosyncratic conception of capital. Capital—the context-appropriate resources available to agents to mobilize within a particular field—links habitus to fields by giving actions a weight or force that is not explainable with reference to the action itself.[17] If actions lacked such force, the world would be reduced to a game of roulette where, just as every bet placed at every spin of the wheel would have equal chance of success, every action would have an equal effect on the world. Clearly, some actions have more impact on their surroundings than others and, more importantly, similar actions by different agents have highly unequal success rates. Further, as a resource underpinning practical strategies within social fields, agents nearly always use capital to accumulate further capital and thereby expand the practical strategies available to them. That is, agents make use of some resources (money, skills, qualifications, and so on) to acquire more.

Embodied cultural capital, in the form of habitus, can be thought of as an agent's biographically specific but contextually structured set of skills. As such, skills are not evenly or uniformly distributed, because the rarest and most useful skills—the skills that are therefore most valuable—require access to familial, educational, and employment contexts where such skills can be mimetically acquired, learned, and often produced through adaptation and adjustment. These skills are the core of the practical political inequality that we need to distinguish from moral equality. Aside from the obvious usefulness of economic and social capital in navigating political terrains, some movement participants gain concrete advantages through cultural capital manifested through, for example, the ability to communicate articulately (verbally and through professional-appearing literature), comfort dealing with elected officials, and familiarity with navigating seemingly neutral organizational practices such as rules of order.

Feminist theorist Jane Ward gives an insightful analysis of how unequal cultural capital can function within movement organizations when there is an influx of "skilled" professionals bearing significant amounts of specific cultural competencies. Looking at the depoliticization of the Christopher Street West Pride Celebration in Los Angeles, she traces how, when the festival ran into financial and operational difficulties, the predominantly working-class board was made to feel unskilled, unprofessional, and unworthy of municipal funding for the pride festivities. Note, however, that skill, professionalism, and financial responsibility are far cries from alternative measures of the qualities that members of a pride board should have. Queers and liberationists, for example, might be expected to value a board member's capacity for community inclusion, their independent thinking, and their commitment to organizational autonomy, as well as their progressive and liberatory political commitments. Nonetheless, Ward's Bourdieuian analysis of the class conflict around the organization of pride celebrations in West Hollywood found that middle- and upper-class efforts to match expressions of pride to their own consumer lifestyles have been articulated as a fundamentally apolitical desire for professionalism in pride festival organization. The result was part of a broader North American trend wherein pride celebrations are becoming decreasingly political.[18]

Queer activists, who have reason to resist this depoliticization, point to how depoliticization is rendered invisible by organizational shifts that legitimate concerns for professionalism and financial responsibility. Often these professionalizing shifts are implicitly supported by community members who are disposed to accumulating the type of capital that conforms with neoliberal visions of good citizenship. For many, this means replacing a vision of pride as a political response to homophobia with a vision of pride celebrations as "positive" cultural festivals that ought to be professionally managed.[19] The benefit of recognition is relief from the enduring devaluation of one's identity. The cost is conformity to a field that depoliticizes and deradicalizes community organization under the ostensibly neutral guise of better organizing and better marketing. "It gets better" by becoming aesthetically pleasing and politically non-threatening.

The skewed nature of the rules of social fields, their tendency to attribute legitimacy to some actions and not to others, is a key form of capital: symbolic capital. Unlike other forms, symbolic capital is less directly a resource. Rather, it is a relation of recognition underpinning symbolic power, the efficacy of which rests on the fundamentally arbitrary nature of fields.[20] Of course, social fields are not historically arbitrary; they are the products of historical struggles over positions within spaces and the rules by which positions are taken. That is, fields are not arbitrary in the way that the spin of a roulette wheel is arbitrary. Fields are, however, *morally* arbitrary insofar as what counts as good or bad, as appropriate or inappropriate, in a given field reflects the historical construction of that object or practice in a space rather than the inherent moral value of an object or practice.

Symbolic power emerges whenever the arbitrary nature of a field's structure and rules is forgotten and misrecognized as natural, and therefore preconsciously accepted as the unthought premises of social interaction, which Bourdieu calls *doxa*. In such conditions, the judgments of dominant agents are accepted—often in advance, through anticipation—by dominated agents, even when those judgments are contrary to the dominated agents' interest. Conceivably, anyone in a field could challenge another's actions by decrying them as arbitrary and of no more moral value than a spin of a roulette wheel. That we rarely do this is a sign that we have come to recognize the actions and the capital supporting those actions as legitimate.

Bourdieu emphasizes the bodily nature of this acceptance and indeed its foundation in preconscious embodied dispositions, organized in the habitus. Symbolic power works by triggering the dispositions in the habitus and thereby provoking a specific response. These responses are most powerful when they indicate a tacit acceptance of the limits that social reality imposes. This acceptance often manifests in bodily emotion (shame, timidity, anxiety, guilt), which is particularly effective in intervening on evaluations of desire and opportunity and deeply rooted in the bodily experiences of childhood.[21] The visible manifestations of submission to dominant judgments can include blushing, inarticulacy, clumsiness, and trembling, but the real power of the symbolic lies in the emotions behind these visible responses.[22] As with habitus, field, and capital, emotional responses are not merely random responses to passing experiences: they express structured, durable relations to social fields.

For good reason, social movement literature is also beginning to pay attention to emotional dynamics. The emotional potency of social movement processes, including collective identity construction, demands to be taken seriously.[23] The structured production of these emotions, however, is marked by power and shaped by the unequal ability of some movement participants to martial pre-existing resources in various forms of capital in morally arbitrary but historically constrained directions. For all social movements, but perhaps particularly for movements rooted in resistance to stigmatized identities, the strategies and unequal resources deployed to direct and transform emotions strongly contradict the neutral language of "negotiation" on which much of collective identity theory depends. The automatic, preconscious, and bodily nature of shame, fear, timidity, and on the other side, aggression, entitlement, and confidence subverts and undoes the rational aspects of debates over movement goals and strategies.

Three concepts at the core of the symbolic are particularly useful in this analysis:

- Symbolic power is the ability to make use of the morally arbitrary rules and distinctions of social space that are to your advantage. In anti-oppression frameworks, this is thought of as privilege and it can operate just as unconsciously as privilege does. So, for example, cisgender individuals make use of naturalized distinctions about bodies and gender in order to have relatively easy access to identification, medical care, and—a recent focus of transphobic politics—bathrooms.[24] Because this ease goes unnoticed, the symbolic power enjoyed here is both an objective benefit and a subjective misrecognition of the fact that it is benefit. Symbolic power entails naturalizing that benefit and deriving psychic comfort from enjoying a world constructed for the sort of person you are. Symbolic power is perhaps most pernicious when agents who are disadvantaged by naturalized, arbitrary rules and distinctions within the social order fail to recognize the arbitrary disadvantages to which they are subjected. Again, Bourdieu calls this phenomenon allodoxia: "mistakenly recognizing oneself in a particular form of representation and public enunciation of the *doxa*."[25]

- Symbolic capital is the recognition agents receive when they perform technically correct and contextually appropriate actions in social space. Agents accumulate symbolic capital in the most banal settings—using the proper fork in a fancy restaurant, or addressing an employer with appropriate deference—but also through technically correct and contextually appropriate use of rhetorical devices and arguments in political debates.[26] The arbitrary rules and divisions of social space extend to what kinds of arguments are viable in a given context, who is able to deploy those arguments persuasively, and which benefits accrue from making them. (I develop this argument further, below.)

- Finally, symbolic violence is the parallel experience of feeling out of place, anxious, awkward, shamed, stupid, and so on because—and this is important—those who experience symbolic violence are both objectively unable to construct appropriate actions (because the resources necessary to do so are unavailable to them) and subjectively committed to, in the sense of recognizing, the very rules of distinction by which they are excluded and dominated. Symbolic violence consists of both the objective hardship and the subjective experience of self-blame, hesitation, self-censorship, and so on.

In the context of collective identity, symbolic power and violence may manifest as a form of epistemic violence. Epistemic violence, generally, refers to the relations of power that allow certain ways of knowing while marginalizing and excluding others. By extension, some ways of knowing authorize "correct" ways of living or of organizing social relations. These authorized ways of living and relating accrue benefits to some groups at the expense of others. If the knowledge in question relates to a collective identity, then excluding some ways of knowing what it means to share in that identity will distort identity-based political projects and claims for justice.

Gayatri Chakravorty Spivak's groundbreaking analysis of epistemic violence demonstrates that even critical intellectuals—Foucault and Gilles Deleuze are her main targets—can remain bound up in imperialist narratives.[27] Following Spivak, the concept of epistemic violence has been taken up in ways that are highly relevant to LGBT/Q collective identity formation. Black feminists such as Patricia Hill Collins and Kristie Dotson have provided invaluable insights into the mechanisms of epistemic violence. The violence they identify takes a number of forms. Dotson points, for example, to "pernicious ignorance," wherein an audience intentionally or unintentionally refuses to communicatively reciprocate with a speaker, producing cognitive gaps and misunderstanding. In the terms I have been using, pernicious ignorance results when an audience is not disposed (via their habitus) to recognize the authority of a speaker, because that speaker lacks the cultural, political, or other capital necessary to establish themselves as legitimately worth hearing. In the face of pernicious ignorance, a speaker may choose to "smother" (restrict or truncate) their testimony because they perceive an audience as unwilling or unable to understand what they want to say. The content may be unsafe or risky, as when speaking about intragroup problems that might be expected to unfairly reinforce negative stereotypes (for example, domestic violence within African American communities); or the conditions for speaking may become unsafe as when an audience finds a testimony to be unintelligible and responds through micro-aggressions (aversive racism; micro-invalidations, micro-insults), which are subtle, possibly non-conscious, non-intentional indications that the audience is unduly sceptical about a speaker's claims.

Again, the affective power of adaptation and anticipation clearly intervenes on what is supposed to be a rational exchange of information and perspectives. Testimonial smothering is closely related to a second quieting of testimony, which occurs when an audience refuses to recognize the speaker's epistemological competence. Before a Black woman is even able to speak, her testimony is disallowed by audiences disposed to overshadow her credibility with what Collins calls the "controlling images" by which Black women are interpreted (mammies, matriarchs, welfare mothers).[28]

A clear parallel exists here with Bourdieu's analysis of linguistic exchange. For Bourdieu, the ultimate measure of linguistic competency is the ability to create speech acts that are not only technically correct, but that are also couched in ways that are sufficiently appropriate to ensure their favourable reception:

> What is called tact or adroitness consists in the art of taking account of the relative positions of the sender and the receiver in the hierarchy of different kinds of capital, and also of sex and age, and of the limits inscribed in this relation, ritually transgressing them, if need be, by means of euphemization....[29]
>
> The definition of acceptability is found not in the situation but in the relationship between a market and a *habitus*, which itself is the product of the whole history of its relations with market.[30]

Every linguistic market—that is, every social space with relatively settled norms about "correct" ways of speaking—carries its own logic of accumulation. Speakers can utter the same phrase in two different contexts and find that in one case they receive approval and reward for the utterance while in another they receive scorn and rejection. Something as banal as a dinner invitation, Bourdieu points out, can be expressed in surprisingly divergent ways. "Where 'If you would do me the honour of coming' is appropriate, 'You ought to come' would be out of place because too off-hand, and 'Will you come?' would be distinctly 'crude.'"[31] Each formation is technically correct, but depending on who is speaking and the context of the invitation, some versions will be subtly or brutally rebuffed while others will be welcomed.

For the most part, linguistic exchanges work. Participants, through habitus, understand the rules and expectations, and they have varyingly sophisticated capacities to follow those rules and to capitalize on opportunities to bolster their position within social hierarchies. Because participants are also heavily invested in the exchange, they are also willing to resort to neutralized, inoffensive language to maintain the structure of a particular linguistic market. They invoke "strategies of mutual accommodation" to maintain consensus about the rules of the exchange and the importance of observing those rules.[32] Put more strongly, in hierarchical settings, linguistic exchanges work because dominated speakers engage self-censorship, quieting, and other truncations in an effort to demonstrate sufficient linguistic capital to win a grudging, temporary recognition from their audience. What a speaker experiencing symbolic/epistemic violence wants to say is not what they end up saying. In the interest of conforming to the rules of a linguistic context, they more or less distort the idea they had hoped to communicate. Most of this occurs preconsciously.

To produce political speech and self-representations, political agents must accomplish two tasks: they must construct technically correct and politically persuasive arguments, and they must do so in a way that is acceptable, or palatable, for the listener. As with any exchange involving symbolic power, the cultural and symbolic capital that is necessary to accomplish these tasks is not uniformly distributed. Self-silencing in the form of euphemization, and in the context of a meeting, quieting in the form of micro-aggressions—dismissive language, intimidation, use of rules of order to prevent speaking, and so on—translate symbolic power into epistemic violence.

In many movement spaces where collective identities are negotiated, fear and shame silence potential speakers. This fear and shame is not a moral shortcoming of the speaker, but a legitimate response to a symbolic space that is constructed to intimidate and exclude those who are not already authorized to speak. It is exacerbated by an audience that is not disposed to lend credibility to voices and arguments that don't already resonate with their own dispositions. Just as professionalization masks patterns of depoliticization within pride organizations, collective identity processes use highly constrained criteria of what constitutes a good argument to present as neutral what is actually a highly exclusionary epistemic scene. As a process of distorted negotiations over the meaning of suffering and its remedy, collective identity production is structured by a circulation of cultural and symbolic capital that legitimizes and misrecognizes arbitrary authority as a natural credibility. This circuit reproduces existing symbolic distinctions within debates over identity and thereby rewards the already well positioned with new sources of symbolic and political capital.

We can label such circuits as epistemic injustice, where credibility accrues to individuals on the basis of their social location and capital rather than on the merit of the knowledge they produce. In short, some individuals (or groups) who ought to be conferred credibility are not, while others benefit from unearned credibility.[33] Insofar as collective identities articulate a sub-episteme to a set of tactics, strategies, and movement goals, any epistemic injustice within the construction of that sub-episteme can act as a proxy for injustice within those tactics, strategies, and goals. This implies the need for a proceduralist conception of justice that is capable of eliminating epistemic violence, rather than the substantive justice claims made by many proponents of LGBT/Q politics. It also points to the recursive nature of collective identity formation and challenge. As I discuss in chapter eight, BLM TO has been successful, in part, because they have collectivized and deployed forms of capital to resist epistemic injustice within Toronto's LGBT/Q communities.

LGBT/Q in North America

Bourdieu did not engage collective identity as an analytic tool. He chose instead to understand processes of group formation through delegation of the authority to speak on behalf of a group, and group members' submission to the spokesperson's political vision. As should be clear by now, delegation of the authority to speak on behalf of a group involves more than a simple show of hands to select a leader. Delegation is always the product of pre-existing struggles and distributions of various forms of capital—particularly cultural capital in the form of the ability to speak well, and political capital in the form of being able to produce successful political representations and actions. Analysis relying on field, capital, and habitus reveals group formation to depend upon repeated acts of symbolic power in which those who speak on behalf of a group have a disproportionate ability to impose their own conception of the group, its environment, and its chances on the group itself.

> What is at stake here is the power of imposing a vision of the social world through principles of di-vision which, when they are imposed

on a whole group, establish meaning and a consensus about meaning, and in particular about the identity and unity of the group, which creates the reality of the unity and the identity of the group.[34]

A Bourdieuian analysis of LGBT/Q politics gains explanatory leverage from identifying the operation of symbolic power and symbolic domination. Hints of these dynamics can be found in Tom Warner's detailed account of Canadian queer activism, particularly in the experience of lesbians in gay male–dominated movement organizations. Warner cites lesbian activists' sense of loneliness, isolation, and powerlessness within movement groups and, tellingly, their frustration at "the conditioning that makes us collude with men in discounting our own experience, our own skills, that makes us feel strangers to power and the use of money."[35] Elsewhere, Warner implicitly links socio-economic status to interest, as for example in the flooding of the liberationist Coalition for Lesbian and Gay Rights in Ontario (CLGRO) with lawyers, civil servants, and professionals interested in relationship recognition, in contrast to lesbians and gays of colour, on low incomes, or with disabilities.[36] The influx of professionals into grassroots liberationist organizations enacted manifestations of symbolic violence in the form of an often unarticulated sense that something has gone wrong, that the debate has shifted or the rug has been pulled out from under early organizers.[37] The shifting of the debate or the reorientation of movement goals was not necessarily the product of a reasoned, objectively reached consensus, though it may have had that formal appearance.

Shifts in movement goals and strategies cannot simply be attributed to the differences in habitus and cultural capital of movement participants. Indeed, Warner's analysis also points to the ways in which the assimilationist orientation of professionals within the movement, much to the chagrin of liberationists, resonated with

> a deep-rooted desire on the part of individual gays, lesbians, and bisexuals—still reviled and viewed as deviant—to achieve mainstream respectability and legitimacy, to have same-sex relationships seen as the same as heterosexual ones—as conventional families—and to be valued in the same way. It was a powerful motivator for the masses of gays, lesbians, and bisexuals who were not politically aware and who had no analysis beyond wanting to make their lives better and to have discrimination removed.[38]

This observation captures the collusion intrinsic to symbolic violence. The flip side of a concern for depoliticization and assimilation is a concern for the ways in which acceding to dominant points of view, norms, and patterns of interaction can relieve suffering in the short run and improve an otherwise dominated position. There is a paradoxical relationship between submission and resistance: if a person's social identity meets with reproach and disapproval (which is to say, with symbolic violence), then it seems obvious that adjusting how they inhabit that identity might diminish their exposure to symbolic violence, even though this strategy—a manifestation of allodoxia—reinforces the symbolic power it seeks to evade. Such adjustments in defence against symbolic violence may explain some of the more assimilationist tactics recommended by certain movement participants. Consider, for example, the complaint, common among assimilationist gays, that media coverage of pride parades gives undue attention to drag queens, nudists, and leather folk. Submission to symbolic violence may also give strategic legitimacy to various versions of "we should be more like straight people" strategies in pursuit of equal rights. Advocates of such strategies for reducing symbolic violence tend to be most vocal around issues of public sexuality.

For example, on June 13, 1999, members of Toronto's 52nd police division raided a somewhat infamous "porn bar" called The Bijou. Toronto's *fab magazine* (which called itself Toronto's Gay Scene Magazine and at the time claimed a circulation of 45,000 readers) gave the raid no news coverage, raising the issue only in its editorial comments and letters to the editor. In his editorial "Just John," *fab* editor John Kennedy argued that the police were justified in raiding the establishment.

> All along our journey in search of respect and equality we assured the rest of society that we didn't want "special" rights, we simply wanted "equal" rights. Now that we have most of the same rights, some of us are asking for special rights—the right to ignore municipal bylaws and liquor regulations, the right to break the laws of the criminal code, and the right to be overlooked during enforcement of these rules.[39]

Kennedy argued that what were dubbed "raids" by some were merely routine investigations. To the extent that this was true, Kennedy argues, police superintendent Aiden Maher was correct to claim that the police could not ignore the public (and therefore illegal) sexual activities occurring in The Bijou. Kennedy's framing of gay collective identity continued in the editorial:

> I think most rational gay men are pleased that police are doing their job and making sure that all businesses—including those gays patronize—are operating within the law. You can bet if 12 men had been killed in a fire at *The Bijou* because it wasn't meeting the requirements of the Fire Act, *Xtra!* [an LGBT newspaper in Toronto that had been critical of the raids] would be criticizing these same officials for overlooking a gay business.[40]

Several significant claims are made in Kennedy's editorial. First, Kennedy invokes previous collective action as a unified "search [for] respect and equality," as though those were the two pivotal demands of a movement reducible to an identifiable "we." Second, Kennedy seems to make an implicit moral judgment about "rationality" and then posits a dichotomy between (rational) gay men who support the police action and those (irrational) gay men who do not. Kennedy's collective identity claim was this: "we" (gay men) are citizens in the same way as anyone else (that is, straight people) and therefore our cultural behaviours (sexual practices) should coincide with certain heterosexual norms (restriction of sexual contact to private locations). This denies a conflict between gay cultural networks and heterosexual legislation, erasing cultural difference behind a claim of moral and ethical equality. Gay men are, in Kennedy's view, expected to identify with heterosexual, monogamous sexual norms.

More recently, Sam Sotiropoulos, then a straight Toronto District School Board trustee, prepared a motion asking that the Toronto Pride Committee ensure that there would be no nudity at the 2014 Pride Parade.[41] His intended goal was to make the event more family-friendly and age appropriate (for Toronto students). Plenty of gays and lesbians in various social media echoed Kennedy's now decade-old claims, some suggesting that nudity was not necessary, is potentially harmful, and constitutes a "special" right. As with Kennedy's support of police raids of The Bijou, LGBT opponents of public nudity at the Pride Parade sought to distance themselves from stigmatized forms of gender and sexual expression, an implicit strategy to reduce discrimination by reducing exposure to symbolic violence.

Opponents of such strategies generally point out that adopting a normalized habitus is not more liberating than being an object of disgust and vilification. Further, they suggest that while adopting a normalized habitus might be liberating for the individual, it can hardly be expected to promote systematic transformation to relations of symbolic power.[42] The deep-rooted desire for recognition held by mainstream gays and lesbians reflects accession to the dominant distribution of symbolic power and motivates the adoption of normalized habitus to reduce the distinctions between gay and lesbian individuals and symbolically more valued heterosexuals. Symbolic power, in the form of a willingness to gain emotional comfort through improved social position, functioned as a resource to bolster the new professionals that Warner identifies. The result is a twofold operation of symbolic power: disparities in symbolic and cultural capital among participants in movement organizations is bolstered by the willingness of LGBT people outside those organizations to conform to the existing rules for accumulating symbolic capital.[43]

Ultimately, an interest in resisting symbolic power provides the grounds for an alternative version to the typical critique of mainstream gay and lesbian politics as assimilationist projects submitting to the normalizing power of the capitalist state. In broad strokes, this version would suggest that access to rights—particularly marriage rights—provides opportunities for accumulating symbolic capital and thereby improving the position of gays and lesbians in social space. This accords with the strategically legitimate but ultimately conformist approach produced by symbolic power's paradoxical implications. In this light, the conformism behind rights-based strategies for accumulating symbolic power is not problematic simply because it is conformist; it is problematic because its success depends on devaluing queer cultural forms, sexual practices, modes of intimacy, and approaches. That is, this strategy's success depends on successfully constructing a sub-episteme that devalues certain ways of knowing and certain knowers based on their relationship to normalcy. Moreover, the ability to make a collective identity oriented toward formal equality rather than queerness and sexual liberation become the nearly official and doxic goal of the movement depended on unequal distributions of the forms of capital needed to impose one vision of collective identity at the expense of another.

Distinction, Not Normalization

Habitus, capital, and symbolic power also give the conceptual tools needed to develop an alternative to queer critiques of the formal equality agenda. In particular, they provide the tools needed to depart from Foucault's logics of normalization and Butler's notion of performativity, both of which I'll explain below. For now, though, it is worth noting that normalization and performativity constitute the conceptual foundation for most queer political and theoretical projects as well as objections to the mainstreaming impulses of gay and lesbian politics. However, symbolic violence and a Bourdieuian conception of power could provide more satisfactory explanatory resources and point to important normative conclusions.

With few exceptions, most queer critics of mainstream politics argue that mainstream movement goals miss out on or actively marginalize alternative political projects, particularly around physical and mental health, community building, and sex-positivity.[44] Implicitly, most critics attribute this distortion to the unequal nature of the negotiations understood to underpin processes of constructing collective identity, and they interpret these negotiations from within a Foucauldian framework. For example, Michael Warner's classic argument invoked the Foucauldian notion of "counter-public" to describe the culture surrounding queer cultural practices.[45] In his account, these queer counter-publics have been sidelined by the normalizing impulses of mainstream gay organizations, media outlets, and opinion-leaders.[46] Such accounts gain explanatory leverage from Foucault's dispersed, capillary notion of power, in which relations of force discipline subjects in accordance with discursive norms.

Canada's Charter of Rights and Freedoms offers an example of discourse in action. In response to the Charter's introduction, gay and lesbian politics reoriented from a focus on mobilization outcomes to cultural outcomes through policy change in the form of integration and inclusion into mainstream social and political institutions.[47] The discursive landscape instituted by the Charter's introduction gave new persuasiveness to equality frames rooted in "rights talk," and helped shift movement goals toward formal legal equality and away from the transformative social and political vision of gay liberation.[48] From a Foucauldian perspective, the Charter is a key discursive resource that facilitated the dominance of an assimilationist collective identity. Famously, though, the normative disciplining Foucault envisioned is never complete and, as Foucault argues, "[where] there is power, there is resistance."[49] Queer political projects, then, have been organized around the claim that queerness itself is a resistance to processes of normalization but that the unequal negotiations on which collective identity has been founded mean the resistive potential of queerness has been swamped by the normative power of, for example, rights discourses.

The normative disciplining that lies at the core of Foucault's understanding of power starts from quasi-laboratory settings—prisons, asylums, schools, hospitals—and expands from those institutions into all corners of the social world. The disciplinary discourses developed in those laboratories construct agents that are incrementally incorporated into the demands and opportunities that those discourses structure. This sounds a lot like Bourdieu's framework, but where Bourdieu's work depends on distinction and difference, Foucault's conception of normalization relies heavily on a logic of homogenization and sameness. (More on this in chapter six.)

The homogeneity implied by Foucault's account of normalizing discourses cannot explain various agents' varying successes within the same discursive fields, nor for the ways in which practices become structurally similar across discursive fields. Butler's notion of performativity appears to offer a way of overcoming these problems, and it is not surprising that many queer theorists and activists explicitly or implicitly ground their analysis in some combination of Butler and Foucault.[50]

In *Gender Trouble*, Butler takes up one of Foucault's most challenging claims: the notion that we have an interior authentic self in contrast to what others see on our surface is itself a product of discourse. The soul, psychic processes, a true self; these are all discourses that create an interiority that simply is not there. We are ultimately only what we are on the surface: our actions, conscious thoughts, and feelings. Our sense of anything "deeper" is a product of discourse, not a reflection of reality. Butler extends this argument to suggest that gender is similarly a product of the incorporation of a specific discourse's disciplinary norms.

> In other words, acts, gestures, and desire produce the effect of an internal core or substance, but produce this *on the surface* of the body, through the play of signifying absences that suggest, but never reveal, the organizing principle of identity as a cause. Such acts, gestures, enactments, generally construed, are *performative* in the sense that the essence or identity that they otherwise purport to express are *fabrications* manufactured and sustained through corporeal signs and other discursive means.[51]

With a genesis similar to that of Bourdieu's habitus (namely, in the "stylized repetition of acts"), Butler argues that gender is not a natural accompaniment to sexual difference, but the sedimentation of norms into bodies that produce binary sets of corporeal styles.[52] If actions and gestures do not represent an inner truth about a subject's gender identity, but merely the incorporation of a norm, then sex, gender, and sexuality bear no intrinsic connection.[53] Like Foucault, Butler finds potential for resistance within disciplined productions of subjectivity. Unlike Foucault, however, Butler argues that the potential for agency against discipline is not produced by discourse directly, but by its necessary failure. She turns to what she calls "the John/Joan case" to illustrate her argument. In infancy, John underwent surgery that severely burned his penis. His parents, after consulting with psychologist John Money, decided to raise their child as a girl (including by removing his testicles). In his teenage years, John insisted on his male gender identity and on living as a man. Butler uses John to argue that invasive and competing attempts to produce John as a girl and then as a man—or more specifically, the failure to compel full incorporation of either—indicates a gap, an "incommensurability, between the norm that is supposed to inaugurate his humanness and the spoken insistence on himself that he performs."[54] For Butler, this gap opens the possibility of political resistance through resignification and recontextualization, which can produce the effect of authoritative communication even where it is not officially sanctioned.[55]

The frame on which Butler's notion of performativity hangs, then, is a largely external (though socially constructed) system of norms and spaces of discursive possibility. In order to become fully human subjects, performers repeat the stylized gestures assigned to them within binary gender and heteronormative social relations.[56] Given the ambivalence and constructedness at the core of these performances, many potential subjects will fail to fully incorporate the expected norms, fail to produce satisfactory gender performances and expressions, and indeed, fail to become fully human. The cost of this failure is significant; it produces symbolic and material suffering experienced as a certain "unlivability."[57]

The model that I have been developing presents two immediate challenges to this conception. First, we lose something when we think in terms of failure to incorporate an external norm rather than in terms of the active production of those failures within social contexts. Symbolic violence as the context-specific imposition of interpretations and definitions of action entails a conception of practice where the "failure" of some agents is in fact the product of other agents' active efforts and success. In the next chapter, I will develop a more direct example of this in relation to diversity of tactics and the alterglobalization movement, but the point here is that failure is more directly linked to success than Butler's performativity allows. That is not to say that fields in which these successes and failures are produced are neutral or unstructured; quite the opposite. What we lose by thinking only in terms of failure is the opportunity to understand failure as the product of the historical struggles that make hierarchically organized positions available to certain agents within a field, and the historical struggles over the forms, quantities, and distributions of capital that both energize social space and give efficacy to some actors' strategies rather than others.

Second, my approach rejects a concept that is central to performativity, the impossibility of closing the gap between norms and subjectivity. Gay and lesbian politics have been successful less because of a disruptive resignification and more because they have turned a failed collective subjectification into a successful one. Put another way, political success did not come from challenging norms to which collective actors were unable to adhere, but from leveraging sources of adherence, in the form of cultural and symbolic capital, into cultural and policy change that tracks with neoliberal patterns of exploitation and individualization. Again, success did not come from failure, but from success. The contours of social space in which LGBT/Q people found themselves directed political action in relatively predictable ways, while those who were already performative failures—but with the most wide-reaching and radical critiques—were remarginalized. Thinking about collective identity in terms of field, capital, and symbolic violence allows a more nuanced account of politics than the queer critiques of failure. Further, it allows for an understanding of the evolving and mutually influencing relationship between structured social space and dynamics of "success."

The difference between gay and lesbian politics and queer politics, then, is not simply a failure on the part of queers to conform to the norms of political space, a failure not shared by gay and lesbian subjects. By examining these issues in terms of collective identity and symbolic violence (in the form of epistemic violence), we can see that queerness as a failure to become a fully political collective subject was erased from the realm of possibility in the processes of collective identity formation, and that this erasure was enabled by the existence of habitus disposed—as most habitus are—to conformity and the presence of cultural and discursive capital oriented toward successfully producing intelligible political subjects.[58]

This observation raises the empirical question of how non-conformist habitus are produced and supported. It also shows that the orientation of LGBT/Q movements toward certain goals and not others is the product of epistemic violence rather than intrinsic interest. Normative leverage comes from critiquing epistemic violence within collective identity production rather than adjudicating between the inherent value of conforming, assimilating, failing, or refusing.

Suffering, Submission, Survival

My intention in this chapter has not been to paint the misrecognizing of dominant interests and submission to one's own domination (allodoxia) as an intrinsic feature of occupying a devalued location in social space. Indeed, objectors might point to the important work of political scientist and anthropologist James Scott as evidence that what may appear to be accession to arbitrary authority in fact masks "false deference" and conceals hidden forms of resistance. Scott argues, essentially, that researchers who limit their understanding of resistance to rebellions and revolutions miss everyday forms of resistance.[59] A number of feminist interlocutors have suggested that Bourdieu misses the types of resistance that Scott identifies because Bourdieu conceptualizes dominated groups entirely in terms of lacking; for Bourdieu, because the working class and feminists lack cultural capital and symbolic power, they are destined to unreflectively submit to the rules of the game established by dominant groups. This oversight, they argue, ignores what feminists have long known, namely that suffering and survival are entirely different things.[60] Indeed, while working-class women may strategically conform to middle-class norms, they do so at the cost of feeling like an interloper. This ambivalence reflects the structured emotional binds that contradictions within fundamental social structures produce through equally ambivalent and contradictory forms of identification and affect.[61]

My argument is that this ambivalence traps dominated groups within a distorting relation to power. Theorists cannot simply revalue working-class and feminist cultural forms as a source of strategic agency, because doing so erases the effects of epistemic forms of symbolic violence and the impact that epistemic injustice has on efforts by dominated groups to resist their domination. At best, this erasure overstates the possibilities for resistance. At worst, it is symptomatic of a tendency to substitute a desire for agency for its actual possibility.

I conclude here with the observation that ambivalence and contradiction are rooted in social structure and therefore amenable to sociocentric (as opposed to linguistic or psychoanalytic) evaluation.[62] Where contradictions and binds foster symbolic and epistemic injustices within social movements, they introduce distortions of justice into justice-seeking movements. The degree to which arbitrary authority is accepted or resisted is an empirical question that is dependent upon the extent to which dominated agents submit to the visions of the dominant. So allodoxia, survival, and false compliance represent points on a continuum of submission and resistance. Social movement research seeking to operationalize the theoretical claims I have made in this chapter will, of course, have to find ways to distinguish between submission and resistance, where relevant, while attending to the complex and distorting nature of social and political domination.

If collective identities suffer from the distortions flowing from strategies based on conformity or failure, they do so no more than the concrete tactics that movements develop and deploy in order to make claims on behalf of those identities. Tactical selection involves its own distortions, though like collective identity they are bound up in the operation of symbolic power. I turn to this form of distortion in the next chapter.

Tactic and Antinomy

As in every well-defined, familiar game, the players know how to modify, improvise, elaborate, even innovate while respecting the ground rules.
 —Tilly, "Getting It Together in Burgundy, 1675–1975"[1]

The Field Is Wrong

Where LGBT/Q politics offer rich insights into relationships among domination, identity, symbolic power, and movement strategies, the alterglobalization movement offers similarly fertile terrain for thinking about the dynamics of domination in the context of movement tactics. In the previous chapter, I suggested that domination within symbolic and political fields (including the epistemic and symbolic power and violence those fields engender), enabled by uneven distributions of various forms of capital, introduces distortions into the long-run positioning and overall orientation that a collective actor takes within the social field. Unequal distributions of cultural and symbolic capital infect collective identity processes with symbolic violence and thereby reproduce relations of domination. To return to the language of critical theory, at the macro level, progressive efforts to negate unjust systems of social relations may contain their own counter-negations; rather than fostering glimpses of a more just world, they obscure justice by distorting the collective lens through which people who share a collective identity view suffering, remedies, and opportunities.

Now I will shift to the micro level to look at how symbolic power distorts movement tactics. Social movements can be short-lived or relatively durable. We can see this relative durability in movement organizations and collective identities. Organizations and identities evolve over time and are deeply contested, but they nonetheless serve as a map to movements' overall trajectories. By "tactics" I mean the individual protests, demonstrations, and actions that movements use in pursuit of their goals. As we saw with collective identity, symbolic power constrains how movements select tactics and, indeed, the tactics that are practically available to movements in particular social and political contexts.

The alterglobalization movement provides a useful illustration of the dynamics of tactical selection because, perhaps more than in any other movement, heated practical and normative debates about tactics emerge from sincerely held commitments to autonomy, representation, and political success. Put another way, in the alterglobalization movement, the moral justifications a participant uses to defend or condemn various protest tactics bear directly on core questions in normative democratic and political theory. In this chapter, I examine a specific protest event—the protests against the 2010 G20 meetings in Toronto, Canada—to demonstrate how a Bourdieuian analysis can bring to light specific challenges that protesters face in neoliberal contexts.

After the Battle of Seattle in November 1999, where demonstrators and Black Bloc activists challenged the World Trade Organization summit, protests around meetings of global economic leaders became the most visible manifestation of the alterglobalization movement. Although the Occupy movement that burst onto the political scene in 2011 had a major influence on how income inequality is discussed, as a tactical practice occupation has been in decline. In the United States and Canada, Idle No More and Black Lives Matter have recently eclipsed the alterglobalization movement, although new movements contesting globalization are sure to emerge in response to the Brexit vote in the United Kingdom and Donald Trump's idiosyncratic version of right-wing populism. With the exception of the Occupy movement, where activists staged weeks-long sit-ins to protest income inequality, the G20 protests in Toronto may have been the last major action of the alterglobalization movement.

The Canadian state—at federal, provincial, and municipal levels—was more than happy to invest a billion dollars to defend state-led economic decision-making from the pesky demands of dissenting citizens. The state's investments ensured extensive police and surveillance mobilizations, massive security infrastructure, and physical separation of protesters from decision-makers. Ramped up police and security measures did not deter thousands of peaceful protesters or a contingent of property-smashing Black Bloc activists.[2] Conflict was inevitable—indeed, at times the police seemed eager for it—and nearly a thousand protesters were kettled (surrounded on all sides by police) and arrested. Nonetheless, the G20 reached an agreement to introduce aggressive austerity measures, further constraining public services and further habituating citizens to devastating neoliberal economic and democratic practices.

For activists and researchers interested in contentious politics, conflicts at the Toronto G20 summit brought into relief tensions between the fact that various groups advocated for and undertook divergent protest tactics, and the practical and moral challenges of maintaining "respect for diversity of tactics."[3] In particular, a small but well-organized group of anarchists making use of Black Bloc tactics were accused of undermining the mainstream People First demonstration that had mainly been organized by the Ontario labour movement. Activists and protesters conflicted not only with the G20 and its defenders, but also with each other. The symbolic terrain of these conflicts reduced the political impact of both peaceful and property-destroying modes of protest to naught. In the face of an apparently inevitable mutual failure, I take up Adorno's observation that "wrong life cannot be lived rightly," to argue that, to a significant extent, debates about the relationships between divergent protest tactics risk neglecting a central feature of domination: adopting a "right" form of protest is impossible in a "wrong" political field.[4] A wrong system cannot be protested rightly.

To make this argument, I move away from the search for positive causal mechanisms that is currently dominant in mainstream social movement studies.[5] Rather than focusing on what works for collective actors, I focus on a negative characteristic of the political space of the Toronto G20 and argue that the structure of symbolic power constituting that space produced what I call "political antinomies" for the G20's opponents. The negative, antinomy-centred approach that I develop is an intentional departure from the contentious politics approach articulated by McAdam et al. that is currently dominant within mainstream research on social movement politics. I described this approach in chapter two; its central project is to identify discrete mechanisms that link together into social movement processes. By bringing symbolic power into the study of social movements, I break from the mainstream research and insist that the various mechanisms described by the contentious politics approach are less causally important than the social fields in which those mechanisms operate and the distribution of various forms of capital within those fields. This leads to an ethical distinction between my approach and that of mainstream research: where the contentious politics perspective is silent on whether possibilities for "success" exist within given institutional arrangements, my focus on political antinomies—the absence of possibilities for success—has normative implications for how we evaluate social movements and their tactics.

In logic, antinomies refer to contradictions between two logically necessary conclusions. Here, I use antinomy to capture the contradictions exposed by the necessary failure of equally plausible but mutually exclusive approaches to protest. When I assert that a wrong system cannot be protested rightly, I am suggesting that the considerable energy that social movements expend grappling with ways to be both ethical and effective is itself a feature of domination. Indeed, just as domination produces distortions in collective identity processes, so too does it produce distortions within tactical selection by turning movement energies inward through impossible efforts to identify "right" protests.

Political antinomies exist when a political field is structured in such a way as to make it impossible for dominated actors to gain sufficient position within that field to alter its basic structures and, therefore, to alter the relations of domination that the field structures. The impossibility of gaining sufficient position to alter a field depends upon widespread misrecognition of arbitrary distributions of capital within social space as occurring naturally or as being morally justifiable. Situations where the contradictory demands of a social field are impossible to satisfy simultaneously constitute practical double binds.[6] Such double binds are produced through the relationships between an agent, the resources the agent carries, and the field in which they act. In the previous chapter we looked at one version of this double bind: gay and lesbian people could improve their symbolic position only by shedding the queerness that might reduce the hierarchies and marginalization that are characteristic of normalized gender expression and sexuality. In the face of overwhelming symbolic power, borne by hostile groups determined to maintain their position in social space, dominated actors are forced into the paradoxical reality that accommodating ourselves to the very system that harms us becomes a practically and morally legitimate strategy. Nonetheless, the degree of individual liberation gained by conforming to unjust relations of power fails to challenge those dominating relations.[7]

To further complicate the moral legitimacy of conformity, there is no reason to believe that the ability to accommodate oneself to relations of power is a skill that is evenly distributed among dominated groups and individuals. Adaptation depends upon pre-existing cultural and economic capital. As I will argue in relation to alterglobalization movements below, the agency purchased by gay and lesbian actors through submission to legal and cultural rules of the game represents an unevenly distributed opportunity for success. To emphasize, success does not indicate the moral quality of a strategy, only the capital that proponents could mobilize and their willingness to play by the rules of the game. Moreover, because accession to the rules appears to prohibit altering the rules, success is partial and distorting; it fails the critical political task of negating the negation. My analysis of LGBT/Q successes can, in the context of tactical selection, be extended to failures of the G20 protests in Toronto, but with attention to the conformist and marginalizing strategies deployed in the People First and Black Bloc actions respectively.

Of course, my claim that the wrongness of the political symbolic field confronting G20 protesters left activists without a right way to protest demands an account of what would constitute a right protest. As rough shorthand, I suggest that right protest would be both ethical and effective. Let me begin with an account of efficacy. Simply measuring efficacy by identifying an action's goals and measuring them against outcomes would run afoul of several conceptual difficulties. Prime among them is the fact that movement goals are almost always multiple both within and among groups and protesters. Individuals and groups almost certainly had ambivalent and possibly conflicting goals, and part of most organizations' preprotest discussions and internal disputes would have centred on exactly this ambivalence, possibly without resolution. Put simply, domination is neither so simple nor so direct that it provokes univocal and unidirectional resistance. I suggest, therefore, that any analysis of the G20 protests must necessarily be selective about what it considers to be relevant outcomes.

An obvious measure might be whether the protesters were capable of stopping the G20 meetings or at least having marked influence on its decisions.[8] Protests against the Free Trade Area of the Americas in Quebec in 2001 were partially credited with the failure to achieve an FTAA agreement, so one might assume that preventing agreement at the G20 could have been a hoped-for outcome of the Toronto protests in 2010. Fully explaining the official decisions made at the G20 in Toronto would include analysis at multiple levels: international political economy, the geography of the summit, the domestic politics of host countries, analysis of policing, as well as mechanisms of contention. Linking protests to decision-making through such a comprehensive analysis is beyond my ambition here. An alternative to measuring efficacy through impact on official decisions is to examine less concrete outcomes such as building a sense of community and common purpose, or developing collective identity even if only in the limited space of the protest. There is certainly room for this type of research.[9]

My interest, however, is in the relationship between protest tactics and power. Therefore, the axis of efficacy I am interested in is the extent to which a movement succeeds in making power visible. While making this argument, however, I recognize that, particularly when it comes to questions of power, visibility is not an all-or-nothing question. Rather, visibility must be thought of as a dynamic process wherein bringing certain features to light will necessarily occlude others. Certainly at the G20 summit, the police response to even the possibility that Black Bloc tactics might make an appearance rendered visible the state's capacity for brute coercive power. It is not clear whether that power would have remained invisible had the Black Bloc not participated. One result of the People First efforts to negotiate with the police might have been to keep the police's power invisible. That is, the state's reliance on coercive power "in the last instance" to ensure the continued operation of economic power, which the Black Bloc exposed, demanded tactics that were designed to render visible that aspect of state power by provoking coercion.

Nonetheless, the Black Bloc's detractors argue that Black Bloc tactics produced distortions in media coverage and public discussion and, in a sense, were therefore also complicit in concealing the G20's economic power from sight: exposing the state's capacity for policing eclipsed the G20's economic violence. In an effort to navigate the dynamics by which power is rendered visible and invisible through protest, I argue that the state's police power and the G20's economic power are separate components of a broader scheme of power that is nearly impossible to render unproblematically visible. Yet, rendering visible the relationship between the arbitrary and disproportionate symbolic power of the G20 and the effects that the use of that power has on people's lives must surely be a necessary condition for confronting neoliberal hegemony.

An account of practical reason as emerging from specific combinations of habitus, field, and capital provides the foundation for this analysis. The imminent, practical demands of fields mediate the dispositions that make up the habitus in at least two ways. First, the overall amount and structure of capital that an agent bears—an objective measure—significantly affects the likelihood of that agent's success in taking action in a social space. Second, the actor's subjective perception of a field as available for successful intervention introduces judgments based on practical reason rather than on mechanistic determinations produced by the structure of the field itself. Actors assess the field, their position within that field, and their capital, and make corollary assessments of other actors within the field. Because these judgments are always undertaken from the actor's concrete position within a field, they are always made from a partial perspective, in two senses: the actor is psychically invested in the assessment, and action is never the result of a rational evaluation based on full knowledge of opportunities and constraints. Action is always strategic (consciously or not) and is the product of context-specific, structured encounters of field and perception.

Bourdieu's notion of symbolic power conceptually links the unequal distribution of a particular kind of capital—symbolic capital—to practical assessments about the field and particularly about the resources one brings to the field. It therefore allows social movement analysts to focus on how symbolic power mediates between habitus and field and to specify the ways in which this mediation facilitates or hinders successful mobilization. It would be a mistake, however, to treat the distinctions through which social space is constructed as giving positive content to specific elements within the symbolic. The "meaning" of labour unions or anarchists, for example, is not derived from a positive ascription of characteristics but by situating them within an interconnected system of distinctions between freedom and constraint, public and private, legitimate and illegitimate. Thus, while protesters clearly disagreed with the G20 state representatives on the meaning of substantive policy issues, the degree to which they adopted doxic understandings about norms of communication, protest, and the public versus private nature of property marks out the terrain and strategy of the symbolic struggle that they waged through divergent protest tactics. It also maps out, in different ways, the constraints on effective symbolic action.

Debates over what is known as respect for diversity of tactics, which emerged after the Battle of Seattle in 1999 and had been fully articulated by the time of the FTAA demonstrations in Quebec City, 2001, usefully illustrate the impact of unequal distribution of resources on tactical selection.[10] Proponents of respect for diversity of tactics argue that the best way to combat capitalism and other modes of oppression is to allow activists to engage in diverse political activities including cultural work, popular education, and grassroots community organizing, but also militant protest activities including property destruction, which can range from stickering, spray painting, and painting guerrilla murals to smashing windows and defacing or destroying signs and other property.[11] It is worth emphasizing that respect for diversity of tactics is both a directive ethic and a permissive one: no activist ought to be forced to throw bricks when they would prefer to hold picket signs, but neither should allies publicly condemn either tactic.

The ethical foundation of respect for diversity of tactics lies in an anarchistic commitment to egalitarian autonomy, an autonomy that stands in stark contrast to the hierarchical order-following characteristic of the state and its disciplinary functions. Autonomy as an ethical principle finds organizational expression in affinity groups: small, independent organizations that determine their own projects and strategies without central movement authority.

Affinity groups demand and retain the right to pursue whatever tactics they consider to be both ethical and effective. The decisive feature of respect for diversity of tactics, then, is an ethical commitment to a respect for tactical pluralism; horizontally organized, independent affinity groups decide for themselves which specific tactics to deploy. Advocates further understand their commitment to autonomous action and organization as creating a duty to refuse to publicly denounce other activists for their willingness or unwillingness to make use of any particular tactic.[12]

At the G20 protests—as at the Battle for Seattle and other summit protests—not all protest participants were willing to endorse a plurality of tactics. While the Toronto Community Mobilization Network defended the rights of all protesters to choose their own protest strategy, many activists were quick to condemn the Black Bloc actions. Notably, Sid Ryan, then president of the Ontario Federation of Labour and one of the central organizers of the People First march, described Black Bloc activists as "cowardly" and "hooligans," while then-president of the Canadian Labour Congress Ken Georgetti issued a statement condemning the Black Bloc activists.[13]

My intention is not to participate in the debate over diversity of tactics directly. Instead, I take that diversity as a fact (that is, I accept that in the near-run at least some activists will pursue property damage, particularly at summit protests). I argue that the structures of possibility into which those tactics are inserted, though, pose considerable risks to the efficacy of any form of protest, and that this risk needs to be taken seriously.

The Ethics of Protest

After several decades of growing neoliberal hegemony, its features are well known, but a few are worth rehearsing briefly.[14] Neoliberal partisans equate economic liberalism and efficiency to democratic freedom, and they link all collectivism, state intervention, and market restraint to archaic forms of totalitarianism. This dual move allows neoliberals to portray their opponents as naively or perniciously fighting hopeless ideological battles against the inevitability and desirability of inequality.[15] As anarchist sociologist Richard Day notes, neoliberalism's shift from Keynesian economics to radically unrestricted markets brought along with it a new common sense, namely:

> those who are oppressed deserve their oppression; everyone (except the rich) must work more for less; the bigger a corporation is the better; the less the state intervenes in the economy (except to bail out

failed corporations and provide them with free infrastructure and the right to pollute at will) the better.[16]

Neoliberals conceive the state's role to be primarily for providing neutral, technical economic management. Prescriptively, they favour austerity financing, state downsizing, and privatization in a concerted effort to roll back the progressive gains of the last century.[17] With a fanatical devotion to technical management rather than democratic oversight and to privatization of public goods, neoliberal restructuring has effectively redrawn the divide between public and private. By limiting the public sphere to a smaller and smaller space, and by rendering what is left in the public sphere increasingly inconsequential, neoliberalism has redrawn the line between what counts as political and the supposedly non-political realm of individual preference and choice.[18] The redrawn boundary between the political and the non-political, particularly as it relates to the authority to oversee the technical management of global capitalism, has profound implications for contentious political action generally and modes of protest specifically.

Despite neoliberalism's extensive and intensive intrusion into the public sphere, neoliberalism is not the sole determinant of the symbolic space within which the G20 protests occurred. Neoliberalism's economic realpolitik has always been accompanied by important trajectories within liberal moral theory, which have sought to delegitimize disruption in favour of "communication societies" free from all traces of structural social conflict.[19] The moral framework behind efforts to eliminate disruption by transforming conflict into communication has roots in both liberal political ethics and deliberative democracy. In both cases, proponents premise mutual recognition and civil negotiation of differences on participants' willingness to eschew actions or modes of communication that either radically question fundamental principles of social organization (such as arguing that those principles legitimize exploitation and marginalization) or that are expressed in ways that are "impassioned, extreme, and the product of particular interests."[20]

For example, liberal philosopher John Rawls advocates a restrictive definition of civil disobedience as "a public, nonviolent, conscientious yet political act contrary to law usually done with the aim of bringing about a change in the law or policies of the government."[21] He then argues that any disruptions falling outside of this definition are morally indefensible. Although the question of what constitutes violence is by no means settled in advance, the requirement that the disobedience be a "political act" takes on particular import in the context of neoliberal restrictions of what constitutes politics.

Moreover, Rawls problematically restricts what constitutes a political act to those actions that are guided by principles of justice regarding social institutions and national constitutions, which is to say that they are not actions based on appeals to personal morality or doctrine. On its own there is little to object to here, except that Rawls argues that in acting politically "one invokes the commonly shared conception of justice that underlies the political order."[22] However, it is a basic premise of critical theory from Marx to Bourdieu that shared conceptions of justice merely reflect adherence to social relations that foster exploitation and domination. To the extent that this is the case and that the powerful have material and dispositional interests in maintaining an exploitative status quo, it is ultimately anti-democratic to argue that activists must restrict themselves to an official conception of justice.

In effect, neoliberalism and liberal political ethics form a double pincer, decisively restricting what constitute legitimate, communicative efforts to eliminate conflict through civil, mutual recognition. Neoliberalism simultaneously conceives of the economic sphere as bearing superior value to democratic practices and heightens liberalism's classic restriction of what policy measures count as political: economic issues are explicitly excluded from the realm of democratic consideration through technocratic management and prioritization of individual choice. At the same time, liberal ethics demand civility while restricting who can legitimately engage in democratic practices to those who either already share conceptions of justice that present little challenge to entrenched forms of domination or who are willing to minimize disruption for the sake of civil public communication.

Neoliberal restructuring constrains the state and anything associated with it as much as possible and organizes as many fields as possible according to market principles. These principles entail particular conceptions of freedom, individuality, and democratic practice. As fields have been objectively structured according to neoliberal classifications that equate the market to freedom and politics to civility, these classifications have been slowly incorporated into the habitus of people living within them.[23] Alongside this habituation to neoliberalism, the symbolic value of political activity has also shifted. While there may never be shared assumptions about specific policy prescriptions, there is increasing consensus about the legitimacy of some forms of protest, namely non-disruptive rallies, clever slogans, and petition-signing, and the illegitimacy of others such as blockades, property destruction, and politically motivated violence. Too often, any action that is merely disruptive, such as a blockade or a strike, is popularly described as violent and an affront to the rights of whomever these tactics inconvenience.

The dynamics between the everydayness of neoliberalism and its consequent incorporation into the disposition of the general public gave ample reason to predict that as Canadians watched the encounters between police and protesters, they would be disposed to perceive and interpret these encounters according to naturalized and misrecognized neoliberal doxa. Not surprisingly, according to at least one poll, the public did not appear to sympathize with either People First or the Black Bloc activists; the majority of respondents expressed disgust, shame, anger, and sadness at the event.[24]

It is worth noting that in other conditions the range of choices facing protesters, the forms of capital they might hope to mobilize, and the potential responses to their actions would be more or less different. The neoliberal and liberal bind I just described is neither universal nor ahistorical. Like any historical moment, the current field of power is a product of previous struggles. Historical analysis akin to what I do here might identify different choices and possibilities; this is inherent in the notion of repertoires of contention—the basket of protest tactics from which movements draw. Neoliberalism is not structural in the sense of bearing determining causal force, but it does shape actions within its ambit. Like any field, the current neoliberal/liberal moment sets out the likely consequences of actions and the more or less predictable outcomes produced by taking one position or another within social space.

The conceptual value of practical reason is its recognition that agents are always situated actors bearing partial perspectives, sedimented dispositions, and specific forms and quantities of capital. This situatedness means that actors cannot make definite predictions in advance. Indeed, a causal chain that seems inevitable in retrospect can only be guessed at in advance. Despite an outcome's apparent obviousness in hindsight, agents' partial perspective makes definite predictions impossible. This uncertainty in the moment fuels debate over strategy, particularly as activists try to match ethical commitments to democratic practice, direct action, autonomy, and peacefulness to their desire for effective, ethical action.

Nonetheless, the symbolic spaces within which the G20 protests struggled were characterized by a neoliberal set of distinctions between public and private, freedom and liberty, and so on. Complementing this schema was a further liberal orthodoxy regarding legitimate and illegitimate forms of communication, which increasingly delegitimizes disruption in favour of a moderate, communicative ethic. Given that a neoliberal public was watching events unfold, the ability to accrue symbolic profit in the G20 field depended, in large part, on choosing protest actions that would resonate with liberal and neoliberal distinctions between legitimate and illegitimate protests, efficiency and disruption, neutrality and bias.[25] Analysis of the symbolic power running through the protest field renders the impossibility of such resonance clear. The G20 field presented protesters with a political antimony: neither conformist, peaceful demonstrations nor refusals (failures) to conform via property destruction strategies could marshal the capital necessary to act ethically and effectively against the G20.

The G20 in Toronto

To assess the actions of G20 protesters, we must first identify the central actors in the protest field and articulate their differences, not as reflections of differing natural properties, but rather as reflections of specific schemes of classification and perception manifested through the actions or position-taking they perform within social space.[26] These position-takings constitute concrete attempts on the part of actors to establish their own self-definitions as well as a definition of the field itself, that is, to establish constructions that in turn have real effects on subsequent developments of the field.

The week prior to the G20 summit included protests and events that focused on issues ranging from Indigenous rights to queer liberation and climate change. Here, I will focus on two major events: the People First march and the Black Bloc Get off the Fence action. The People First march was organized by labour unions (primarily the Canadian Labour Congress and the Ontario Federation of Labour) as well as a number of allied groups (such as the Council of Canadians, Greenpeace, Oxfam Canada, and the Canadian Federation of Students) and—depending on whose count we give credence to—attracted between four thousand and thirty thousand participants.[27] Organizers of this event negotiated with police and attempted to gain symbolic leverage through their visibility, their numbers, and the moral content of their message.[28]

By contrast, the Get Off the Fence action intended to join with the People First march until the march turned away from the fence behind which G20 negotiations were happening, toward the police-sanctioned "free-speech zone." At that point, Get Off the Fence activists intended to break off and engage in "a militant, confrontational demonstration where [they would] challenge the global apartheid and injustices the fence represents."[29] As promised, where the People First march was stopped by three rows of police, Black Bloc activists broke off and undertook a highly choreographed burst of property destruction. Activists engaging in Black Bloc tactics insisted on maintaining anonymity, framed the police as singularly hostile and violent representatives of state power, and sought to gain symbolic leverage through the destruction of the "symbols of capitalism," primarily storefronts of big businesses such as Starbucks and various banks.

Politics of Disruption
An obvious place to begin seeking political antinomies is to examine the use of so-called violent actions by Black Bloc protesters. Property destruction fits comfortably within Black Bloc activists' commitment to respect for diversity of tactics, although at the 2002 NATO summit in Prague, one Black Bloc protected a police vehicle as it, perhaps provocatively, made its way through a three-thousand-strong rally of anarcho-communists.[30] At bottom, destruction per se is not the goal:

> [By] participating in a Bloc, activists offer up their semi-protected bodies to state-sponsored violence, in the hope not only of saving other protesters from physical harm, but also to provoke shock, horror and perhaps event dissent among liberal citizens who hold to values like freedom of speech and the right to legitimate protest.[31]

Nonetheless, at the G20 protests, Black Bloc activists did make use of politically motivated vandalism, and therefore its value as a tactic bears consideration. A number of features of political property destruction are worth briefly recounting here. Supporters of the tactic argue that property destruction is a continuum of actions from stickering to window-smashing and that some actions on the continuum (graffiti, billboard "corrections," and stickering in particular) are well accepted as legitimate forms of protest. Some also argue that any protesters who act outside legitimate, routinized, and bureaucratized forms of dissent are indiscriminately deemed "violent" and that the term ought only to be applied to situations where people actually get hurt. They also suggest that people engaged in this type of property destruction distinguish between private (capitalist) property and personal (use-value) property, and only target the former. The intention in doing so is to unsettle reified middle-class attitudes about private property and thereby open up debates about alternative ways of organizing ownership and material goods.[32] Finally, some anarchists observe that the use of force in direct action political events has positive emotional effects for protesters, namely, an increase in the sense of well-being and reduced levels of depression. This motivates a demand for the "right to be angry"; the deliberate (and deliberated upon) use of force becomes a legitimate mechanism for combining emotion and rationality in political action and contrasts with liberal and academic efforts to restrict legitimate political action to the realm of rationality.[33]

These justifications appear to have been at play in the G20 field. Media reports contain claims such as, "This isn't violence. This is vandalism against violent corporations. We did not hurt anybody. They (the corporations) are the ones hurting people."[34] Mathieu Francoeur, of the Montreal-based Anti-Capitalist Convergence, called the vandalism "a means of expression [that] doesn't compare to the economic and state violence we're subjected to."[35]

To understand the place of these tactics in opposition to neoliberalism, we need to break from substantialist thinking about violence. Substantialist thinking wrongly treats violence as a determinate object with moral properties. Instead, we ought to treat "violence" as a site of struggle over how to understand relationships between individual or group actions, structural conditions, and those people and objects that are somehow damaged by those relationships. That is, thinking about violence should focus on process and relationships surrounding action rather than the action itself. Analysts ought to avoid joining Black Bloc activists in arguing for a different definition of violence, which would treat violence itself as an object of study rather than focusing on the conditions under which definitions of violence are produced. The task is to objectify the structures by which violence itself is objectified, which is to say, constructed as an object of study. In this way, we can interrogate the viability of activist attempts to impose a new definition of violence or even to open up the question of violence in the minds of the watching public.[36]

In Bourdieu's view:

> The specific efficacy of subversive action consists in the power to bring to consciousness, and so modify, the categories of thought which help to orient individual and collective practices and in particular the categories through which distributions are perceived and appreciated.[37]

The question, then, is the conditions under which vandalism has the power to modify conscious beliefs about property and its relation to capitalist exploitation. However, modifying consciousness is not a simple task of changing ideas that people have about the world, it entails changing the embodied dispositions—the habitus—through which people perceive the world. There is reason for concern, then, that Black Bloc tactics may be too discursive. That is, the logic behind Black Bloc tactics appears to rely on the philosophical lineage associated with Butler and Foucault that I critique elsewhere (see chapters four and six). In such approaches, discourse appears as something that is universally available and amenable to resignification. By contrast, attention to field and capital shows how symbolic power both structures and unevenly distributes the capacity for resignification on which Black Bloc strategies appear to rely. Black Bloc tactics need to be understood in terms of the field in which they enter and the form and quantity of capital that they mobilize within that field.

The antinomy that disruptive protesters faced at the G20 centres on the question of violence. Black Bloc activists sought to subvert the category of violence without having sufficient symbolic and material capital to do so. Symbolic domination is not simply the result of framing or messaging; it comes from the complicity between neoliberal schemes of classification, the physical space occupied within the G20 field—the fence, the police lines, the kettles, the protest crowd—as well as from the symbolic and material capital that all participants bring to the field and the disposition of the public toward activist attempts at resignification. Therefore, while Black Bloc activists sought to unsettle and transform reified valuations of the tactical and ethical value of "violent" property destruction, their use of tactics already devalued by reified conceptions could never have resonated with a neoliberal public. As a consequence, the action itself diminished their capacity to accrue sufficient symbolic capital to impose a new definition of violence on the field. Fundamentally, the relationship between the tactics and the symbolic structures into which the tactics were inserted foreclosed any possibility that the tactic would succeed.

This analysis in no way represents a commitment on my part within debates about the value of property destruction as a political tactic. Rather than taking sides, I am trying to demonstrate the importance of distinguishing between the moral leverage upon which movement actions implicitly rely and questions of tactical efficacy. De-objectifying violence and other movement tactics entails reconceiving moral leverage as symbolic capital. This kind of political contention requires a two-stage struggle. First, property destruction needs to be endowed with adequate moral content to be recognized as a legitimate action within the political field. Only then can violence be deployed against specific objects. The close relationship between habitus and field, on which social intelligibility depends, means that agents cannot simply force their way into a field and make socially intelligible actions that disregard the entire scheme of distinctions according to which that field operates. Put another way, discursive efforts to disrupt reified conceptions of property risk short-circuiting the relationship between symbolic power and property destruction.

The question could be raised of whether Black Bloc activists are properly considered as part of the political field, or rather, whether they conceive of themselves in this way. If submission to the rules of the political field entails a commitment to routinized and legitimate forms of political action (including demonstrations that are expressive but not disruptive), then Black Bloc tactics might suggest a different political project, one where the political is subverted in favour of a performative freedom to resignify the value of property and the symbols of capitalism. This argument would suggest that Black Bloc activists have freed themselves from symbolic violence precisely because they reject the doxic rules of the political field.

To respond to this objection, I turn to Bourdieu's observation that action cannot be understood solely on the basis of the conscious intentions of the actors involved. The meaning and cause of action depends not only on conscious calculation but also on subjective dispositions and the objective conditions of the field within which action takes place.[38] I would go beyond Bourdieu to suggest that participation in a field itself may not be entirely intentional, and that even anarchist Black Bloc activists who intentionally reject participation in "legitimate" political processes get caught up in a political field without necessarily intending to do so.

Black Bloc activities—if they are distinguishable from random or merely criminal acts of vandalism, and surely they can be—entail a communicative relationship with an addressee. Indeed, the highly symbolic nature of the vandalism implies an audience in a way that attacks on the materials of capitalism (machines, factories, and so on) or upon capitalists themselves, do not. While the intended audience might be Starbucks and bank CEOs, the unlikelihood of CEO conversions to anti-capitalist perspectives suggests that the actual audience of Black Bloc property damage is more likely some combination of fellow protesters and the wider public. Insofar as it is the wider public, this indicates a reliance on mass media (although such a reliance must be hopelessly troubled), and reliance on appeal to the dispositions of a wider public that misrecognizes, and therefore accepts as natural, neoliberal doxa about property and democratic behaviour.[39] This is the moment at which Black Bloc activists—intentionally or not—become bound up in the rules of the political field and submit—consciously or not—to a regime of symbolic value that delegitimizes the very strategy by which they entered into the field.

To summarize, the objective possibilities inscribed in the G20 protest field—as part of a broader political field constructed on neoliberal doxa and the combination of dispositions and capital upon which the protesters construct their actions—conspired to create a set of impossibilities for Black Bloc protesters. Despite themselves, Black Bloc activists sought symbolic leverage where there was none to be had, a position-taking occasioned by the resolution of their ambivalence toward the political field through their forced incorporation into the very scheme of legitimacy and accumulation that their tactics hoped to undermine.

Politics as Pluralism

To appreciate the impossibilities facing the People First march, we need to break from the democratic sensibilities of expressive protests and relocate protests within the non-democratic space of symbolic markets. The difficulty lies precisely in accomplishing what mainstream approaches to social movement research fail to do, which is to understand protests in terms neither of their own self-conception nor of their function within democratic structures, but rather in terms of the relationship between self-understandings within the protest field and the structure of the field itself.

Observers of social movements have already begun to point to the diminishing effectiveness of demonstrations. Demonstrations have become relatively normalized, encouraging movements to shift their strategies away from efforts to make trouble for powerholders—through strikes and blockades, for example—and toward efforts to show popular support by mobilizing large crowds. In doing so, movements accept and reinforce the devaluation of disruption generally, as communication takes priority over exposing social conflict.[40] However, even large protests that fail to cause a disturbance tend to have minimal affective impact, at least in the North American context, precisely because the tactic has become so institutionalized. This creates upward pressure on how many people need to be mobilized in order to be taken seriously and creates significant disadvantages for smaller groups with less institutional capacity behind their mobilizing efforts.

Organizers of the People First rally pursued a strategy that, at least in part, attempted to increase their symbolic capital by distinguishing themselves from the activities of the relatively resource-poor anarchists using Black Bloc tactics. Sid Ryan polemically equated the threat to democratic space posed by Black Bloc "hooligans" to the threat posed by the state's massive police presence, and boasted of working to create a democratic space—the so-called free-speech zone—by working with police.[41] In fact, prior to the summit, organizers argued somewhat ironically that they were providing a safe place to express dissent that was "free from the overblown security presence that's become so commonplace during meetings of the world's most powerful heads of state" precisely by working closely with representatives of the overblown security presence on details of where the demonstrations would take place.[42]

Close co-operation with security forces can be understood as precisely the kind of paradoxical manoeuvring that agents undertake when they are faced with impossible situations. Instead of looking at co-operation with police as a mechanism for facilitating democratic participation, co-operation is better understood as a mechanism—intended as such or not—for accumulating symbolic capital by producing a distinction between People First and Get off the Fence. By demonstrating that People First was not Black Bloc, People First organizers accumulated symbolic capital at the Black Bloc's expense. The organizers' ability to produce this distinction depended materially on their organizational resources; they also brought to bear important symbolic resources. They used their institutional stability to maintain relations with police and thereby portray those relations as supporting legitimate protest. Further, organizers' commitment to non-disruptive politics conformed to the neoliberal equation of efficiency and order to progress, to liberal pluralism, and to liberal conceptions of conflict as located in, and resolvable through, democratic and communicative spaces.

The resources needed to establish the permanent bureaucratic organizations on which this strategy depends are not evenly distributed.[43] Compared to the Black Bloc, the relatively large organizational and economic capital mobilized by the labour movement and its allies, combined with the normalization of mass protests, reproduced a symbolic distinction between the ideological value of two sets of political goods. First, those produced by the social democratic claims of People First, with its accompanying politics of representation. Second, the anarchistic challenges posed by Black Bloc activists and their accompanying politics of affinity. Again, Bourdieuian attention to the political economy that characterized the institutional background and symbolic space in which they mobilized (in this case, a naturalized valuation of a particular form of protest) allows us to track the symbolically mediated production and consumption of political goods. In addition, we can do so without reference to the substantive content of the claims being made. The question remains, though, whether People First could mobilize sufficient material and symbolic capital to render visible the G20's economic and political power, or whether rallies merely indicate accession to a field structured precisely against the possibility of such change.

The People First organizers sought to achieve symbolic leverage by repeatedly emphasizing the size of the protest and the moral virtue of their claims and their means of expression. These strategies rely on a state and public disposed to appreciate the value of a particular size of demonstration and the claims being made, that is, on a shared understanding of the structure of the social field and positions taken within it. Implicitly, the strategies rely optimistically on the potential for a combination of size and virtue to provoke reflection in the watching public and to thereby make that public available for subsequent mobilization against neoliberal projects.

There are good reasons for thinking that these strategies were doomed to failure in the G20 field; they miss out on the fact that neoliberalism has, wherever possible, shifted decision-making out of the democratic arena and into technical ones. Attempting to confront neoliberalism from within democratic space fundamentally misrecognizes the semi-autonomous operation of different subfields within the field of power. As discussed above, one of neoliberalism's primary achievements has been to consolidate the apparent obviousness of the need to technocratically protect an expansive capitalist economy at the expense of all other considerations. As a result, the ability to question the underlying premise of the G20—technical global economic management—has been removed from the democratic field. The doxic, unspoken, and misrecognized character of this removal makes the expressive demands of the protesters politically (though not literally) unspeakable. Or to be more accurate, such demands are unintelligible in a democratic field where socially motivated intrusions into the market have become, in practice, unthinkable.

Thus, the commitment to liberal pluralism that underpins the expressive politics of demonstrations—a commitment that imagines groups making rational and moral claims for justice in a democratic arena, and entails expressive protesters submitting to the rules of democratic engagement that restrict allowable appeals to those based on reason and shared moral values and presented in non-disruptive, reasonable ways—misses a critical feature of contemporary political struggle. Conflicts within the democratic field are at best minor skirmishes in the broader field of power, and they have been highly marginalized by the neoliberal reorganization of the relationship between economic management and democracy. This constitutes a political impossibility. The field in which protesters are competent to protest, the field in which they have the requisite practical knowledge, organizational capacity, and symbolic legitimacy, is a field in which neoliberalism is sufficiently dominant symbolically to have already excluded anything protesters might say from the realm of the politically thinkable.

Affinity and Representation; Protension and Project

The Black Bloc and People First rallies illustrate ethical and practical characteristics of both affinity-based politics and representative politics. In essence, affinity-based politics bring together individuals solely for the purpose of a short-term project based on a shared willingness to work together, without committing to any form of long-term association. Once an action is complete, the group dissolves, although it may re-form for the next project. Every participant expects full autonomy to withdraw, but the focus is on consensus-building in order to maintain participation without eroding autonomy. By contrast, representative politics depend on organizations with greater durability. Decisions are often based on a combination of majority voting and authority delegated to leaders and committees. Both forms of mobilization claim to have transformative potential and both justify themselves on ethical and practical grounds. However, neither mode can claim both transformative potential and respect for tactical autonomy, because transformation and autonomy operate according to separate political and ethical logics.

Anarchist archaeologist David Graeber suggests that Black Bloc activists and other anarchists who are willing to use force during political protests are interested in creating a new language of protest, one that is less restrictive than strict non-violence but without the unethical violations of bodily integrity that are caused by armed insurrection.[44] Insofar as this is true, Black Bloc activists participate in a lengthy struggle over the communicative aspects of how repertoires of contention evolve. The key issue, in this case, is how such evolution occurs and what strategies activists can take to affect this new language. Fundamentally, the ability to transform the language of protest depends upon access to the same resources needed to transform any field: sufficient authority, in the form of symbolic and other forms of capital that are specifically valuable in that field, to impose a new system of meaning, a new scheme of classification, common to or shared by other participants in the field. Like any participant in a field, Black Bloc activists, labour activists, and other civil society actors seek to accumulate (all at once or, more likely, over a considerable period of time) the capital necessary for their actions to make sense within the relevant field. I have argued above that anarchists' considerable deficit in symbolic capital makes such accumulation within the political field an uncertain enterprise, but the logic of prefigurative and affinity-based politics may also restrict this project in ways that raise broader ethical questions.

Contemporary anarchist politics centre on tactics that refuse traditional left-wing strategies aimed at seizing state power. Instead, they seek to expose the coercion at the heart of the state in order to delegitimize its authority, while building autonomous political, economic, and social space.[45] For most anarchists, tactics are intended to be prefigurative socially and individually; the processes by which tactics are selected and the tactics themselves reflect the kind of society participants seek, while also having profoundly transformative effects on participants.[46] Most importantly, however, unlike sectarian models of mobilization that demand ideological uniformity—the labour movement and partisan politics loom large in such models—the alterglobalization movement seeks diversity. Anarchists focus their debates on action, not ideas, because participants have no hope or desire to convert everyone to a single point of view. This means that debate is also usually focused on the task at hand without trying to force the action into a long-range (beyond the predictable future) program.[47]

The problem of anarchist interest in linking prefiguration to respect for diversity of tactics is that the logic of diversity of tactics does not operate on the same level as logics of either prefigurative or representative transformative politics. Diversity of tactics depends on refusing to bind activists to the long-run trajectory of social change in order to unite ethical commitments to autonomy and immediacy to organizational form, expressed through affinity. This is not to say that anarchists do not engage in projects over time, only that the ethical foundations of affinity require them to engage that trajectory using specific tactics at snapshot points in time rather than as a coherent long-term strategy.

Husserl's distinction between "protension" and "project," introduced in relation to the anticipatory function of habitus, provides a means of conceiving how ethics, organization, and time relate to each other. Recall that fields are relatively stable but nonetheless evolve as a result of internal struggles. Habitus-bearing agents are only able to undertake meaningful actions within a field because its stability allows them to anticipate how those actions will be perceived by other agents, what actions other agents are likely to take, and what cumulative effect these actions will have on subsequent opportunities. This predictability allows for investments in, and if successful, accumulation of, the form of capital specific to that field.[48]

Such "anticipation" takes two primary forms. On the one hand, an agent might anticipate an event that is so close in the future as to be, for all intents and purposes, in the present. As in the tennis analogy (introduced in chapter three), when an athlete sees a competitor hit a ball across a court, their "practical" sense of gravity, wind conditions, and so on gives them such a clear sense of where the ball will be that it might as well be there now. The future is so imminent as to be practically present. Indeed, phenomenology rests on such a relationship between time and space: agents do not stop at every moment to recalculate where a moving object is going to be in space and adjust accordingly; they simply preconsciously move to where it is going to be, based on embodied practical sense. This matches Husserl's notion of "protension": a preperceptive anticipation and reaction, based on a practical relation to the evolution of a field of objects and agents rather than on conscious deliberation and intentional mobilization. There is certainty inscribed in a field, which can only unfold in one way—because the timescape of unfolding is so short that there is no room for alternative actions or intervening variables. Bourdieu likens it to the certainty of knowing that the sides of a cube are present without actually seeing them.[49] At the individual level, protension is the least reflective mode of action; as in the case of a skilled athlete responding to the exigencies of a game, it represents a habitus perfectly in tune with the field it encounters.[50]

By contrast, a "project" entails marshalling capital and resources to some long-range goal. At a minimum, such marshalling requires making assessments about the field in which action is to take place and within which resources are marshalled, and it will therefore have an element of conscious consideration about it. Such consideration, though, is likely to be practical and strategic rather than reflexive consideration of the doxic assumptions underpinning the field. The practical consideration that underpins projects does not eliminate the role of habitus in action; practical reflection always occurs within the realm of considerations perceived by those disposed to perceive them. An important challenge that affinity-based politics pose to representation is that what could be described as the organizational habitus of a representative body unduly restricts the tactics under consideration and thereby undermines the autonomy of participants whose dispositions might lead them to alternative forms of protest.

Nonetheless, the value of distinguishing between protension and project is not to determine which is more radical, more just, or more practical. Instead, the usefulness of the distinction comes from specific assumptions inherent to projects but absent in protensive action. First, projects depend upon a reasonable faith in the morphology of the field in which the future resources are to be deployed. That is, they require a relative certainty that, although the field will evolve and various actors will manoeuvre within it over time, thereby amending its shape, the fundamental rules of the field will not be overthrown and the species of capital being marshalled for a future intervention will remain relevant. It would make no sense for political parties to fundraise, for example, if they did not have a reasonable expectation that they would be able to use those funds for campaigning, advertising, organizing, and so on.

Protension requires no such commitment precisely because it entails action on the field as it is currently unfolding, in an imminent future that is so near as to be essentially present. In this vein, affinity-based politics that refuse to think beyond the predictable future have two advantages: the restriction of tactical reflection to questions of immediate resources eliminates the need to protect investments in specific forms of capital, and protension allows for the use of capital that does not necessarily submit to the logic of the political field. By narrowing its horizon to the value of autonomous action and its apparently transformative effects on individual protesters, affinity refuses investment in the—admittedly hierarchical and arbitrary—norms of credibility, authority, and legitimacy that structure political interaction and political projects. Again, a diversity of tactics is perfectly compatible with this self-constrained conception of the political.

Second, political projects, in contrast to political protension, require an identity between the collective actor that makes investments in the current field in order to benefit from those investments in future field interventions and the collective actor who will act in the future. This is part of why the formation of collective identities involves such high political stakes. Collective identity depends on an ability to perceive duration, and to establish a relationship between past and future, and action and effect.[51] For agents to identify with a collective identity they must engage in constructive work by which suffering, opportunities, goals, and strategies are articulated into an overall movement trajectory. In turn, these shared perceptions of duration, the effects actions are likely to have, and the relationship of those actions to suffering—all of which are necessary for collective identity—are also necessary to collective action in the form of intentional and strategic uses of capital over time.

Because collective identities, by their nature, do not enjoy the unifying corporeal consistency that we associate with individual identities, their mechanisms for unifying perceptions and strategies across time are organizational and cultural. Identity therefore not only relies on the logic of representation and on delegation to institutional mechanisms like leadership roles and institutionalized channels of authority (which are anathema to anarchist commitments to organizing through affinity), but it also relies on an implicit commitment to maintaining the value of its capital by supporting the current morphology of the political field. This is accomplished primarily through excluding and disavowing tactics that jeopardize the field itself. Thus, insofar as diversity of tactics depends on a protensive disavowal of representation in favour of an immediate connection between autonomy and organization, it is compatible with affinity-based politics but incompatible with representative politics and long-range political projects. Equally, insofar as representative politics engage in long-run strategies, collective actors must protect their investments by truncating the autonomy of individual participants and excluding in advance certain forms of protest.

Respect for diversity of tactics, then, troubles or obscures the diversity of political logics that underpin affinity and representation. On its own, that is not sufficient for rejecting it entirely. The fact remains that political antinomies wreak havoc on both protensive and project-oriented political strategies, and the experiences of protesters at the G20 show how easily protension and project come into conflict. If diversity of tactics requires an ethical commitment to allowing such conflicts to arise as expressions of activist autonomy, then it remains a constant component of protest fields that representative organizations must anticipate and act upon. Therefore, diversity of tactics raises questions about the ethical duties protesters have toward one another, given reasonable disagreement about the value of autonomy and affinity on the one hand, and representation and investment on the other.

In the previous chapter, I pointed toward the presence of symbolic power and epistemic violence as potential markers for whether collective actors are replicating patterns of domination. At the G20 protests, labour organizers clearly made an effort to exploit the distance between themselves and Black Bloc activists for symbolic gain. They thereby reinforced a classificatory scheme (peaceful, non-disruptive marches are legitimate; political vandalism is illegitimate) that jeopardizes the Black Bloc efforts to stake their own symbolic claims. This may constitute a form of epistemic violence. Yet, the Black Bloc's wilful refusal to consider the effects of vandalism on media representation of the protests as a whole similarly jeopardizes People First's efforts to speak and be heard.

Fundamentally, however, the problem lies—as I have been arguing—in the nature of symbolic space. It is impossible to select effective ethical action within unethical space. One effect of such spaces is to direct the frustrations of dominated agents toward themselves and their fellow sufferers. In the next chapter, I return to a close examination of how symbolic power and violence relate to justice. The specific conception of justice I offer will provide a preliminary roadmap for practical strategies that movements can adopt to resist the distortions exemplified by the alterglobalization and LGBT/Q movements.

Suffering and Justice

> *Not truth and certainty are the opposite of the world of the madman, but the universality and the universal binding force of a faith; in sum, the non-arbitrary character of judgments. And man's greatest labour so far has been to reach agreement about very many things and to submit to a law of agreement—regardless of whether these things are true or false. This is the discipline of the mind that mankind has received; but the contrary impulses are still so powerful that at bottom we cannot speak of the future of mankind with much confidence.*
> —Nietzsche, *The Gay Science*[1]

Distorted Energies

Social movements resist what they take to be unjust social, economic, and political arrangements. Resistance demands navigating complex and contentious processes including, above all, the construction of collective identities and the selection of tactics. Progressive allies benefit from this work as movements provide us with glimpses into how a fully just social field might function. In the language of critical theory, by working through collective identity and tactical selection processes and by struggling against various forms of exclusion and oppression, movements show how we might negate the negation. They open windows on to how to cancel out (negate) the patterns of domination that frustrate, stunt, and distort human and social potential (the negation). To borrow Melucci's language, social movements are prophets that reveal both suffering and possibilities for alleviating that suffering.[2]

The complexity of culturally, politically, and institutionally entrenched domination, however, makes direct negation of domination impossible for any movement—no matter how broad-based, virtuous, and effective it may be. As illustrated by LGBT/Q and alterglobalization mobilizations, processes of collectivization and strategy inevitably founder on the impossibility of directly negating domination, and movements gravitate seemingly inevitably toward conformity or failure. The conformity and failure of movements do not indicate their official commitment—or lack or commitment—to sweeping changes. Rather, they are competing strategies that agents pursue, rooted in the participants' habitus, played out within objectively structured fields, and dependent upon the various forms of individual and collective capital that movements can mobilize within those fields. In this light, both conformity and failure bear strategic and moral value, but they also bear high costs in the form of distortions that replicate the very patterns of domination that movements struggle to negate.

Critical theorists may reflect these distortions back to movements to describe the processes by which domination cancels and distorts movements' efforts to negate the negation. Given their commitment to keeping suffering at the centre of their philosophical and political projects, most seek to reflect on domination in a collaborative spirit intended to contribute to those movements as both allies and participants. Critical theory's general project of exposing negations becomes more like traditional political theory when we refuse to be satisfied with analyzing negations and attempt—tentatively—to expand the insights that movements provide about suffering into more general claims about the nature of justice. These claims can form the basis on which new forms of political practice are organized, though with full awareness of the likelihood that they too will be distorted and therefore require their own negations. Even if there is no direct route to a justly structured social field, progressive activists and critical theorists can work toward arrangements that are less unjust, and then toward negating those in favour of arrangements that are less unjust still. The proceduralist account of symbolic democracy that I develop in chapter seven is designed to help movements move in that direction.

Traditional political theory begins by identifying the site of justice. That is, theorists seek to identify the kinds of individual and social phenomena that are appropriately governed by principles of justice.[3] My own judgment of the site of justice relies on two claims. First, justice is intrinsically social. That is, justice is about how we relate to one another and, collectively, to our environment. Sociologically, this claim is rooted in the nature of action itself, the possibility of which depends upon the equally social phenomena of habitus, capital, and field. As I have argued, the dispositions that orient our actions originate through our entrance into the social. Therefore, it would be difficult to describe an action that is *entirely* individual or isolated. This is not to imply that every action is subject to a justice-based critique simply because every action is conceptually social in origin. It does, however, root justice sociologically rather than in naturalistic or a priori terms.

Second, not everything is a question of justice. Not all forms of suffering are the products of injustice. Not all interactions among groups or individuals ought to be described as either just or unjust. Beyond the logical problems involved in an all-encompassing conception of justice, because justice is intrinsically social, to force everything to become a question of justice would risk prioritizing an abstractly defined collective interest over individual practices and actions. Critical theorists would not need to fall back on a liberal concern for liberty or individual autonomy to find fault in an absolute prioritization of collective interest over individuals; such an overarching claim would inevitably lead to homogenization and regimentation. The task for political theory—and of this chapter—is to identify forms of suffering that are normatively significant and recommend principles or practices that might alleviate that suffering.[4]

What, then, ought to be the site of justice? What kinds of suffering are normatively significant to theoretical investigations of justice? In the first chapter, I suggested that a defining characteristic of critical theory is its refusal to treat questions of justice as abstract, formal problems. Critical theorists centre their analysis on experience, particularly the experience of those facing various forms of exclusion and domination. In this spirit, this chapter articulates a conception of symbolic suffering. By connecting Bourdieu's conceptual tools to insights gained from the LGBT/Q and alterglobalization movements, it provides the basis for a preliminary account of justice that can help researchers and activists identify and assess impasses and distortions in social movement politics. Attention to suffering provides a means of conceptually linking adaptive and socially invested accounts of habitus to the aspirations and distortions of collective identity and collective political action.

Therefore, I want to turn now from specific cases to the more general question of suffering, not to render suffering as an abstract theoretical question, but to connect suffering's sociological roots and social movement manifestations to the concrete political theoretical task of making claims about justice. Out of the myriad ways in which I could have critiqued LGBT/Q and alterglobalization movements, I used a set of conceptual tools that brought into focus the operation of symbolic power within these contexts. I did this to sketch out a roadmap with which to navigate contemporary social theory's uneasy tension between structural forces and the active interpretation and practical strategies that agents rely on to act within those structures. Field, habitus, and capital allow us to recognize the constraints that structure imposes on agency while providing tools to track those constraints with context-sensitive nuance. Accepting the centrifugal pull of conformity and failure as a background condition, while recognizing that hierarchically organized social fields mean that people in various locations do not experience this pull uniformly, allows us to make normative claims about justice within movements.

From my analysis of LGBT/Q and alterglobalization struggles, I arrived at two conclusions. First, where movements engage in collective identity processes in a context of radically divergent cultural capital and a field that punishes difference, agents' disproportionate access to symbolic power produces epistemic and symbolic violence, which distort a movement's overall strategic orientation. Second, certain political fields, those particularly prone to differences in symbolic power, produce political antinomies. These antinomies render tactics based on either conformity or failure equally unlikely to succeed within short-term protest-based encounters. Symbolic power infects the processes by which movements commit to both short-term tactics and longer-term strategies. Therefore, in this chapter, I investigate the basis on which symbolic power works by focusing on its experiential level. I examine how the symbolic interacts with affect to influence agents' active construction of the possibilities and obstacles that they face.

For social movement analysis and normative thinking about justice, symbolic power manifests as affective suffering and logical conformism. Logical conformism refers, generally speaking, to the areas where differentiated schemes of perception and differentiated dispositions nonetheless agree, particularly regarding the likely outcomes of social actions and the value of social objects around and upon which strategies are developed. It depends fundamentally on agents bearing a homogeneous conception of time, space, number, and cause. Symbolic power colours the lens through which agents perceive the value of the capital that is available to them, the value of various positions within the social field, and the feasibility of various strategies for achieving or defending those social positions. Therefore, symbolic power is both an effect and a stake. In short, symbolic power sets out the terrain on which agents (individually and collectively) act out of and upon their suffering and its causes, as they understand them. Based on arguments about symbolic power, suffering, and strategy, I suggest in this chapter that justice entails both suffering and the universal distribution of the means of overcoming suffering. In the next chapter, I operationalize that claim by developing a procedural, deliberative account of collective reasoning about strategy and tactic.

A Cry of Distress

Critical political theory, oriented toward normative reflection provoked by, as Young suggests, "hearing a cry of suffering, or distress," seeks to develop and defend conceptions of justice that are interested in ameliorating suffering and therefore, implicitly or explicitly, to foster robust opportunities for all members of society to pursue their full human potential.[5] This approach has not, however, ever been dominant within normative political theory. The mainstream of political theory is dominated by liberal theory, with critical theorists either directly confronting liberalism or trying to construct entirely independent alternatives. Before engaging directly with symbolic power as it relates to suffering and justice, let us look at the major forms of justice on which mainstream political theory has typically founded its arguments.

Unjustified vs. Legitimate Coercion
Liberal political theory—particularly within the social contract tradition and, more recently, in debates about deliberative democracy—has given considerable attention to the moral foundations of political legitimacy.[6] At their core, questions about the social contract and democratic practice ask what moral justification there might be for compelling obedience to the law, for punishing those who disobey, or more simply, why an individual ought to be bound by decisions made by or on behalf of a group. To put it in terms of suffering, this tradition argues that morally unjustified coercion of individuals by the state constitutes a politically relevant form of suffering. Thinkers grappling with these questions will often recognize and consider other forms of suffering, but within the confines of these debates, prescriptions about justice require moral justifications that are capable of legitimizing the state's coercive power. In particular, liberal thinkers are concerned with the extent to which the obligation to obey the law infringes on the individual's sphere of autonomous decision-making.

Liberals tend to remain neutral on suffering that results from individual choice or unavoidable happenstance. They prefer to focus on the relationship between individual freedom and the appropriate distribution of the benefits and burdens of social existence. Justice in this view is established through one of several means: a rationally justifiable constellation of formal equality, the universal application of the law and protection of individual freedom through some combination of legal rights, or for democratic theorists, through a morally legitimate method of collective decision-making.[7] State coercion in matters ranging from criminal prosecution to economic regulation and redistribution is legitimate only insofar as that coercion can be morally justified through reference to equality, universality, pluralism, and the protection of liberty.[8]

There are, of course, many critiques of liberalism, and there is a vigorous debate within liberalism itself on how best to hold together its constellation of central commitments. However, political theorist Steven Lukes's analysis of the kinds of power provides a useful starting point for understanding why liberal conceptions of political legitimacy are insufficient for making claims about justice. Liberal and pluralist conceptions of politics, legitimacy, and democracy typically limit themselves to what Lukes calls one-dimensional and two-dimensional views of power. In one- and two-dimensional understandings, power is thought to exist only when there are conflicts between the interests that political agents articulate as preferences, particularly when they translate these preferences into concrete political actions. In such cases, power manifests as the ability of one individual or group to realize their preferences at the expense of another.[9] Lukes's key insight, however, is that power is more than the mechanisms by which competing interests are politically adjudicated: power's most important dimension lies in the mechanisms by which it obtains consent by controlling the desires upon which interests are constructed. He calls this the third dimension of power.[10]

Field and habitus can make Lukes's critique concrete while also extending its reach. In the adaptive understanding of habitus that I set out earlier (see chapter three), I emphasized Bourdieu's attention to the role of mimesis and correction in producing the generative schemes of perception and dispositions through which agents act on the natural and social worlds. The twin foundations of this conception are a phenomenological commitment to practical mastery developed through exposure to the world, and a structuralist commitment to differentiated but relatively durable social fields. The result is a conception of agency as the strategic effort to defend and improve one's store of various forms of capital through successful actions within the prevailing rules of the relevant social context.

Remember that agents implicitly understand the rules of most social fields rather than consciously recognizing and agreeing upon them. As a result, agents' schemes of perception and dispositions are structured preconsciously according to doxa and logical conformism. For instance, the state regulates the major events of the social calendar (school calendars, fiscal years, public holidays, and so on), and imposes principles of classification such as gender, age, and qualification through diverse mechanisms (voting age, age of consent laws, educational credentialling and institutional regulation). Over time, the social categories that the state constructs through official classifications become reified and naturalized cognitive categories through which agents perceive and act upon the world.[11] We looked at this process in relation to the LGBT/Q and alterglobalization movements. The Charter of Rights and Freedoms fostered a doxic commitment among gay and lesbian activists to individual liberty and equality-as-sameness at the expense of collective freedom and equality-as-difference. At the G20 protests in Toronto, politicians and the police alike used state levers to support distinctions between legitimate and illegitimate forms of protest, but also to devalue disruption more generally.

At the heart of habitus, then, lies agents' misrecognition both of the arbitrary nature of distinctions based on age, race, and protest tactic (though these distinctions may become the objects of political contests) and of the arbitrary origins of the state's power to underpin these distinctions.[12] Thus, the bulk of obedience to the modern state derives from neither mechanical coercion nor conscious consent to rational forms of legitimate authority. Rather, the state is a particular instance of social calls to order that trigger dispositions predisposed to notice them.[13] In this view, legitimacy is therefore not a question of lucid consciousness (à la Weber and the social contract theorists) but an agreement between social and political structures that are incorporated into the body through habitus and the objective organization of the political and state fields. Playing on David Hume's astonishment at the ease with which people submit to rule, Bourdieu argues that the problem of legitimacy is the fact that for the most part it is not a problem.[14] Conceptualizing normatively relevant suffering as illegitimate coercion, then, misses the point. There is no such thing as an agent that would be completely free if it weren't for the interventions of the state. The idea of presocial freedom is nonsensical because our sense of freedom and action is produced socially, largely through state and cultural doxa internalized as habitus.

My refusal to accept suffering as illegitimate coercion as the primary site of justice is not an anarchist argument; states have a role to play in promoting just distributions of economic and symbolic capital. It is, however, an explicitly anti-liberal argument. Just as pluralist conceptions only recognize power when it affects observable decision-making and thereby mask power's prior effects, liberal conceptions of justice as the partial redress of suffering achieved by limiting the state's coercive power to its morally justified exercise mask the myriad ways in which suffering is socially produced and organized. In short, centring unjustified state coercion as the most relevant form of suffering masks the sociological—rather than moral—foundations of consent and legitimacy. Justice as legitimate coercion therefore supports a status quo circularity: questions of legitimacy are bound up in one-dimensional or two-dimensional conceptions of power, yet they rest on a state-fostered, doxic consensus over what counts as coercive use of power.

Material Exclusions
The Occupy Wall Street protest in New York and the occupations of public space that it inspired in cities around the world in the fall of 2011 point to the ongoing political relevance of disparities in wealth and income. Inspired by

the successful 2011 occupation of Tahrir Square in Cairo, Egypt, by activists demanding the resignation of then-president Hosni Mubarak, the "culture-jamming" magazine *Adbusters* issued a call to action: "On September 17, we want to see 20,000 people flood into lower Manhattan, set up tents, kitchens, peaceful barricades and occupy Wall Street for a few months."[15] Although Occupy Wall Street protesters refused pressures to present a coherent and unified list of demands, they quickly came to be associated with the slogan "We are the 99 per cent," a reference to the economic and political distortions that surround the consolidation of significant amounts of wealth in the hands of the richest 1 per cent of the population.

A report from the United States Congressional Budget Office, released shortly after the occupations began, confirmed many of the claims that protesters were making about income disparity. The report found that between 1979 and 2007, overall average real household income in the United States increased by a modest 19 per cent. However, this average increase was not evenly distributed; those in the top 1 per cent enjoyed a tripling of their income over the period.[16] The rise of various forms of precarious employment has contributed considerably to these disparities, as it tends to put a downward pressure on wages by making unionization more difficult and individual workers less able to demand higher wages. A 2013 study found that, in the Greater Toronto Area, nearly 40 per cent of workers report some form of precariousness in their employment, meaning they are working part-time, casually, or on temporary contracts.[17] Not surprisingly, researchers investigating income inequality in Canada found that in both the most prosperous growth era of the last generation (1997–2007) and the decade with the slowest growth (1987–1997), Canada's richest 1 per cent, whose average annual income was $404,500, took almost one-third of the national growth in income.[18]

Given the massive upward redistribution of wealth that developed economies have experienced over the last several decades, and neoliberalism's remarkable proclivity for producing wealth at the expense of the large segments of the population that are condemned to precarious employment, poverty, and material suffering, economic exclusion constitutes an immediate and obviously political form of suffering.[19] Certainly, there is ample evidence that low-income and precarious employment is associated with a range of negative impacts on wellness, including barriers to social mobility, loss of time with family, social isolation, and poor health outcomes. Centring normative thinking about justice on economic exclusion would therefore fit with critical theory's commitment to starting analysis with cries of distress rather than with abstract metaphysical questions. Nonetheless, attention to material inequalities may not give a sufficiently robust foundation on which to make general prescriptions about how social movements ought to pursue justice.[20]

Egalitarian debates remain within the distributive paradigm and, although they pay important attention to material suffering, they occlude the importance of symbolic violence and distinction-based suffering. Domination, as it is conceived in the model I am proposing, is about active constructions, struggles over meaning, and subjective adjustments. If justice is a question of distribution, then it is not material goods that require egalitarian consideration—or at least not primarily—but the power to shape and apply value to the constructions, meaning, and subjective adjustments through which agents experience and act upon their suffering. Naturally these entail reference to relevant material realities, particularly as those realities articulate into more or less durable class structures. Moreover, it is the hierarchical distribution of symbolic power that (as we saw in the previous chapter) frustrates efforts to redress material inequality and material suffering.

Distributive justice alone is insufficient for an account of justice that is sensitive to the relationship between suffering and accumulation. Instead, justice demands a more thorough account of the relationship between adaptation to the demands of fields (whether provoked by injury or reward) and the distribution of potential for accumulation within economic, cultural, and symbolic fields. Examining a third form of suffering—what I call incidental suffering—might help to illustrate this point further.

Incidental Injuries
At first glance, it might seem as though the incidental injuries of everyday life—stubbed toes, boredom, minor disappointments, and so on—are normatively and politically irrelevant. Indeed, these kinds of injuries are generally not the stuff around which social movements organize. On the other hand, just because incidental injuries appear to be relatively minor in isolation does not mean that they bear absolutely no relation to justice. Appreciating the social and political context of everyday injuries opens the door to a more thorough understanding of the forms of suffering that are traditionally considered to be normatively relevant. Therefore, it is worth considering the relationship between distribution and justice generally and the account of agency on which these conceptualizations depend in order to contrast such accounts with Bourdieu's more nuanced account of embodiment, hurt, and the distribution of chance.

Indeed, the pressures and perspectives that practical engagement with the world entail—the fact that we are exposed to physical and emotional injury, suffering, and death—force us to take the world and its dangers seriously and to orient ourselves, preconsciously, through the habitus toward adapting to, avoiding, and overcoming the dangers that the world poses. Injuries and traumas are central to how habitus is formed: the corrections and adjustments that provoke adaptation may take the form of positive rewards, but they are more likely to manifest in psychological and physical suffering. Short of injuries that are sufficiently traumatic as to cause ongoing distress or mental illness, minor psychological and physical suffering is beneficial insofar as it provokes the adaptation necessary for habitus to incorporate the dispositions that agents rely on for successful struggle over stakes in various fields. Such adjustments, to emphasize, have nothing to do with adopting an objective perspective from which a list of all possible choices and outcomes can be drawn. They have everything to do with the overall set of injuries a person faces and the classed, gendered, racialized, and otherwise hierarchical distribution of both the quantity and quality of those injuries. If habitus reduces suffering by adapting to the demands of the physical and social world, injury itself is not normatively relevant: normative stakes lie in the highly contingent distribution of the kinds of injuries that are typically experienced and the adjustments that those injuries produce.

Think, for example, of the indignity routinely caused to young Black men through policies such as stop and frisk in New York City and carding in Ontario. In both cases, police routinely stop people; in the latter, they also record information about the encounter. Even if police do not behave in an intimidating or threatening manner during these encounters—although they often do—there is a clear injury here. In and of itself, the fact that Black men are disproportionately stopped and interrogated is humiliating and threatening.[21] Insofar as daily humiliations, injuries, and exclusions are structured into the fields that people navigate—which are also fields that they must adapt to or resist—and insofar as these fields systematically injure and humiliate some but not others, they constitute a potential site of justice.

Critical theorists have long pointed to the markedly different subjective experience of the social world by members of dominated or oppressed groups. Iris Marion Young and Marilyn Frye point to the structurally produced experience of being closed in on all sides that is common to members of oppressed groups and foreign to the experience of privilege.[22] Everyday, banal incidents of suffering are not uniformly experienced because they cannot be entirely abstracted from broader distributions of frustrations, exclusions, and (as I will further discuss below) misrecognized and subtle incidences of symbolic violence. Visions of justice as related to material exclusions are wrong to separate questions of power from questions of material well-being, precisely because this separation abstracts the distribution of material goods from the subjective experience of acting in a social world that hierarchically organizes people's ability to enjoy, accumulate, and derive psychic and symbolic benefit from those goods.

To make my argument about justice—that justice entails both suffering and the universal distribution of the means of overcoming suffering—I tease out two distinctions: the conceptual differences between Young's conception of oppression and Bourdieu's symbolic violence, and then the conceptual differences between Foucault's and Bourdieu's theories of power.

Normalization and Generation

Young's classic conception of oppression as a way of understanding how suffering is socially organized provides a useful contrast to Bourdieu's claims about symbolic violence. It is worth considering both for its own conceptual merits and because of its considerable influence over the ways that social movements have understood themselves.[23] Young's reliance on a Foucauldian conception of power in her articulation of group-based politics foreshadows much in contemporary identity and post-identity political movements. Nonetheless, Bourdieu's notion of symbolic violence offers important explanatory and normative resources that are missing from Young and Foucault.

Young conceives of justice as the absence of domination and oppression, where domination consists of institutional constraints on agents' self-determination, and oppression consists of institutional constraints on self-development. Young seeks to maintain liberal commitments to individuals' ability to autonomously select and pursue whatever life goals they value. She rejects, however, liberal conceptions of power that ignore the structural and group-based social contexts that differentially distribute opportunities to select and pursue one's conception of the good life. In short, Young measures social justice by the degree to which institutions and norms allow agents to develop and exercise their capacities, express their experience, and participate in determining their actions and the conditions of their actions.[24]

This argument relies on establishing a social ontology—in contrast to liberal individualism—that recognizes both the existence of groups and the structured power relations that produce those groups. Although democratic participation (non-domination) is important to Young's account, her treatment of oppression is particularly relevant because it is an overtly political attempt to understand the organized suffering of various groups. It describes various forms of suffering—such as racism, sexism, and homophobia—without reducing them to a single, unified axis (as has been typical of Marxist conceptions). To that end, Young recommends five overlapping categories for understanding oppression: exploitation, marginalization, powerlessness, cultural imperialism, and violence.

Young's conceptualization of oppression is motivated by a number of normative and theoretical goals. Primarily, she is interested in establishing the grounds for justifying group-based policy and representation. Focus on group-based relations to structures of power, for Young, draws attention away from the substantive, pattern-based conceptions of justice that are typical of distributive paradigms and toward proceduralist accounts that link participatory deliberation and decision-making to positive evaluations of group difference.[25]

There are several obvious similarities between some of what Young describes as oppression and what Bourdieu might label symbolic violence. Young's cultural imperialism, for example, "involves the universalization of a dominant group's experience and culture and its establishment as the norm."[26] The universalization and imposition of dominant groups' judgments is central to symbolic violence as well, but where cultural imperialism appears to connote specific, substantive beliefs about groups and individuals, symbolic power operates through deeper divisions and homologously organized sets of distinctions. In a sense, Bourdieu is concerned with deeper cognitive classificatory structures that are both more misrecognized and also, therefore, more resistant to transformation. Indeed, this is why distortions plague social movements: consciously rejecting the substantive, superficial definitions imposed through symbolic power does not transform the bodily dispositions by which underlying schemes of classification gain affective hold over dominated agents.

Admittedly, the kinds of suffering that Young labels oppressive and Bourdieu describes as everyday humiliations and exclusions are, for the most part, the same phenomena. Where these two approaches diverge is not on the substance of the suffering, but on the conception of power that explains how that suffering comes to be institutionally and contextually organized. The relevant distinction, therefore, is not just between oppression and symbolic violence, but between Young's use of Foucault's disciplinary power and Bourdieu's conception of symbolic power.[27]

Relying on Foucault's conception of power, Young rejects theories of justice that treat power as an object to be distributed, wielded, or shared. Foucault argued for treating power as positive, as productive, as intrinsic to and circulating among "relations of force," which is to say that power operates in the minutiae of spontaneous strategies available to subjects through multiple overlapping discourses.[28] Foucault was particularly interested in how institutions—prisons, schools, and psychiatric hospitals provide paradigm cases—produce subjects through constant surveillance and discipline.

We can use Bourdieu's insistence on the connection between seemingly trivial details of daily life and social behaviour—which is superficially similar to Foucault's method—as an opportunity to distinguish between the two thinkers. Foucault was interested in how institutions produce subjects through discipline and confessional moments; Bourdieu argued that this was a mistake. Subjectivity truly emerges, according to Bourdieu, in the everyday minutiae of social interactions, what he calls the "ordinary order of things," rather than through power's officially authorized—that is, institutional—manifestations.[29] Therefore, Bourdieu was less interested in normalization and the production of variously disciplined subjects—the psychiatric subject, the prison subject, and so on—and more interested in how the ordinary order of things and the continuous stream of corrections and adjustments to which agents are exposed in ordinary life operate on the body to instill a preconscious sense of social space and its rules through the habitus.[30]

In so distinguishing his own conception of power from Foucault's, Bourdieu neglects a central feature of Foucault's approach: Foucault treated institutions as laboratories, where strategies of control and techniques of normalization are developed and subsequently exported beyond the institution. Bourdieu, and some who take up his approach, mistake the laboratory focus of Foucault's description of power as the entire picture.[31] In fact, for Foucault, modern power gains its efficacy precisely when techniques developed in prisons, schools, and psychiatric hospitals—above all the techniques of surveillance and discipline that these institutions enact directly on the body—are exported outside those institutions into everyday life. That is, the laboratories, on which Bourdieu charges Foucault with being overly focused, develop techniques of power that become available for articulation to "discourses"—organized sets of knowledges and practices that constitute the means by which subjects understand themselves and the strategies that are available to them.

This constitutes Foucault's key insight about power: institutions are unnecessary for surveillance and discipline because individuals, in adopting and incorporating discourses, become the agents of their own normalization. Foucault offers the paradigmatic example of families, caught in contradictions between sexuality and alliance. Families experience conflicting demands produced by psychiatric and medical discourses, but for rescue from these contradictions they turn to psychiatrists and doctors as the experts authorized by these discourses. They become, as Foucault says, "the chief agents of a deployment of sexuality which drew its outside support from doctors, educators, and later psychologists."[32] Bourdieu is wrong, therefore, to suggest that Foucault's conception of power is overly institutional. Power gains its efficacy precisely at the moment of export when the institutional discipline of subjects is taken over, through accession to the discursive demands of normalization, by subjects outside of institutions themselves.

In the Foucauldian schema, discourse performs two key functions: it organizes knowledge and it produces strategies. In a poststructuralist conception of power, these functions are distributed and decentred, emptying them of the determining causal power that structuralism had previously assumed. Nonetheless, discourse runs the risk, conceptually, of ossifying into another form of structuralism. Insofar as discourse is produced at the macro level, but internalized and activated at the micro level through the subjects it produces, subjects appear to have no choice but to enact the knowledges and strategies by which they are produced. Discourse becomes a linguistically and institutionally based determining structure comparable to the old determining class structures of orthodox Marxism.[33]

A Foucauldian response could legitimately suggest that strategic action is not simply a mechanistic response to the demands and opportunities produced by a single discourse; rather, it must involve selection among multiple discourses. That is, subjects are not only produced by discourses about sexuality or only by discourses about citizenship or only by discourses about ethics and religion. They are produced by all of these discourses simultaneously. Subjects act, therefore, from within multiple discourses simultaneously and according to the demands of a given context. Further, any given subject might turn to one or more discourse depending on the imminent demands of the situation. One might turn to psychiatry, while another turns to religion. Neither discourse can, strictly speaking, be said to be determinative because neither has a monopoly on the production of subjectivity or on the strategies to which subjects turn.

This points to a more fundamental problem with Foucault's approach. If families turn to psychiatry as agents of their own normalization, then we need to explain why they make that particular turn as opposed to a turn to religion, nihilism, politics, or some other discourse by which they might understand and seek to resolve the contradictions they experience. What makes one discourse more appealing than another? Or rather, to avoid the voluntarist implications of a word like "appeal" here, what brings subjects to one set of normalized practices rather than another? Moreover, there is no room in Foucauldian conceptions of power and discourse for explaining why various agents, pursuing exactly similar strategies from within the same discourses, are likely to have different levels of success.

Bourdieu's framework does, however, provide a mechanism for understanding behaviour within discourse: namely, practical reason. Fields set out the terrain within which specific agents are objectively related to each other and determine the value of all of the objects and practices within that field. Habitus provides a hierarchically produced and therefore highly differentiated set of dispositions and cognitive distinctions through which agents perceive that social field, the value of what is at stake in the field, and the strategies available for pursuing those stakes. Capital, finally, provides resources that not only improve or diminish an agent's chances for successful action, but also orient an agent toward strategies that are appropriate for the amount and type of capital they have available to them. Practical reason is the interaction of field, habitus, and capital, manifested through strategy.

The essential difference between Bourdieu and Young/Foucault hinges on what gives structures their durability and thereby conditions the kinds of resistance that are available to groups and individuals within them. Young remains somewhat abstract in her definition of structure, preferring instead to describe structure in terms of institutional context and linking it to "the unquestioned norms, habits, and symbols, in the assumptions underlying institutional rules and the collective consequences of following those rules."[34] Elsewhere, Young argues that power is relational, but non-dyadic, which means that, with Foucault, Young suggests that power exists only in relations between groups and individuals and that the exercise of power depends on the position one holds, an agent's nodal point within a network of force relations.[35]

In Young's network-based conception, structures derive their durability from the homogenizing and ever-deepening operation of normalization. Therefore, insofar as Young's conceptualization of oppression depends on Foucault's understanding of power, oppression risks the same conceptual problems: either oppression is determinative, or we need a more nuanced account of resistance to oppression than Foucault can provide. Given that agents have demonstrably refused to be determined by their oppression, the latter option seems more fruitful to pursue, and Bourdieu's framework offers the required nuance.

The distinctions between oppression and symbolic violence and conceptualizations of power come down to the difference between the incorporation of norms (Foucault) and the incorporation of schemes of classification (Bourdieu). The contrast between the operation of an incorporated norm and an incorporated scheme of classification—between normalization and habitus—lies in the fundamentally homogenizing nature of the former and the generative nature of the latter. To clarify the conceptual, strategic, and normative implications of the distinction between homogenization and generation, I will now undertake more detailed analysis of symbolic violence, the forms of suffering it generates, and the implications it has for social movements and political action.

Symbolic Violence

Bourdieu grounds his analysis of the effects of neoliberalism in a distinction between material poverty (*la grande misère*) and the daily, ordinary suffering that social exclusion and domination produce (*la petite misère*). This Rousseauian conception of social life suggests that suffering increases within "multiplied social spaces" created by capitalist social inequalities, even when overall poverty has been somewhat reduced.[36] We have already looked at elements of symbolic power and violence in previous chapters; in this section I will emphasize the affective life of symbolic violence and its implications for suffering and political mobilization. Just as habitus is a general set of dispositions that generate action in response to immediate demands of social fields, affect is a structured set of dispositions that produce emotional responses. Emotions such as fear, shame, and pride are neither rootless nor spontaneous. They express at the emotional level general orientations—affect—that are essential to how habitus navigates the symbolic. There are three components to my analysis of the affective life of symbolic violence:

- the dynamics of stratification, recognition, and misrecognition that are central to Bourdieu's conception of agency;
- the mimetic origins of affect; and
- the constant practical and strategic pursuit of symbolic capital that is central to Bourdieu's conception of agency.

Bourdieu's account of symbolic suffering hinges on his treatment of the symbolic as a structured construction of a shared classification of the social world, which is to say a shared scheme of perception and meaning by which agents understand the value of objects, agents, and actions within social space. Here, three central features of the symbolic give it its affective power. First, the symbolic depends entirely on recognition. If a symbolic object did not meet with agents bearing a habitus that is disposed to perceiving and appreciating that object, then it would have no social value or effect. Dispositions function as an energy repository, triggered into action (or reaction) by the symbolic. Without the recognition that appropriate dispositions afford, the habitus's energy would remain merely potential, and representations would have no meaning.[37]

Second, the symbolic depends on relational logic to ascribe meaning and value to all objects within a symbolic system. The fact that Bourdieu was writing, in part, against structuralist linguistic and anthropological methods means he relied on the "principle of difference" developed by Swiss linguist Ferdinand de Saussure. According to the principle of difference, the meaning of every object within structured space (or in Saussure's work, the meaning of each word and phrase within language) can only be determined in relation to all of the other objects within that space. This means that the value of any object, agent, or form of capital in social space is determined not by its intrinsic value, but by its value compared to all other objects, agents, and forms of capital. Such structuralist means of tracing value represent an important shift away from substantialist thinking. As discussed earlier in relation to violence (see chapter five), substantialist thinking ascribes positive properties to objects and agents rather than treating such properties as emerging from dynamic processes and the relationship among objects and agents.[38] Therefore, the symbolic is a representation of the world, but not a direct, positive representation of individual objects that names some essential truth about the objects represented. Rather, the symbolic represents the relations among objects. The symbolic is laden with power because it naturalizes the historically produced but morally arbitrary distinctions by which social fields are hierarchically organized. To the extent that agents recognize and accept this hierarchical organization, they also recognize the differential esteem or value the symbolic assigns to various individuals, groups, objects, and practices.

Finally, the symbolic is a scheme by which agents act upon the world and engage in struggles over the construction and shape of this structured system of meanings. The constructed systems of meaning that organize the symbolic are not spontaneous, random, or easily transformed—they exist durably in buildings and in the physical structures of human geography, and they are incorporated into the durable dispositions of habitus. Further, these schemes of classification, produced through long histories of struggles over interpretations of the world, having been objectified in habitus and geography, produce logical conformism. This shared logic enables agents bearing reasonably different habitus to reach sufficient agreement about the meaning of the natural and social worlds that they are able to act upon them in socially intelligible ways.[39] This phenomenon manifests in the dispositions of the habitus as preconscious structures underlying cognition that are the basis on which agents encounter the world. Classed, gendered, and embodying unequally distributed capacities for participating in social fields, but nonetheless sharing fundamental logical and normative assumptions and vested in social participation, habitus encounters the practical exigencies of the social world (and the possibilities and obstacles it contains), and it reflects the schemes of classification that organize that world back onto the body in the form of emotional experience and evaluation.

Turning to the mimetic origins of affect, we see how logical conformism and differentiated habitus underpin symbolic power. Symbolic power operates through the body to replicate the tension between conformity as agreement about the social world and habitus as unequally distributed chances to act successfully in the world, to be recognized by it, or conversely to suffer in it. For this reason, Bourdieu emphasizes the close relationship between the mimetic, cognitive, and affective aspects of habitus:

> The body believes in what it plays at: it weeps if it mimes grief. It does not represent what it performs, it does not memorize the past, it *enacts* the past, bringing it back to life. What is "learned by body" is not something that one has, like knowledge that can be brandished, but something that one is.[40]

What is "learned by body" is the entire cosmology of the body's social environs; the body learns schemes of classification that articulate power and authority to value, in the sense of what is desirable, beautiful, and good. Affectivity, then, involves a two-stage process. First, agents acquire, in the form of habitus, a practical bodily knowledge capable of giving them a sense of their present and potential position in social space (a sense of one's place), which is also a sense of placement (awareness of rank, how to behave to keep that rank, and how to keep within it).[41] Both deeply embodied and laden with emotional content structured by the structured dynamics of recognition, these senses of place and placement are then retriggered in social situations where bodies are re-placed in concrete relations of power and judgment. Bourdieu writes:

> The practical recognition through which the dominated, often unwittingly, contribute to their own domination by tacitly accepting, in advance, the limits imposed on them, often takes the form of bodily emotion (shame, timidity, anxiety, guilt), often associated with the impression of regressing towards archaic relationships, those of childhood and family.[42]

Sense of place and placement take the form of emotion (unease when out of place, comfort when in one's place). When repositioned in subordinate postures, the habitus expresses unease through behaviours such as avoidance or unconscious adjustments of speech; visible manifestations may include blushing, inarticulacy, clumsiness, and trembling.[43]

When I introduced habitus and symbolic capital (see chapter three), I focused primarily on our exposure to the world and on our capacity to adapt to the dangers and opportunities our world presents. At the same time, agents undergo a founding pedagogical achievement—the capacity to make a binary distinction between self and other, which, in turn, allows subjects to take on the point of view of others and thereby act in accordance with their expectations. Adaptation and the cognitive capacity to act as social agents combine to allow agents to develop normative classifications about what they value.[44] Nonetheless, the uneven distribution of skill that attends the categorically differentiated production of habitus allows for a gap, for some agents, between the norms and evaluations that structure social space and an agent's sense of their ability to meet those norms. Produced through an agent's internalization of other agents' real or perceived judgments, shame is exemplary among emotional responses to this gap. Shame indicates that we are deeply interested—recall that the power of the symbolic depends on releasing energy from the habitus through recognition of value or interest—but that we are also painfully aware of how short we have come from meeting other agents' real or perceived expectations, now internalized as our own. Shame is therefore deeply social, though it is experienced individually, and its tendency to remain unarticulated makes it a particularly powerful embodied re-enactment of the past.[45]

Describing what is arguably the flip side of the same coin, sociologist Steph Lawler points to disgust as a visceral mechanism by which social hierarchies are reproduced through a preconscious and affective evaluation of the self in relation to people in different areas of social space. Disgust is a particularly strong indication that a norm is presently operative and is being violated. This is by definition a social evaluation, an evaluation based on internalized collective judgment. Like shame, however social the origin of the evaluation, the experience is individual and visceral; in limited cases, disgust can result in an actual physical expulsion—vomiting—in response to a norm's violation.[46]

The implications for identity-based movements are clear. It is one thing to consciously recognize the formal equality of all individuals; it is another thing entirely to transform the shame produced by the gap between, for example, the aspiration to lead full, affirming, experimental, and egalitarian queer sexual lives and the perceived expectation that doing so depends on establishing mature, monogamous, respectable relationships. People in any particular dominated group are more than aware of the disgust their lack of capital creates in dominant agents, and most could list off the ways in which members of dominant groups freely broadcast that disgust.

Homonormative calls from conservatives such as Andrew Sullivan and liberal activists who want formal equality because "we are just like everybody else" depend, in a sense, on lesbian and gay interest in reducing shame by reducing the gap between aspiration and expectation. That is, they call for a reduction in shame through a reduction in exposure to disgust. At the same time, queer activists, who seek to reduce shame by freeing themselves from homo- and heteronormative calls to order need to be more explicit in their attention to providing the psychic resources necessary to reorient deeply embodied normalized dispositions and to be aware that this task is more manageable for the bearers of certain forms of capital (for example, the security derived from economic and cultural capital in a tenured university appointment). It is unfair to expect LGBT people to bear the cost of failure without providing resources and strategies to support them in doing so. This is precisely why a critical theory of social movements cannot simply adjudicate between conformist or failing strategies: symbolic power, in this case as manifested at the affective level, operates to undermine both.

The Politics of Experience

It would be easy to make direct connections between suffering, politics, and justice, but making those connections too quickly bears conceptual and practical danger. Indeed, where these connections seem most obvious there is the greatest danger that doxic thinking and arbitrary logical conformism underpin common sense responses to suffering: LGBT/Q people's suffering *must* be reduced through formal legal equality; capitalist exploitation *must* be reduced through peaceful protest.

At the same time, when we link justice to suffering, there is a risk of treating suffering itself as an object with normative status rather than as an expression of tensions between skills and expectations, or put another way, as an unequal distribution of the jeopardies that the world presents us with and the resources required to confront those jeopardies. There is a danger that suffering itself could be fetishized. Taking up Nietzsche's psychological notion of *ressentiment* is useful here. When an individual or group is unable to physically prevent someone else from harming or exploiting them, it becomes an appealing strategy to convince an attacker that they are morally wrong, or in the alternative, to convince enough other people that this harm is morally offensive so that they defend you themselves or by proxy.

Postmodern political scientist Wendy Brown argues that politics based on substituting moral codes for action valorize suffering as a social virtue. It leads politicized identities to invest in their own subjugation and, ultimately, to prefer political powerlessness and generalized impotence to collective liberation through empowerment. She argues that political projects that substitute morality for agency are destined to remain complicit in the legal, cultural, and discursive structures that produce suffering.[47] I don't disagree with Brown on this, but I would suggest that the greater problem, from a Nietzschean perspective, is that ressentiment trades action and creativity for a sheltered security. Indeed, ressentiment is the opposite of action, insofar as it uses morality to short-circuit conflict. Ressentiment deadens and constrains, it makes life smaller and more narrow; action enlivens and invigorates.

For LGBT/Q communities in particular, but also for alterglobalization and other activists, the choice between ressentiment and direct action matters: in turning in one direction or the other, movements cultivate a collective disposition and accompanying skills. When movements work with police to demonstrate the legitimacy and "peacefulness" of their protest, as the People First march did at the G20, or rely on courts to win legal rights, as the North American LGBT movement has done, they invest in state-produced security at the expense of their ability to engage in autonomous disruptive action.

Given that it matters how movements translate experience into strategies and tactics, experience alone cannot provide reliable insights for making claims about social being and, therefore, for making claims about justice. Instead, experience must be understood in relation to action. Because experience is constructed through relations of power, political theory can make normative claims about the moral value of various ways in which those relations are structured and the resulting distribution of suffering, privilege, and so on. However, there is no vantage point—for theorists or for activists—from which either experience or the relations of power that produce it can be assessed. Agents respond to their suffering and to opportunities to act upon that suffering based on the partial and perspective-bound assessments that their dispositions and capital permit. Theorists, insofar as they are committed to avoiding justice claims based on formal abstractions, rely on the strategies agents develop for glimpses into how a more just society would be organized. This constitutes a dialectical relationship in which suffering produces action, which is available for critique, which in turn helps inform new strategies and new actions.

Moreover, theorizing the relationship between experience and justice must remain rooted in action because the possibility of action in response to experience remains intricately bound to relations of power. More than simply a strategic question of how to gain sufficient power to improve one's position within a field, the experience of power—or its lack—is part of what the habitus incorporates. As a result, habitus develops dispositions toward power and a tendency toward certain kinds of action. Ressentiment is a mode of action that responds—however problematically—to the relationship between powerlessness and action.

The close relationship between experience and action could appear to recommend treating habitus as a site of justice. After all, in Bourdieu's theory of practice, habitus emerges from practical experience of the world (including suffering) and functions to unite the various resources that an agent bears to the range of objectively structured opportunities and necessities they confront. Habitus is both a fundamentally relational concept and Bourdieu's way of uniting agency in a dialectic of experience and action. Further, I have emphasized habitus's adaptive nature and its strategic deployment of the capacities that it mobilizes. It is tempting, therefore, to treat habitus as the site of a capacities-based account of justice. Political theorists could endeavour to describe a desirable or most desirable habitus, perhaps focusing on its strategic skill or its ability to identify and resist symbolic violence. Alternatively, mechanisms could be sought for enhancing the adaptability of the habitus, a sort of focus on reconciling even dominated agents to the conditions of their domination, although it seems particularly undesirable to respond to unjustly organized social structures with adaptation rather than reorganization.

Treating habitus as the site of justice depends on making use of relational logic—an improvement over substantialist thinking—but nonetheless attends to the wrong relation. Habitus is an explanatory concept that captures the relationship between distributions of capacities and the objective structures within which those capacities are deployed. As I've noted, focusing on capacities alone is dangerous because, short of a just distribution of those capacities, the adaptive origins and development of habitus could recommend an account of justice that is based on adaptation to domination. However, it is also insufficient to simply attempt to identify a "just" set of institutional arrangements (as in the distributive debates within liberalism) because the most perfectly just institutions would still require agents who are disposed to adhering to the institutions' strictures.

Thus, a conception of justice ought to focus on promoting a relationship between habitus and field founded in fair terms of play: a distribution of capacities such that each has access to the universal and to political participation, and objective structures that both reproduce that distribution and allow for innovation, conflict, and conflict resolution. Reproduction is key here because the conception of politics that I am relying upon does not imagine an end-of-history type teleology wherein a "perfectly just" society is achievable. Rather, I rely on a basic assumption that the nature of interest and our induction into the social means that agents will generally try to secure their own profits even, though not necessarily, at other agents' expense. The relationship between objective conditions and the distribution of capacities ought to be such that political struggle ensures the reproduction of fair terms of play.

Justice, in this view, is a procedural requirement wherein suffering is politicized, recognized as socially organized, and acted upon within the context of the relationship between field and habitus. The absence of both the field conditions necessary for this relationship and of habitus disposed to participate in these conditions produces distortions. These distortions manifest primarily through schemes of symbolic meaning that prioritize some forms of suffering while marginalizing others, and in strategic political efforts to alleviate the suffering of some while replicating the suffering of others.[48]

Prophets of the Present

Suffering is a politically and socially mediated experience; our understanding of suffering, therefore, has explanatory and normative implications. At the explanatory level, social movement research's consensus on the importance of collective identity in mobilizing processes points to what Melucci calls the "prophetic function" of social movements.

> Contemporary movements are prophets of the present. What they possess is not the force of the apparatus but the power of the word. They announce the commencement of change; not, however, a change in the distant future but one that is already a presence. They force the power out into the open and give it a shape and a face.[49]

Social movements make existing conflicts and suffering publicly visible. Importantly, movements do not directly represent conflict and suffering; they construct it, mediating both how it appears and how it is experienced. However, while social movements might serve a prophetic function in forcing symbolic power out into the open by making visible the suffering it produces, symbolic suffering is not just an object on which social movements act, but also a mode of domination that they replicate. To attend to symbolic suffering, as I have argued, we must shift from an account of group formation based on negotiation and collaborative meaning-making to an account based on domination.

To conclude this chapter, I want to revisit the core distinction that I drew between Foucault and Bourdieu. While the former articulated a conception of power based on normalization, the latter's vision was rooted in a differentiated, generative habitus capable of practical reason. Normalization's totalizing ambition derives its efficacy from the ever-deepening submission of the subject to the bounds and limits of discourse. Foucault emphasized the subject as the product of discourse. Subjects are compelled to present themselves and to construct a sense of self-knowledge through discursively informed introspection. This mode of power does not operate, strictly speaking, through either violence or consent, but by "action upon actions."

> In itself, the exercise of power is not a violence that sometimes hides, or an implicitly renewed consent. It operates on the field of possibilities in which the behavior of active subjects is able to inscribe itself. It is a set of actions on possible actions; it incites, it induces, it seduces, it makes easier or more difficult; it releases or contrives, makes more probable or less; in the extreme, it constrains or forbids absolutely, but it is always a way of acting upon one or more acting subjects by virtue of their acting or being capable of action.[50]

The crux here is that for power to be action upon action, it requires a subject who acts. In fact, for Foucault power and freedom are not mutually exclusive, because power's operation depends on the existence of a free subject whose actions can be acted upon.[51] But where his claim in *History of Sexuality* that "where there is power there is resistance" seemed to rely on an incomplete account of the source of agency (again, because it is not clear how subjects "choose" to turn to one discourse or another), his account of resistance appears to be tautological. Foucault's turn to a political strategy based on the ethics of the self, through aestheticized experiments in living without the expectation of freedom from power, is therefore deeply problematic. In particular, it provides no conceptual ability to distinguish between radical aesthetic gestures and pseudo-individualistic replications of power.[52] That is, it remains impossible to tell whether, or in what ways, gestures challenge or merely rework power creatively but superficially.

By contrast, the Bourdieu-inspired framework that I have developed lets us trace radical and conformist strategies as well as whether those strategies challenge or fail to challenge hierarchically organized fields of power. Foucault's conception of agency depends both on the discursive production of individuals and on the totalizing effacement of individuality through normalization and population-level constraints on action. This ever-intensifying normalization provides no conceptual grounds for understanding how subjects strategically shift from one discourse to another. Unlike normalization, habitus works through non-specific incorporation of general schemes of classification. These classificatory schemes and the dispositions they engender reflect the coexistence of homologously structured fields and thereby describe a mechanism by which action is generated. The fields in which agents find themselves demand practical action. The habitus's classificatory schemes generate action according to practical strategies appropriate to those fields. The relative durability of fields in Bourdieu's framework derives from the coincidence between the specific rules and demands of a particular field and the dispositions of habitus-bearing agents who participate in a field precisely because they are disposed to accept and therefore reproduce the existing structure of that field.[53] The extent to which an agent's strategy fails to meet the demands of a field, refuses to meet those demands, or meets them in such a way as to incrementally change that field is normatively relevant and empirically measurable. This is the central conceptual advantage that habitus, field, and capital provide and that normalization fails to deliver.

As importantly, fields are reproduced when agents deploy certain kinds of strategies underpinned by the kinds of capital they bring to those fields. In particular, the cultural capital and the general range of skills and competencies that an agent is able to mobilize depend on the conditions of the production of their habitus (for example, their class and ethnic background, position within gendered divisions of labour, access to time in educational institutions), and it is always linked to both an agent's own symbolic evaluation of what kinds of strategies and positions are "for us" and the evaluations of all other participants in a field as to whether or not a strategy or position is "for them."

The dual face of action—the opportunity created through the right combination of resources and symbolic permissibility—depends on two instances of differentiation:

- differentiation produced through the various socially structured conditions of the acquisition of dispositions; and
- differentiation within the field of action, produced by symbolic distinctions and manifested through the rules of division and action that inhere in particular fields.

This dual face and dual differentiation contrasts with Foucault's description of the homogenizing operation of disciplinary power through norms. It also means that the hierarchical organization of power and therefore the uneven production and distribution of suffering has already operated prior to the operation of oppression through Young's categories of exploitation, marginalization, powerlessness, and so on. Indeed, the operation of oppression depends on prior incorporation of the rules and divisions that underpin symbolic domination.

Not surprisingly, attention to oppression derives different claims to justice than attention to dynamics of symbolic violence, though the distance between the two conceptions of justice is much smaller than the distance between either of these models and the redress for suffering offered by liberal attention to legitimacy. Because Young maintains a normative commitment to the value of allowing every individual to achieve their full human potential, justice requires the elimination of oppression and domination. In turn, this requires a group-based "politics of difference" in which decisions are made through deliberative and participatory procedures that are capable of recognizing and valuing group differences. Young takes social movement politics as the origin of both the critical insights that justify her normative vision and the vehicle through which this vision is most likely to be achieved.

Attention to symbolic power similarly demands procedural remedies, but it fundamentally requires a prior step, namely the universalization of political capacities. For Bourdieu, the political field is a specific context in which specifically political stakes are exchanged and accumulated and where the tendency for agents to be dominated through arbitrary rules and divisions is particularly pernicious. This vision demands the exposure of the arbitrary divisions of the political field—and other fields in which domination can be said to produce suffering—primarily through the conceptual tools of sociologists and what he calls the "ordinary means of political action—creation of associations and movements, demonstrations, manifestoes, etc." aimed at setting up the proper relationship between field and habitus.[54]

In the next chapter, I will operationalize what the Bourdieuian vision of "ordinary means of political action" implies for procedurally based justice. However, I go beyond Bourdieu to argue that it is insufficient to universalize political capacities because symbolic power—operating at the level of affect and orienting dominated actors toward some modes of action rather than others—requires a specifically symbolic response. I attended closely to the affective life of symbolic power earlier in this chapter, because the turn from ressentiment to action is rooted in affective orientations toward risk rather than security. Given the affective and dispositional stakes in symbolic power, justice requires a response to power that is capable of operating at the affective level to orient agents toward a creative, overcoming relationship to suffering, rather than remaining at the level of political contest. I consider this response to be as follows: justice is suffering combined with a universal distribution of the means of overcoming one's suffering.

7 New Stakes and New Strategies

> *Now that the great utopias of the nineteenth century have revealed all their perversion, it is urgent to create the conditions for a collective effort to reconstruct a universe of realist ideals, capable of mobilizing people's will without mystifying their consciousness.*
> —Bourdieu, *Acts of Resistance*[1]

Toward Symbolic Democracy

Twin principles of critical theory motivate my critique of social movements: centre analysis on suffering; and develop conceptual tools that reflect back and potentially inform active efforts to negate existing structures of domination. The first principle ethically grounds the second. Starting from suffering and returning to it again and again inoculates against formalist accounts of justice. In the face of suffering, gripped by how viscerally suffering is experienced along a range of measures—from overt physical coercion to the more subtle but nonetheless damaging effects of symbolic violence—normative political theorists are hard pressed to justify abstract commitments to liberty and equality without a concrete account of how hierarchically organized fields of power distribute the practical opportunities and skills necessary to enjoy the benefits that those fields offer.

For the study of social movements specifically, critical conceptual tools contextualize the struggles through which movements seek to transform the conditions that cause suffering. If, to borrow Butler's language, domination negates the possibility of enjoying fully livable lives, then social movements seek to negate that negation. The approach I advocate insists that movements bring no guarantee of social arrangements free from domination and negation, but they offer potential glimpses into how such a world might look. The role of activists and analysts alike—with full recognition of the porous boundary between the two—is to amplify such glimpses.

By the same token, I opened this project with a rejection of what I see as a kind of metaphysical thinking: the deep-seated and often misrecognized belief that the world is fundamentally morally well ordered and that injustice is a symptom of departure from that order. Having followed my argument about the pitfalls and betrayals that both conformist and failure-oriented strategies offer, readers might understandably feel like it fosters a sort of hopelessness. In a sense, that is correct. My argument does intend to do away with hope, with faith in a just universe and the implicit faith held by many activists that just actions can produce just results. In short, a movement's good intentions are no guarantors of justice—neither in the sense of promoting positive transformation (goals) nor in the sense that movements are capable of acting in accordance with the justice of the situation (that is, protesting rightly). However, hopelessness is not the same as helplessness.

So far, my strategy has been to elaborate a specific feature of power, namely the distorting effect that domination has on efforts to transform suffering. Because efforts to negate the negating effects of domination emerge from within hierarchically organized social fields, such efforts are never unaffected by the unjust relations of power that they oppose. Further, because domination distorts transformative struggles, the glimpses of a world free of domination that movements offer also need to be critically assessed. In this chapter, I argue that the recursive nature of domination and its distortions need not leave progressive forces entirely bereft of hope. More accurately, I argue that by giving up the hope for movements freed from domination, we can develop practices that may diminish the life-negating effects that domination engenders, without first finding a political or theoretical grounding outside of distorting structures.

Fundamentally, social movements embody diverse interpretations of the value of collectivization itself: as a strategy for counteracting disparities in material and symbolic capital between claimants and powerholders; as an emotional accomplishment and resource in the face of the individualizing tendencies of domination; and—especially in the anarchist mode—as a temporary site of autonomous action in the company of like-minded groups and individuals. The various ideas and interpretations that participants bring to movements, and the suffering to which they respond, are elements that collective actors—constrained by the social facts of habitus, field, and capital—combine into specific constellations through which participants understand and justify their actions. All too easily, though, activists and observers alike reduce complex interactions between values, dispositions, and resources to simplified visions of political projects as either radical or reformist, and then credit symbolic value to their preferred pole.

The conflict between the Black Bloc activists and the labour-led march against the G20 could be interpreted as a radical/reformist polarization produced by the incompatibility of political projects rooted, respectively, in autonomy and in empowerment through representation. Conflicts between queer and lesbian/gay visions of collective identity are rooted in conflicting conceptions of the value of immediate, integral responses to the suffering experienced within heteronormative North American socio-political systems. Queer and rights-based strategies show similar radical/reform polarization. Because such polarizations are ultimately rooted in alternative accounts of suffering and political value, any radical-reformist contrast is deeply unstable. Such a contrast might be configured differently at the level of identity, strategy, and tactic, depending on the opportunities and constraints presented by a specific field and the resources that individual and collective actors within that field are able to mobilize.

Nonetheless, given the energy expended on such debates, and the internal animosity these debates tend to produce, one might say—parallel to Bourdieu's claim that the subjectivist/objectivist division is "the most fundamental, and the most ruinous" opposition that divides social science—that the radical/reformist split is the most ruinous to progressive social movements.[2] Arguably one symptom of dysfunction among many (including the violence and antinomies we have looked at in previous chapters), antagonism between bearers of reformist and radical visions is a primary source of conflict and needlessly wasted energy in social movements. Certainly both LGBT/Q and alterglobalization movements (not to mention feminist, anti-racist, environmentalist, disability, Indigenous, and worker movements) have been plagued by this symptom.

It bears emphasizing that the recommendations I set out will not resolve debates in advance. They will not settle once and for all the value of property destruction or same-sex marriage. Rather they are intended to serve as a tool to help dominated agents challenge dominant groups and to push them toward new justifications for action. Activists ought to ask, within the matrix I develop, whether building a campaign that makes claims for same-sex couples because they are "the same" as opposite-sex couples will make it easier or harder to act differently from opposite-sex couples in the future? If we submit to police co-ordination in planning protest activities now, will doing so make it harder or easier to act against police preferences in the future? Naturally, it is impossible to know the answers in advance. Instead, these questions will generate arguments, arguments that need to be protected from the distorting effects of epistemic violence and unequal distributions of cultural capital and material resources.

Revaluing the Universal

Movement participants and researchers need to explicitly treat social movements themselves as sites of justice and locations of democratic practice, rather than simply as the vehicles through which claims for justice are made. This position flows directly from the argument I have set out thus far. First, movements as they currently exist are social fields, and as such, they reproduce the morally arbitrary but historically produced nature of broader fields. Second, given the conservative and predisposed nature of habitus, there are no grounds for thinking that movement participants could avoid dominating and being dominated simply through a collective act of good will. Indeed, habitus only operates within the context of fields and capital; therefore, we cannot expect movement participants to act differently—to disrupt patterns of domination—without altering in advance how capital is distributed and the field in which they act.

However, the morally arbitrary but historically conditioned nature of social fields does not condemn those spaces to inevitably express only hierarchy, power, and domination. Fields can offer a route out of the morally arbitrary, but only if they are structured in a way that promotes the universal. By universal here, I mean, as Bourdieu did, negating the subjective in favour of the transpersonal, the objective, the disinterested. The goal, then, is to foster political spaces where agents receive symbolic, political, and other rewards insofar as they sublimate individual goals and preferences in favour of the universal. Just as business fields value money and artistic fields value beauty, the political spaces that I envision must value the universal above all else. To achieve this, political spaces need to be fields constructed according to specific features (which I describe below). Moreover, the agents struggling within those fields need to act through habitus that are disposed to pursue the universal within the rules and confines of these fields.[3]

This is not an argument for prefigurative practices, in which the just social relations envisioned by a movement are incorporated into the activities and strategies of the movement itself. Prefigurative politics, by definition, rely on already-decided visions of what just social relations should be. My interest is in taking a step back to ensure that decisions about what ought to be prefigured are produced from within a normatively defensible framework.

Recall that the distinctions through which social space is structured and the rules for position-taking within that space are established in two ways. On the one hand, they are institutionalized in the space itself, the shape of which is the result of historical struggles and position-taking. On the other hand, they are instituted in the habitus of the participants. Indeed, bearing a habitus disposed toward recognizing the rules of a particular social space as well as the stakes involved in that space is a prerequisite for participation in the field. As an agent participates more fully in a field, their habitus undergoes continuous and often unnoticed adjustments to become more compatible with the demands of the field. To be consistent, pursuit of universality must therefore be conceived of as an appropriate distribution of the dispositions needed to orient agents toward the transpersonal and the disinterested. Further, these dispositions must also orient agents toward, and encourage them to participate within, political spaces that reward pursuit of the universal.

In short, I argue for a form of symbolic democracy where the constraining conditions within which struggles over vision and tactic take place constitute a decision-making system capable of orienting participants toward the universal. This orientation depends upon the universal itself being a prize garnered in the form of political capital and esteem. To make this argument, I will compare two specific fields: the political field, in which actors use whatever forms of capital they can to universalize their particular interests and perspectives; and the scientific field, in which actors sublimate their particular interests according to rules that make successful accumulation of economic and symbolic capital dependent upon pursuit of the universal.

The Political Field

As with aesthetic, scholastic, and other dispositions, political dispositions are products of specific relations to the world and mobilize specific forms of political capital. Unsurprisingly, political dispositions and skills are not evenly distributed throughout populations.[4] I have gone to some pains to situate this account within Bourdieu's framework because his conceptual tools—habitus and field—prohibit a purely liberal, individualistic, or pluralist reading of the democratic model that I sketch out below. The classed, gendered, racialized, and otherwise hierarchical production of habitus, and the corollary classed, gendered, racialized, and otherwise hierarchically distributed opportunities for success that fields offer, render impossible a vision of political struggle in which autonomous individuals do their best to rally other individuals around the best idea, the best argument, or the best justification. This is why my account focuses on the relationship between habitus and field and the pursuit of universality; hierarchical distributions are morally arbitrary, institutionalized redistributions of social benefits to particular agents and groups. Democratic practices within movements, if they are to have moral value, must be explicitly oriented toward reversing this dynamic.

Democratic political fields consist of struggles among individual and collective agents that bear various kinds of resources, or capital, and that are invested in gaining control of the specific resources and advantages that the state offers through elections, lobbying, or other forms of influence. Naturally these resources include not only economic capital, but also social capital in the form of organizations capable of mobilizing members and supporters as well as cultural capital in the form of the skills needed to communicate effectively (crafting political messaging; appearance and mannerisms) and possession of the political instincts that are needed to perceive and capitalize on opportunities that the field presents at any given time.[5]

Analysis of political fields, then, begins with assessing what Bourdieu calls the "political economy" of "political goods" such as commentaries, analyses, partisan proposals, communications strategies, and messaging produced within the field and the division of labour and consumption within and external to the field itself. Bourdieu insisted on understanding the production, circulation, and consumption of political goods—and the mobilization of supporters (itself a form of social capital) that this circulation seeks—as conditioned by constraints of symbolic power (which establishes the rules of production and the value of political goods, and which is an artificial construct mediating the value of political goods without reference to the truth or coherence of their claims) and the institutional arrangements that structure the political field.[6] The speeches, laws, and other products that are produced within the political field are fundamentally "instruments for perceiving and expressing the social world (or, if you like, principles of di-vision)."[7] As with any instrument, various groups and classes will have different access to political products and therefore different access to the capacity to formulate and articulate political opinions, to circulate those opinions, and to have them treated credibly. In effect, unequal distribution of the ability to appropriate and produce political products limits what is thinkable and unthinkable politically and, moreover, who is authorized to speak credibly.

The relationship between location within a field and the success of various strategies within that field is worth exploring somewhat more closely. If we say that the central stake involved in a democratic political field is control of state resources, we bring into focus a diverse range of strategies for influencing what the state does.[8] These strategies will generally be understood as relatively legitimate or taboo. That is, some actions—campaigning, lobbying, demonstrating—are clearly permitted, while others—bribing, bombing, fraud—are officially prohibited. Within that context, participants bring into play various resources (capital) in order to make their actions more successful. Although social fields are social spaces made up of people and objects that are related by a shared interest in particular stakes and bound by the rules of legitimacy and taboo, the rules of the field are skewed to value actions that are supported by some forms of capital more than by others.

For example, while demonstrations and rallies are legitimate strategies (or more precisely, strategies that are legitimized by the field in which they are deployed), they don't offer the same direct access to decision-makers as, say, lobbyists enjoy. Therefore, because the capital required to demonstrate is relatively widely distributed, while the capital required to lobby is not, lobbyists can be said to occupy a better (higher) position within the field than demonstrators. Further, lobbyists are better positioned to ensure that the kind of capital they enjoy remains both legitimate and effective. Naturally, this dynamic is not the complete story. Political fields are infinitely more complex than a rudimentary contrast between demonstrators and lobbyists would show. Politics are not simply about exchange of ideas or expression of public opinion; they are about strategy and resource within the confines established by the political field's rules of legitimacy and taboo.

Alongside the division of labour between political producers and political consumers, the conditions of entry into the political field are central to understanding its dynamics. Most political consumers appear within the field as producers only through delegated production of political goods, that is, through representatives rather than directly. Political parties, organized interest groups, and movement organizations are cornerstones that structure the political field.

In this regard, Bourdieu identified two broad trends. First, that the more dispossessed of various forms of cultural, economic, and symbolic resources a category of people is—he had working-class people in mind here—the more they rely on acts of delegation to representatives in the form of organizations, parties, and spokespeople. These representatives aggregate the comparatively scarce and diffused resources of dominated groups and transform them into political products that are appropriate for exchange within the political field. However, as anarchist critics argue, this delegation always threatens to become dispossession. Although spokespeople are representatives in the sense of having delegated authority, they are also representative in the sense of portraying a concrete vision of the group's concerns, ambitions, and self-image. Because representation in the latter sense is articulated by a delegate whose authority to speak on behalf of the group emerges from systems of symbolic power and unequal capital distribution, and through representatives' production of goods oriented toward a specific state of a political field, it is always a mediated representation. All too easily, representatives stray from mediated representation into outright misrepresentation, and delegation becomes dispossession.

Tellingly, the second trend that Bourdieu identifies is the monopolization of the means of political production and the accompanying increase in the esoteric nature of political discourse, which intervenes between how dominated groups experience the world and how that experience is manifested in the political field.[9] Leaders typically don't just want to speak on behalf of a group: they want to be the only speakers on behalf of a group. This is particularly true the more professionalized a representative organization becomes, the more closely it is integrated into the political field, and consequently, the more a group has invested in message control, branding, and other efforts to accumulate and defend symbolic capital.

The monopolization of representation is particularly at stake in competing visions of the alterglobalization movement (as I argued in chapter five). Here I want to point to two levels at which anarchist concerns about representation might be expressed in this context. First, as a means of resisting domination by consolidating various kinds of capital, anarchists may simply prioritize one value, autonomy, over a competing one, representation-based collective action. Second, many anarchists argue at a more fundamental level that representation entails a false imposition of identity. For example, John Holloway, following Adorno, argues that capitalism reifies processes (actions, doing things) into concrete states of being (static, unchanging, fixed). This reification is characteristic of capitalism's tendency to hypostatize the present. By treating the present as all there is, as discrete and separate from structural and historical processes, capitalism separates people from processes and action. Capitalism naturalizes the present and makes it appear inevitable. From this perspective, because collective identity and identity-based politics fail to escape reification, representation turns lived individuality into something deadened, static, stagnant, and alien.[10]

In both versions of anarchist critique—valuation of autonomy over consolidating resources, and fear of deadening lived individuality into reified collective identities—the central concern is that the delegation that is intrinsic to representation entails a loss of the ability to act for oneself without coercion. Increasing monopolization of the capacity to produce legitimate political products by movement organizations, labour unions, and official political parties diminishes the potential for autonomous political action. Effectively, monopolization of the ability to produce legitimate political goods dispossesses already marginalized agents of the ability to refuse delegation and appear in the political field on their own behalf.

As political scientist Francis Dupuis-Déri argues, the ephemeral nature of affinity-based organizing negates the possibility of consolidating power and thus prevents the official imposition of will on subordinates.[11] Political fields are rife with symbolic violence, which potentially justifies treating representation as a negative constraint on freedom, as this anarchist critique implies. (That is, my freedom is constrained insofar as social movement organizations prevent me from undertaking actions that are not officially sanctioned.) Representation may also be treated as a constraint on positive freedom, insofar as representation involves the imposition and acceptance of political projects that are contrary to the interests of those for whom representatives claim to speak. When dominated delegators come to accept an imposed vision not on its merits, but because of the epistemic and symbolic authority of its advocates, it is impossible to treat delegation as an authentic expression of autonomous political agents. On the contrary, in this view, representation begins to appear exploitative as political organizations mobilize the energy of activists not for the sake of improving the lives of all participants, but for the sake of improving the lives and capital of dominant individuals and interests within a social movement. In this light, the dispossession that underpins monopolization in the political field appears to be incompatible with pursuit of the universal.

Worse, as in any political economy, accumulation favours those who already have the most capital and, in the context of political fields, dispossesses the most marginalized of the ability to refuse delegation. The trend toward monopolization and increasingly disproportionate control over the capacity to produce political products is not limited to the so-called 1 per cent or to the political elite; it is endemic to mainstream social movements. Given that these trends are not (necessarily) products of the bad faith of political actors but are, in fact, expressions of the logic of economies of practice that underpin social fields, movement participants have a highly constrained capacity to avoid the reproduction of domination within movements as they are currently organized. The way out of this dilemma requires finding normatively grounded principles for democratic practice adapted from a field that, when it functions properly, unites particular interests with universal ones—the scientific field.

The Scientific Field

Is there a model of social action that promotes the universal while avoiding exploitative delegation? If so, can this model be translated into prescriptions for political practice? For Bourdieu the field that is most closely aligned with the universal and therefore embodies the most potential for avoiding the distorting effects of dominant interests is the scientific field.[12] Because the field of science (understood, like any field, as a norm-based space of action) is intrinsically bound up in dialogue among invested participants, and because its participants agree to common standards for this dialogue, science provides a model for escaping the relativism that is implicit in Bourdieu's conception of fields as quasi-autonomous spaces where agents undertake evaluations and actions based on the arbitrary rules of that space.

Crossley describes Bourdieu's approach to science as founded on what he calls "communicative rationality." In this view, reason progresses through human interactions rather than through individual, private deliberation; rationality depends upon such interactions being based on logic and evidence rather than on coercion or bribery; and where the previous two conditions prevail, there exists the possibility that particular perspectives may be replaced by universal ones.[13] In contrast to the scientific field, agents within artistic and political fields are not bound by shared conceptions of logic and evidence. As a result, the artistic field falsely universalizes a particular aesthetic gaze, and the political field remains oriented toward particular claims rather than universal visions.

Because competence within any given field is closely connected to having a habitus disposed to participating in that field, competence entails being disposed to follow the rules and recognize the distinctions of that field. Disposition is not the same as uniform adherence; it only marks out a general tendency in terms of action and a psychic commitment or investment in the field. In this light, the relationship between field, habitus, and competence is somewhat circular. An agent's habitus disposes them toward participation in a field. Participation leads to adjustments in the habitus, including (with varying success) accumulation of the cultural capital that is necessary to participate in that field. This cultural capital then further disposes the agent toward participation. In academia and scholastic settings, disposition and competence appear as practically synonymous, and successful participants in those fields must preconsciously adopt specific orientations and ambitions in order to succeed.

Bourdieu characterizes scientific fields as similar to others in that participants are mobilized by selfish interests and engage in conflicts over resources, but as exceptional in the degree to which the use of reason is instituted in the structures, dispositions, and rules that make up the field. Specifically, participants in scientific fields mobilize technical competence and scientific knowledge for the sake of accumulating symbolic capital, but the weapons they use in this struggle must be sanctioned principles of proof (generalizable evidence, rational argumentation, peer review, citation, and so on). In the scientific field, social constraints take the form of logical constraints. Naturally these standards and norms are highly contentious and debated, but those debates—struggles, really—also recursively rely on reason, logic, evidence, and persuasion.

Science advances because it has available to it habitus-bearing agents who are willing to sublimate their drives and interests to the "censorship of the scientific field," namely its rules of methodology, proof, and so on. This means that there must be reasonably high entry barriers to participation in the scientific field. Otherwise, the norms of reason and proof by which the field advances could be jeopardized. For Bourdieu, truth is rescued from relativism by the relationship between well-disposed habitus and the struggle over specific (scientific) forms of symbolic capital that is undertaken in the context of high entry barriers and participation rules that emphasize reason, method, and proof.[14]

Elements of Symbolic Democracy

Contrasts between the dynamics of scientific fields and political fields are readily apparent. The political field has low entry barriers—anyone with an opinion can participate at some level—and norms of participation have more to do with advertising, rhetoric, framing strategies, and emotional manipulation than rational debate. Bourdieu argues:

> If one wants to go beyond preaching, then it is necessary to implement practically, by using the ordinary means of political action—creation of associations and movements, demonstrations, manifestoes, etc.—the *Realpolitik* of reason aimed at setting up or reinforcing, within the political field, the mechanisms capable of imposing the sanctions, as far as possible automatic ones, that would tend to discourage deviations from the democratic norm (such as the corruption of elected representatives) and to encourage or impose the appropriate behaviours; aimed also at favouring the setting up of non-distorted social structures of communication between the holders of power

and the citizens, in particular through a constant struggle for the independence of the media.[15]

It should by now be clear that the "creation of associations and movements, demonstrations, manifestoes, etc." on which Bourdieu's *Realpolitik* rests is itself contentious because core components such as collective identity formation are already sites of domination. This immediately presents a twofold conceptual challenge: How do we identify domination/submission, and on what grounds can we say whether movements arising from patterns of domination are distorted?

Conceptually, the recognition of symbolic domination allows the observer to identify distortions, but it does not provide objective grounds from which to contrast "true" interests with disingenuous or harmful representations. The existence or absence of external measures capable of assessing the extent to which adopting a particular point of view or scheme of classification is in accordance with, or in opposition to, one's interests is an important problem for normative social theory. It also indicates a core tension. For example, on the one hand, most queers—that is, those who resist imperatives to live according to standards of "normalcy"—would be rightly suspicious of an externally derived conception of justice, given the horrors realized through twentieth-century revolutionary and utopian movements.[16] At the same time, exactly such an external moral standard appears to operate in accusations that mainstream gays and lesbians who accumulate symbolic capital through strategies based on conforming to dominant patterns of symbolic power are misguided, traitorous, and complicit in entrenching relations of power.[17]

Treating the sites of collective identity formation—social movement organizations, movement media, and so on—as sites of justice could help resolve this tension. More specifically, by extending Bourdieu's realist philosophy of science to social movement politics, justice could be conceived according to procedural rather than substantive measures. The key features of the model of democratic practice that I am suggesting can be summarized as follows:

- Legitimacy derives from a correct relationship between habitus and field wherein the dispositions of participants fit with a logic of practice that rewards certain kinds of actions and where participants openly struggle with one another for the rewards that that field offers.

- The "correctness" or quality of this relationship depends on the degree to which, in Bourdieu's words, "there are profits in rationality and universality so that actions which advance reason and the universal advance at the same time the interests of those who perform them."[18]
- An equitable distribution of key resources, especially those potentially embodied in habitus (political opinions, instinct, communication, strategy) ensures as nearly universal as possible an access to both the dispositions to participate in the field in universalizing ways and to the capacity to do so.
- In contrast to efforts to achieve consensus, conflict's value is recognized insofar as it encourages agents to actively mobilize resources to engage in struggles that are constrained toward the universal; struggle over the rewards of the political field (in terms of state power, but also of symbolic recognition, esteem, and other rewards) energizes the relationship and renders it dynamic.
- Above all, normative evaluation is system-centred rather than agent-centred or outcome-centred.

Within this framework, analysis would not ask whether a movement goal or outcome sufficiently moves the movement toward the universal by adequately representing the interests of all of the affected participants. Rather, analysis would focus on whether there are procedural mechanisms in place within social movements that ensure a general trend toward universality. Researchers would ask, in the struggle over a vision of the world—a vision that explains queer difference and exclusions, global economic injustice, or other forms of suffering—whether and to what degree that vision is confounded by epistemic violence (particularly, but not exclusively, in the form of symbolic violence) at the expense of communicative rationality. Researchers could take seriously the various stakes and interests involved in partisan debates that are internal to social movements, assess internal movement outcomes, and draw clear conclusions about processes of domination without relying on external, theoretical judgments about objective interests.

For a field to be structured in such a way as to permit communicative rationality, it needs to be relatively autonomous, which can be measured in two ways. First, autonomy correlates to the extent to which only other participants in a field consume goods that are produced in that field.[19] On this measure, for example, the literary field is less autonomous than the field of avant-garde art. Participants in the former typically intend their works to be widely read, whereas avant-garde art maintains its distinction in large part by remaining unintelligible to the uninitiated.[20] It is an open question how much politicians, pundits, and pollsters speak only to each other, but in general we would want the political field to produce and circulate goods fairly widely.[21] Indeed, a central benefit of distributing political skills widely is precisely to permit more widespread participation, recognizing that the inequality of chances to obtain the cultural capital needed to participate is at the core of the distinction between moral and practical equality, and lends normative force to the pursuit of remedies to this maldistribution.

A second measure of a field's autonomy is the extent to which only the forms of capital that are relevant to a field are able to gain purchase within that field. In the scientific field, for example, autonomy is measured by the extent to which agents are only able to use scientific capital (argument, evidence, research design) and not economic or political capital in order to advance their interests. In claiming the scientific field as relatively autonomous, Bourdieu probably envisioned an ideal, purified version; he certainly recognized that any given scientific field is embedded within a broader scientific and academic context and that its autonomy is therefore relative.[22] Nonetheless, one can say that scientists undertake research (and are open to condemnation if they don't) for scientific reasons, not economic ones. They struggle for various rewards, including symbolic capital in the form of scientific authority, and in that struggle, scientists must rely predominantly on logic and evidence.

For democratic theorists, especially deliberative democrats, it would appear normatively valuable to exclude non-political forms of capital. However, it is a tricky thing to determine what exactly constitutes political capital. An electoral mandate would certainly be a relevant form of capital and (depending on the quality of the electoral process, which is a separate question) one that is normatively desirable. Many would also see the value in restricting or at least limiting the role of economic capital in strategies for accumulating political power. But what about social capital, which is the networks that an agent can mobilize on behalf of a project or goal? Lobbyists, social movement organizations, neighbourhood phone trees, social media, and social movement organizations all depend on various kinds of social capital to promote political causes. In fact, the value of collectivization lies primarily in social capital, which can act as a mechanism to compensate for maldistributions in habitus and other forms of capital. Collective action is, at its core, an effort to resist unequal distributions of power. As it turns out, then, the value of excluding non-political forms of capital from the political field, and from democratic practice, is conceptually uncertain, particularly in contrast to the value of such exclusions from the scientific field.

Bourdieu moves too quickly from his idealization of the scientific field to democratic practice. Aside from the obvious need to go beyond ensuring the independence of the media, Bourdieu elides, in the passage cited above, the normative difficulties of simply transposing scientific practice onto democratic fields. A fully autonomous political field seems unlikely; it may also be conceptually incomprehensible and normatively undesirable. Further, Bourdieu's own lengthy discussions of the class-differentiated hierarchies of political skills raise the possibility that high entry barriers would, on his terms, almost certainly exclude the entry of working-class and other dominated groups into the political field. The exclusion of people with low levels of the requisite capital may be necessary for the scientific field to function, but it is difficult to justify normatively for political participation. That is, scientists may be required to have scientific skills and background knowledge to properly participate in the scientific field, but people should not be barred from political participation simply because they lack political skill.

In fact, Bourdieu's own political commitments point to how we might resolve this tension. Bourdieu's main political project can be summarized as an interest in universalizing the capacity to engage in politics.[23] Yet, if cultural capital, embodied in the habitus, is necessary for such universalization, and cultural capital is distributed in accordance with existing fields, how can this vision be accomplished? The first step is a robust defence of collective action and, implicitly, of representative politics. To be clear, I am not suggesting a naive endorsement of collectivization. I acknowledge that, just as deliberative democrats have drawn attention to important elements of democratic practice—the importance, for example, of fostering changes in opinions rather than simply expressing a fixed interest—anarchists have made important critiques of identity politics and representative politics.[24]

Nonetheless, political strategies based on representation by political parties, social movement organizations, or even temporary coalitions can provide important grounds for addressing concerns about the autonomy of the political field and the conceptual difficulties of redistributing cultural capital. Indeed, the solution to the question of the autonomy of the field is not to reduce the relevant capital to political capital, but rather to expand what constitutes political capital. Labour movements are rooted in an effort to counter power imbalances between workers and capitalists by collectivizing the scarce resources that workers have.[25] Social movements, at their best, mobilize participants in order to tap into economic, symbolic, and social capital that is insufficient for affecting political change when left in the individual hands of the most dominated actors. Early efforts at gay and lesbian mobilization were oriented almost entirely toward building up social capital by creating spaces for gays and lesbians to gather and to express themselves.[26]

Further, there is ample evidence that participation in collective struggles provides an opportunity to acquire cultural capital that might not otherwise be available due to class and other positions.[27] Membership in activist networks may also provide psychic resources that allow participants to continue mobilizing and struggling even in the face of short-term political defeats.[28] Finally, participation in various forms of collective action helps foster skills and dispositions that Bourdieu's entry barriers were intended to encourage. Collective action allows gradual entry into the political system and therefore demonstration of an embodied commitment to the norms of the field without absolutely prohibiting anyone from participating.[29] To emphasize, given the impossibility of immediate redistribution of the cultural capital that is required to participate in politics, collectivization in the form of political parties and social movements can fulfill a compensating function. For democratic theory, this entails reorienting attention from face-to-face deliberation to the macro level. Further, to prevent macro-level politics from simply becoming a war of all against all, the terrain of struggle must be properly constrained.

What might this look like? An exhaustive list of characteristics is impossible, but we might note that a field that encourages universality would discourage goals and tactics that move beyond disruption and onto a spectrum of violence. However, it would also recognize that the difference between rallies or demonstrations and disruptive actions such as blockades and property damage is, in part, a response to unequal distributions of various resources.[30] Therefore space needs to be made for disruption, provided—and this would require additional normative inquiry—that such disruption is itself oriented toward transcending the particular. Notwithstanding the results of such inquiry, the framework that I recommend here suggests that disruption can be a good thing insofar as it is a manifestation of conflict and it energizes struggles over political goods. The point is not to eliminate conflict or disruption, but to channel it toward the transpersonal, the objective, and the disinterested.

Increasingly restrictive state responses to collective claims, particularly through policing and legal restrictions on protest, should also be interrogated in these terms. Do police tactics pose threats to civil liberties in the name of order? If so, does that order benefit particular groups or a general interest? I take it as a central tenet of the tradition of critical theory in which I situate my work that order is understood to unequally benefit the most powerful groups in society. Order itself, then, needs to be reconsidered in light of universality versus particularity. Finally, my approach would also suggest that non–social movement actors bear a moral duty to facilitate social movement activities. This would include news organizations censoring racist and other particularizing remarks in their comments sections, and for political figures to refrain from using political tactics that are designed to undermine credibility rather than confront issues.

There is, however, a danger to the procedural approach that I just outlined. In particular, by emphasizing the norms by which the scientific field forces participants to sublimate their interest in symbolic power and submit to the demands of evidence and logic, Bourdieu approaches a more Foucauldian vision. The logic of norms and normalization (as I argued in chapter six) is fundamentally homogenizing. By praising norms in the scientific field, Bourdieu attempts to escape the power-laden imposition of difference through distinctions that he finds to be arbitrary and devastating in social fields, but he does so at the expense of internal diversity.

Bourdieu was not naive about the power relations that surround academic institutions, nor about the economic power that underpins scholastic dispositions. Nonetheless, his reliance on economistic models of accumulation, tied to institutions that distribute scarce productive capacities (access to labs, publication opportunities, research grants), means that scientific economies remain, ultimately, political economies. The danger of mechanism-based, or procedural, approaches to justice within social movements in keeping with Bourdieu's vision of universality, then, is that the homogeneity underpinning the norms operating in "properly structured" fields—both in the rules of the fields themselves and in the embodiment of those rules in habitus—may undermine creativity, dissidence, and independence. Absent such diversity, a highly normalized and proceduralized field returns to rough and unequal political economies.

Collective actors, therefore, need something more than a habituated orientation toward universalist procedures. The collective actor that I envision requires more than the Bourdieuian vision's ability to conform. Although conformity to rules that are oriented toward the universal can channel agents' pursuit of symbolic power toward a political project that transcends particular interests (even particular group interests), there remains the danger that investment in conformity will foster overidentification with the existing system and therefore reproduce distortions and domination that predate that investment. In noting this danger, I am intentionally shifting from the economic sense of investment (that is, long-run accumulation of symbolic power by developing capacities and especially the dispositions necessary to sublimate particular interests) to the psychoanalytic sense, both of which senses Bourdieu collapsed into his use of the term.[31]

Revaluing conflict within movement spaces provides a small part of the answer to this problem. Democracy is not served by eliminating conflict; properly organized conflict promotes democratic legitimacy. Conflict ought to be regulated, oriented toward the universal, and played out on the most even terrain possible, but it should also encourage participants to break with dogma and to refuse to conflate playing by the rules with consensus and homogeneity.

Resistance and Democracy

> *What gives habitus its particular force, in this context, is that power is conceptualized as working such that it is not what you do or what you have, that is marked as wrong or right, but who you are. This is not to deny that subjects can resist such a positioning, nor that habitus may be imperfectly aligned with the field. However, it is important to note that there are some people who, by virtue of their habitus, are able to pass judgement, implicitly or explicitly, on others, and to make that judgement count.*
>
> —Lawler, "Rules of Engagement"[1]

The argument I have presented here has been about rethinking and enlivening the practices of collective struggle without relying on metaphysical fantasies about hope and justice. It would be a mistake to think, simply because we want to overcome domination and because the realities of injustice are viscerally and urgently felt, that there must be a mechanism by which we can do so. Mistaking desire for possibility binds us more and more tightly to the distorted and irrational systems that movements fight to dismantle. Agency, whether individualized through the relationship between habitus, capital, and field, or collectivized through social movement processes, is fundamentally strategic and adaptive. We are disposed to act because we are exposed to the world, and at individual and collective levels, we incorporate a distorted world's contradictions and jealous pursuits of capital—symbolic capital, above all—into how we perceive, judge, and act. When we take our desire for something better as a sign that we can effectively create something better, we act on the world as we want it to be, not as it is.

There is a danger, for movements that are fully aware of the world as it is, of becoming what psychologist Matthew Adams calls "reflexivity losers." A reflexivity loser is an individual or group that is marginalized, dominated, and excluded, that is fully aware of their marginalization and the structures of power maintaining their exclusions, but that possesses none of the resources necessary to change their situation. Without such resources, reflexive consciousness of power is simultaneously a blessing and a curse.[2]

Critical theory risks leaving social movements in danger of remaining reflexivity losers at a collective level. We begin with attention to suffering. We experience our own suffering and empathize with the suffering of others, and begin struggling to negate that suffering. Through that struggle, social movements become highly reflexive, but they generally remain at the level of practical reflexivity. They develop sophisticated strategic analyses and novel political tactics but nonetheless remain trapped in questions of radicalism and reformism. The argument I have made in this book pushes movement reflexivity beyond practical debates toward awareness of how structures of domination infiltrate movement strategies and tactics. That is, my argument pushes activists toward an awareness of how domination forces movements into seemingly inevitable choices between conformity and failure.

The paradox of submission and resistance that is implicit in Bourdieu's logic of practice comes from the fact that conformity to the rules of social spaces is necessary for successful action within such a space. However, by unevenly distributing the resources that agents require for success, these rules naturalize domination within social spaces and ensure that that domination reproduces itself indefinitely. To the extent that dominated actors conform to these rules in order to mitigate their suffering in the short run—without challenging the rules themselves in the long run—they remain complicit in their own ongoing domination. Nonetheless, efforts to combat domination in social fields without conforming to the rules of those spaces appear unable to garner sufficient traction to affect major changes to structures of domination. Both reformist and radical political projects—measured either in terms of movement goals or strategies—are captured by this paradox. Movements invested in the capital needed to succeed in hierarchically organized political and cultural fields risk reducing political imaginations and projects to logics of success. These logics always demand submission to the very relations of power that produce and reproduce domination in the first place. Movements that refuse such investments disavow the long-term collective subjectivity that is needed to resist domination.

Given this paradox, the distorted visions that movements offer provide only pale reflections of how a post-domination world might look. Worse, the problem of reflexivity losing remains: even if movements internalize a reflexive awareness of the dangerous paradox posed by submission and refusal, there is no guarantee that they can self-immunize against power's distorting effects. There is no easy way out of the paradox. However, maintaining a clear distinction between desire and possibility should not demobilize us entirely. Quite the opposite, it should push movement participants to find greater clarity about the world as it is, to find strategies for piercing through the logical conformism that we internalize through participation in the world.

A modest plea implicit in my argument, then, is for continued attention to theoretical and practical debates about democratic practice. Problems of epistemic violence within social movements in particular—which are most readily apparent in collective identity processes—necessitate attention to internal democratic practice. Dominant trends within democratic theory, deliberative and radical, offer some guidance in such a project. Deliberative advocates tend to emphasize three features of deliberative democratic theory: it is a normative theory intended to enhance democratic practices and provide a more just method of managing pluralism than is offered by aggregative or realist models (which are seen as overly general and inattentive to community-based politics); it is centred on communicative processes rather than on voting; and it argues that accountability ought to replace consent in determining the legitimacy of concrete policies and institutions.[3]

At its core, deliberative democracy pursues a specific moral economy: in giving reasons for decisions, citizens and representatives should try to find justifications that minimize their differences with their opponents. Democratic practices organized in this way foster consensus and a willingness to continue with deliberation.[4] In short, rather than gaining legitimacy from capturing the preferences of the largest number of participants in a vote (as is done in aggregative democracy), deliberative democracy gains legitimacy through the mutual accountability of participants as expressed through reason-giving, a willingness to change one's preferences, and an orientation toward consensus.[5] Deliberative approaches fall short, however, because they rely on an overly narrow conception of legitimate forms of expression, underestimate the extent to which social authority (based on race, class, gender, and so on) displaces rational justifications in deliberation, and fail to attend to the importance of confrontation rather than consensus in democratic practice.[6]

Radical democrats, on the other hand, emphasize the problems that are created by deliberative democracy's insistence on moving toward consensus. Proponents insist that because power is endemic and because relations of domination produce interests that do not merely diverge but also actively conflict, consensus is either impossible or is achievable only by suppressing dominated groups' perspectives.[7] Radical democracy seeks mechanisms by which potentially hostile, antagonistic relations are transformed into adversarial (what Chantal Mouffe calls "agonistic") relations. In this framework, participants share a commitment to recognizing each other's legitimacy as democratic agents, without expecting to persuade opponents through rational discussion. Instead, participants establish temporary compromises without seeking to annihilate or dominate adversaries.[8]

The model of symbolic democracy that I began sketching in the previous chapter could add to this debate. Democratic practices are potential sites of communicative reason. Activist dispositions and movement spaces need to be oriented toward fair but robust conflict. These conflicts need to have the universal itself as a desirable form of symbolic capital, and they must dispose participants toward rules of fair play and open—rather than subterranean or misrecognized—conflict. Are there concrete democratic mechanisms that might mobilize participants' self-interested pursuit of symbolic capital in the interest of universal principles? Properly organized, struggles to accumulate symbolic capital in democratic spaces might promote the universal if participants must rely on strategies based in norms of impartiality, fairness, and so on to do so. Democratic theorists could work out a model of symbolic democracy that can integrate deliberative democracy's attention to formal constraints on participation (in the form of justifications, public reason, and so on) and radical democracy's recognition of the inevitability of struggle (as opposed to consensus) through the relationship between habitus, field, and norms of democratic struggle.

A model of symbolic democracy would also require increased sophistication in the conceptual and empirical tools used to identify instances of allodoxia. That is, there must be a means of identifying when the rules of democratic spaces are opposed to the interests of certain groups and, further, when that opposition of interests remains unrecognized and therefore unchallenged by those groups. Symbolic power is not an absolute phenomenon, but it does underpin all social interaction. As such, the submission and misrecognition at the core of symbolic violence is difficult to operationalize. At what level does agreement about social space and distinctions operate? Is it social, cognitive, affective, or some combination thereof? How comprehensive does the logical consensus underpinning symbolic power need to be?

Researchers could investigate the disparate ways in which symbolic salience operates within social movement fields, as social psychology has done with identity salience. That is, given the transferability of the habitus's dispositions as well as the competing and sometimes contradictory roles that agents must take on, we need a clear picture of the mechanisms that orient various embodied responses—the affective and practical responses necessary for symbolic power—within social spaces. From there, we can continue thinking about how political actors can intervene upon those mechanisms.

In 2016, Black Lives Matter–Toronto demonstrated that meaningful protest tactics are still possible. While marching as the Honoured Group for the 2016 Pride Parade, BLM TO staged a brief sit-in, temporarily bringing an event dominated by whiteness, corporate sponsorship, and consumerism back to its political and activist roots. BLM TO organizers presented Mathieu Chantelois, then the executive director of Pride Toronto, with a series of demands. Chantelois accepted those demands on behalf of Pride Toronto, though he quickly recanted, saying he only agreed in order to get the parade back underway. One demand in particular continues to generate controversy: a prohibition on uniformed police marching in the parade and hosting booths in the accompanying fair. Before unpacking the action and subsequent debates, it is worth acknowledging the demands in their entirety.

> Black Lives Matter–Toronto, along with various community groups, including BQY and Blackness Yes have the following demands:
> 1. Commit to BQY's (Black Queer Youth) continued space (including stage/tents), funding, and logistical support.
> 2. Self-determination for all community spaces, allowing community full control over hiring, content, and structure of their stages.
> 3. Full and adequate funding for community stages, including logistical, technical, and personnel support.
> 4. Double funding for Blockorama + ASL interpretation & headliner funding.
> 5. Reinstate and make a commitment to increase community stages/spaces (including the reinstatement of the South Asian stage).
> 6. A commitment to increase representation amongst Pride Toronto staffing/hiring, prioritizing Black trans women, Black queer people, Indigenous folk, and others from vulnerable communities.
> 7. A commitment to more Black deaf & hearing ASL interpreters for the Festival.
> 8. Removal of police floats/booths in all Pride marches/parades/community spaces.
> 9. A public townhall, organized in conjunction with groups from marginalized communities, including, but not limited to, Black Lives Matter–Toronto, Blackness Yes, and BQY to be held six months from today. Pride Toronto will present an update and action plan on the aforementioned demands.[9]

I was honoured to participate in the action as an ally and float marshal, and I witnessed not only the inspiring power of solidarity (Indigenous activists immediately joined BLM TO), but also the power of refusal. BLM TO leaders refused to be moved and insisted on their right to call out racism in the mainstream gay and lesbian community. I also witnessed first-hand the fury of white gays enraged by the disruption to their party.

Perhaps more than QuAIA's participation in the parade six years earlier, BLM TO's action unleashed a wave of debates about collective identity and protest tactics. In August 2016, Pride Toronto held a town hall meeting to discuss BLM TO's demands including the demand that police floats and booths be excluded from the parade. At Pride Toronto's annual general meeting in January 2017, members voted to remove police floats from future festivals. Shortly afterward, the chief of police announced that Toronto police would not participate in the Pride Parade (other than by providing security). Pride Toronto's official statement on the issue noted:

> LGBTQ+ police officers and their allies are not banned from the parade. We welcome and encourage their participation to add to Pride this year as members of our community. LGBTQ+ police officers and their allies can march in the Parade with community groups, with the City of Toronto, or even create their own group. We are simply requesting that their participation not include the following elements: uniform, weapons, and vehicles.[10]

Inspired by BLM TO, similar protests and demands for banning police floats have sprung up in Vancouver, Seattle, New York City, and elsewhere. For the 2017 parade, BLM TO did not register a float but, maintaining an activist approach to pride, marched in the parade anyway. As co-founder Rodney Diverlus argued, "Pride is actually ours. Queer and trans people of colour actually started this. We don't need to register for a deadline, we don't need to tell you we're coming, we don't need to pay money for a float. We're just going to take up space."[11]

I was not part of the collective identity processes within BLM TO that led up to the 2016 or 2017 parade actions, nor have accounts been published that would provide insight into those processes. However, the reaction from white gay and lesbians opposed to the action has been public and vocal. Facebook, Twitter, and other social media have been flooded with debates about BLM TO and it has become nearly impossible to participate in LGBT/Q spaces (including bars and parties) without the issue coming up.

Opposition to BLM TO has largely tracked along two rhetorical strategies. First, opponents have relied on an explicitly racist disavowal of BLM TO as part of "our" community. Because explicit racism has very low symbolic value, white gays have denied the racism of this position almost as forcefully as they deny the right of "them" to crash "our" party. Generally, this type of argument has been expressed by contrasting the supposed openness of the Pride Parade to the alleged homophobia of Black communities. The recurrent refrain became, "Why don't they go protest Caribana instead of disrupting our celebrations?" (Caribana is an annual festival of Caribbean culture, a celebration of and for the sizable Caribbean diaspora living in Toronto.) The racism of this refrain is twofold: it denies the existence of racialized LGBT/Q people (some of whom are leaders of BLM TO itself); and it marks racialized communities—especially Black ones—as other, homophobic, backward, and dangerous. In chapter five I described how the People First march distinguished itself from Black Bloc activists in order to augment its own symbolic capital. By distinguishing the Pride Parade from Caribana, advocates of this position hope to secure their own symbolic capital by portraying themselves as inclusive and open in contrast to party-crashing BLM TO activists and their communities. Although it is difficult to know definitively how much traction this rhetoric has gained, it is beginning to appear that the high (though diminishing) value of activism and the low value of explicit racism within the pride field has made this distinction less successful than the one drawn by the People First march. This failure may indicate space for further discussions about racism within LGBT/Q communities and strategies for eliminating that racism.

The second rhetorical strategy builds on the first. Here, largely white detractors accuse BLM TO and their supporters of contravening pride's core value: inclusivity. In May 2017, city councillor John Campbell (who had never actually attended a Pride Parade himself) introduced a motion to make the city's annual $260,000 grant "conditional upon Pride Toronto reaffirming its core value of inclusivity by welcoming uniformed officers from Toronto Police to participate as they wish in the parade celebrations."[12] In contrast to the low value of violence in the G20 field, inclusivity enjoys high symbolic capital because of its association with liberal commitments to formal equality.[13] However, the meaning of inclusivity, in practical terms, is far from settled. For supporters of BLM TO, it is galling that commentators equate inclusion of police to inclusion of racialized queers, Two-Spirited people, queers experiencing poverty, and trans people. These communities are overpoliced and often experience the police as agents of violence rather than keepers of peace. It makes a mockery of pride's roots and the diversity of queer communities to prefer formal inclusion that, in practice, supports the police while further marginalizing the very groups Pride Toronto is mandated to serve. Debating councillor Campbell's motion to defund Pride, councillor Neethan Shan succinctly expressed the difference: "Inclusion is not about letting everybody in every time. It is about removing barriers and making things accessible." Ensuring marginalized people are not retraumatized by seeing armed and uniformed police celebrated during Pride is a humanizing strategy for removing barriers. Despite the attempt to mobilize inclusivity on behalf of the police, this strategy was not successful. Campbell's motion was defeated and backlash against the exclusion of police in 2017 was muted.

Although I support BLM TO's actions, my intention is not to wade too far into this specific debate. Instead, I want to capture some of the ways in which sensitivity to field and capital can be used to understand the success of BLM TO's action and to see whether the tactic can be evaluated according the vision of symbolic capital that I sketched out in the previous chapter. In that light, it is worth noting that BLM TO entered the parade already bearing considerable symbolic and cultural capital. Their cultural capital comes largely in the form of considerable organizing skills, developed in part through a number of actions earlier in the year, including camping outside Toronto police headquarters to demand accountability for overpolicing Black communities. In fact, Pride Toronto institutionalized BLM TO's cultural capital by giving it an official place in the parade as the Honoured Group. As an Honoured Group, BLM TO was able to mobilize cultural and symbolic capital through a tactic (a sit-in on Yonge Street) that has been used by LGBT/Q and HIV/AIDS activists numerous times before. I would suggest that what gave such tremendous energy to the debate following their sit-in is the fact that BLM TO deployed their considerable capital within a social space characterized by anti-Black racism and a collective identity centred on whiteness. Using their capital in this way, BLM TO forced open space within the pride field for reflection on structural racism and how it manifests in LGBT/Q communities. Fulfilling social movements' function as prophets of the present, BLM TO brought racism to the surface and forced LGBT/Q communities to address (though perhaps not resolve or eliminate) that racism.

The primary goal I set out for symbolic democracy is to encourage participants to reject the personal in favour of the universal. Symbolic democracy is about ensuring a correct relationship between field and habitus, and in that light it is worth noting that the social field surrounding Toronto's pride festivities does appear to have rewarded BLM TO's pursuit of barrier-free participation in queer celebrations by recognizing its specific forms of cultural and symbolic capital. It is not surprising that an organization disposed toward a universalist political vision should include demands supporting youth, queers with disabilities, and Indigenous peoples. Although hotly contested, the activist history of pride celebrations helps construct a field wherein these types of demands, put forward by groups with considerable activist capital, can gain a foothold.

I want to close, however, by critiquing what I would characterize as an attempt at deliberative democratic practice to illustrate how far Pride Toronto's response fell from the demands of symbolic democracy. For its August 2016 town hall, Pride Toronto used an open-mic format. What struck me about the format was the facilitator's insistence that attendees neither applaud nor boo speakers. The do-not-clap, do-not-boo rule was justified according to arguments that are fairly typical of deliberative democratic practice and its commitment to "civil" discussions. Applause, we were told, provides an incentive to speakers to be more emotional, more dynamic, and more rhetorical than they might otherwise be. Booing intimidates and potentially silences speakers. In short, the facilitator argued that reactions from the crowd would distort the discussion and prevent the town hall from obtaining rational, objective arguments. The approach fails in a number of ways.

First, banning applause only makes speaking easier for a specific type of speaker: one who is uninvested, non-anxious (comfortable speaking publicly), and who bears the privilege of assuming that most spaces are already designed for them. It fosters a space that is deferent to authority (that is, to the authority of whoever is speaking), and rewards speakers whose lives are already free from the quotidian ways in which non-dominant groups are stopped and interrupted. Because these privileges disproportionately accrue to white men, the ban on applause disproportionately supported white cisgender male and middle- or upper-class speakers. The ban ignores the importance of community in supporting those who speak truth to power. It ignores the daily psychic and emotional tolls incurred by oppression and the importance of not only communicating that emotional expression, but also—in order to make expressing that experience as safe as possible—allowing fellow-travellers to amplify descriptions of that experience. Although applause may provide incentives for more rhetorical flourishes, insisting on meeting speech with silence breaks the connection between a speaker and their community.

Second, the town hall was organized as a scene where speakers spoke and Pride board members listened without responding. Banning applause, had it been successful, would have created a dyadic speaking scene between speaker and board only. That is, it would have individualized speakers and artificially restricted their audience to the board itself. It is arbitrary to assume, in a moment of collective identity production such as this, that speakers should speak only to the board and not to fellow audience members. Whether or not it was a good idea to have board members listen without responding (and it wasn't), intervening between speakers and other participants by denying those participants a role as a communicative partner supports the production of falsely individualistic, unemotional, rationally neutral speakers. When grappling with oppression, individualism, coldness, and neutrality are the opposite of justice.

Third, the ban on booing failed to fulfill the organizers' intention to promote inclusion by creating a safe space. A commitment to safe space is both a practical principle (movements are stronger with more participants) and a normative one (movements ought to make everyone they claim to represent feel safe, at home). However, the town hall could never guarantee such a space, particularly because what makes a dominant group feel safe may make a dominated group unsafe. The fact that a central goal of the town hall was to address the impact of anti-Black racism in policing should have woken Pride organizers to the need to create safety through an anti-oppression lens, rather than a liberal anti-censorship lens. The facilitator prohibited booing apparently on the liberal principle that collective reasoning is best served when all opinions are heard. Such a liberal anti-censorship perspective valorizes the least popular opinions precisely because they challenge accepted views and force all speakers to articulate themselves better, to rethink their premises.

As with many liberal principles, however, enforcing a freedom-of-speech prohibition on booing was both individualizing and context-denying. Like the prohibition on applause, the prohibition on booing severed the speaker from the audience. Unlike the prohibition on applause, which undermines the community's ability to support and reflect the speaker, the prohibition on booing undercut speakers' accountability to the community they addressed. When one speaker articulated a racist denial of oppression and followed it with "fuck you, BLM TO," the facilitator refused to censor him while trying to silence audience members who vocally objected. Ostensibly neutral anti-censorship rules intended to create a safe space predictably sided with the anti-Black racism that had precipitated the town hall in the first place. In short, prohibiting booing did not ensure safety, but officially devaluing racism might have. As a counter-principle, symbolic democracy would forgo official neutrality in favour of rules that promote the safety of vulnerable groups even if (or especially if) that causes discomfort for dominant speakers voicing oppressive ideas. This might entail explicitly censoring racist speech, but it should also encourage identifying and implementing a discussion format that rewards universality and accountability.

Ultimately, procedure alone can never be sufficient to give us glimpses of social arrangements that are more just than the ones we currently endure. If the paradox of submission and conformity seems suffocating, then surely a call to conform more closely and explicitly to a set of procedural rules—even for the sake of well-regulated conflict—will offer little relief. If, as has been a guiding principle of my argument, there is no natural order or natural justice, then an end to domination is not a matter of just synching up with how the world ought to be. There is no "ought."

If meaning does not come from metaphysics, neither does it come from strictly ordered social spaces. Movements with sufficient creativity and the ability to harness scepticism of rules while nonetheless accumulating and deploying appropriate forms of capital may find strategies to allow them to pry open the bindings of conformity and failure. Cultivating the transformative power of movements requires, above all, continuous critique of the morally arbitrary but historically determined hierarchies and maldistribution of resources and authority. Acting collectively against these structures of domination does still offer the possibility of slightly diminishing symbolic power's suffocating grip. Symbolic power works because we give it power, but that "giving" is a non-intentional effect of habitus and social fields sedimented with long histories of inequality and oppression. In that light, reducing the internalization and operation of symbolic judgments may offer as much opportunity to empower dominated groups as formal democratic procedures.

As I said earlier: social change is amazing. It can be beautiful, inspiring, devastating, or all these things at once. Unfortunately, a few short months after BLM TO's 2016 pride action, another movement began to show similar capacity to translate capital accumulation and political refusals into movement successes: the racist alt-right movement in the United States. If BLM TO provides hope that social change can be beautiful and inspiring, then the alt-right reminds us that it can also be fragile and that racial, sexual, and class hierarchies are not easily undone. The work of negating unjust social and political systems remains as urgent as ever, as does the critical goal of opening up glimpses into better, more livable fields of action.

Notes

Preface
1. Friedrich Nietzsche, *Beyond Good and Evil*, trans. Walter Kaufmann (New York: Vintage Books, 1989).

Chapter One: Power and Struggle
1. Pierre Bourdieu et al., *The Weight of the World: Social Suffering in Contemporary Society*, trans. Priscilla Parkhurst Ferguson et al. (Stanford: Stanford University Press, 1993), 64.
2. Peter Weltman, "Assessment of Planned Security Costs for the 2010 G8 and G20 Summits," ed. Office of the Parliamentary Budget Officer (Ottawa, 2010), ii; Canadian Press, "Conservatives Make No Apology for High Cost of G8-G20," *Toronto Star*, www.thestar.com, Sept. 24, 2010; Adam Radwanski, "A History of Violence: The G20 Barrier That Wasn't," *Globe and Mail*, July 2, 2010, A9.
3. André Marin, "Caught in the Act: Investigation into the Ministry of Community Safety and Correctional Services' Conduct in Relation to Ontario Regulation 233/10 under the *Public Works Act*" (Toronto: Office of the Ombudsman, 2010); Toronto Police Service, "G20 Summit, Toronto, Ontario, June 2011: Toronto Police Service after-Action Review" (Toronto: Toronto Police Service, 2011); Wendy Gillis, "G20 Commander Apologizes after Being Convicted of Misconduct," *Toronto Star*, Aug. 25, 2015.
4. I am conscious here of the use of the LGBT/Q. There is no consensus about which letters ought to be included in the acronym. Although LGBTQ is currently used by The 519, Toronto's centre for services supporting sexually and gender-diverse communities, those letters exclude Two-Spirited people, intersex communities, and allies. In this book, I use LGBT/Q to capture the political differences between mainstreaming tendencies, particularly among lesbian and gay groups on the left side of the slash and the radical, anti-normal political project of queers on the right. It would be hard, though, to overstate the extent to which the language of inclusion in the acronym is contested, complex, and bound up in exactly the kinds of strategies and erasures I explore in this book. Trans people in particular have often been given token inclusion via the acronym, and queer-identified people have often overstated how radical and/or inclusive their politics are. My thanks to Tobias Wiggins for these insights.
5. Giorgio Mammoliti and David Shiner, "Notice of Motion MM49.12: 2010 Funding to Pride Toronto," ed. Toronto City Council (Toronto: City Council, 2010). Pride Toronto describes the potential loss of municipal dollars as having put the organization into an "operational crisis." Pride Toronto, "Pride Toronto Disallows Phrase 'Israeli Apartheid' in 2010 Parade" (Toronto: Pride Toronto, 2010).

6. "Pride Toronto to No Longer Restrict Language in the Parade" (Toronto: Pride Toronto, 2010).
7. Matt Thomas, "First-Person Account of the Toronto G20 Protests," *Xtra!*, June 28, 2010; James Burell, "Queer Journalist Seeks Answers," *Xtra!*, July14, 2010; Tor Sandberg, "Eighteen-Year-Old Detainee Recounts Experience of Being Held inside G8/20 Police Cage," rabble.ca, June 28, 2010.
8. For those unfamiliar with the differences between sociology, political science, and political theory, a brief explanation might be useful. Sociology typically focuses on the behaviour of groups in society and how social structures and processes impact people's lives. Political science, on the other hand, tends to concern itself first and foremost with the exercise of power within society. Understandably, there is considerable overlap between the two disciplines. Political *theory* is a subset of political science. Some political theorists try to explain why political events occur; this is called *explanatory* political theory. *Normative* political theorists tend to be more interested in whether political events or institutions are just or unjust, legitimate or illegitimate. My argument is based in normative political theory (it is concerned with justice), but it relies heavily on sociology and explanatory political theory.
9. What exactly to name the collection of efforts to resist the intensifying and global neoliberal project has not been settled. Early mobilization was called "anti-globalization," but given the movement's efforts to establish transnational networks of resistance, particularly through the World Social Forum and its regional and local versions, the movement is clearly not anti-global. Movement for Global Justice, anti-corporate globalization, and other terms have also been used. In this discussion I use "alter-globalization" to capture both the movement's attention to global issues and what I take to be the movement's most urgent task: to resist the doxic, neoliberal assertion that alternatives to corporate-dominated globalization are both impossible and undesirable. For excellent discussions of the terminology related to these movements see: David Graeber, "The New Anarchists," *New Left Review* 13 (Jan./Feb. 2002), 62–63; Richard Day, *Gramsci Is Dead* (London; Anne Arber, MI: Pluto Press, 2005), 4.
10. Theodor Adorno, "Sociology and Psychology ii," *New Left Review* 1,47 (1968), 78.
11. Iris Marion Young, *Inclusion and Democracy* (Oxford/New York: Oxford University Press, 2000), 10.
12. Loïc Wacquant, "Critical Thought as Solvent of *Doxa*," *Constellations* 11,1 (2004), 97.
13. Pierre Bourdieu, "Forms of Capital," in *Education, Globalization and Social Change*, ed. Hugh Lauder et al. (Oxford: Oxford University Press, 2006), 106; *The Logic of Practice*, trans. Richard Nice (Stanford, CA: Stanford University Press, 1990), 54. Although Bourdieu situated his work within a theoretical space dominated by the structuralism of Lévi-Strauss and Sartre's existentialism, his intellectual project owes a considerable debt to classical social theorists particularly in terms of his synthesis of Marx, Durkheim, and Weber. See: Rogers Brubaker, "Rethinking Classical Theory: The Sociological Vision of Pierre Bourdieu," in *After Bourdieu: Influence, Critique, Elaboration*, ed. David L. Swartz and Vera L. Zolberg (New York: Kluwer Academic Publishers, 2005), 30.
14. Lois McNay, "Agency and Experience: Gender as a Lived Relation," in *Feminism after Bourdieu*, ed. Lisa Adkins and Beverley Skeggs (Oxford: Blackwell Publishing, 2004), 184.
15. David Swartz, "Pierre Bourdieu and North American Political Sociology: Why He Doesn't Fit in but Should," *French Politics* 4,1 (2006), 94. See also: Mary S. Pileggi

and Cindy Patton, "Introduction: Bourdieu and Cultural Studies," *Cultural Studies* 17,3/4 (2003).
16. Swartz, "Pierre Bourdieu and North American Political Sociology," 87.
17. Nick Crossley, "Pierre Bourdieu (1930–2002)," *Social Movement Studies* 1,2 (2002), 15; *Making Sense of Social Movements* (Buckingham; Philadelphia: Open University Press, 2002), 189.
18. Swartz, "Pierre Bourdieu and North American Political Sociology," 93. See for example: Rogers Brubaker, *Nationalism Reframed: Nationhood and the National Question in the New Europe* (New York: Cambridge University Press, 1993); Joel S. Migdal, *State in Society* (Cambridge: Cambridge University Press, 2001); Susanne Soederberg, "Cannibalistic Capitalism and the Current Crisis," *Studies in Political Economy* 86 (2010).
19. Michele L. Crossley and Nick Crossley, "'Patient' Voices, Social Movements and the Habitus: How Psychiatric Survivors 'Speak Out,'" *Social Science and Medicine* 52 (2001), 1477, 1487; Nick Crossley, "From Reproduction to Transformation: Social Movement Fields and the Radical Habitus," *Theory, Culture & Society* 20,6 (2003), 51.
20. Elizabeth A. Armstrong and Mary Bernstein, "Culture, Power, and Institutions: A Multi-Institutional Politics Approach to Social Movements," *Sociological Theory* 26,1 (2008); Chares Demetriou, "Political Violence and Legitimation: The Episode of Colonial Cyprus," *Qualitative Sociology* 30,2 (2007); John Girling, *Social Movements and Symbolic Power: Radicalism, Reform and the Trial of Democracy in France* (New York: Palgrave Macmillan, 2004); Randolf Haluza-Delay, "A Theory of Practice for Social Movements: Environmentalism and Ecological Habitus," *Mobilization* 13,2 (2008); Yousaf Ibrahim, "Political Distinction in the British Anti-capitalist Movement," *Sociology* 45,2 (2011); Steph Lawler, "Rules of Engagement: Habitus, Power and Resistance," in *Feminism after Bourdieu*, ed. Adkins and Skeggs [originally published in *Sociological Review* 52 (2004)].
21. An important exception is Alan Topper's work, which I examine briefly in chapter four.
22. Nedim Karakayali, "Reading Bourdieu with Adorno: The Limits of Critical Theory and Reflexive Sociology," *Sociology* 38,2 (2004), 358–59.
23. Michael Grenfell, "Interest," in *Pierre Bourdieu: Key Concepts*, ed. Michael Grenfell (Stocksfield: Acumen, 2008), 153.
24. Pierre Carles, "Sociology Is a Martial Art (La Sociologie est un Sport de Combat)" (New York: First Run/Icarus Films, 2001).
25. Barbara Ehrenreich, *Bright-Sided: How the Relentless Promotion of Positive Thinking Has Undermined America* (New York: Metropolitan Books, 2009).
26. Friedrich Nietzsche, *The Gay Science*, trans. Walter Kaufmann (New York: Vintage Books, 1974), 343.

Chapter Two: Critical Theory and Social Movement Research
1. Wacquant, "Critical Thought as a Solvent of *Doxa*," 101.
2. Theodor Adorno, *Minima Moralia: Reflections from Damaged Life*, trans. E.F.N. Jephcott (London: Verso, 2005), 15.
3. For excellent overviews of these issues, see: Crossley, *Making Sense of Social Movements*; Donatella Della Porta and Mario Diani, *Social Movements*, 2nd ed. (Malden, MA: Blackwell Publishing, 2006).

   Like empirical researchers, normative theorists ought to be clear about when questions of justice are relevant. They also need to be clear about whether claims they make about justice in the context of social movements—about protest tactics and violence, for example—are intended to apply in other social and political contexts.

Arash Abizadeh calls this the "site and scope" of justice; it will be a key question when I examine suffering more closely in chapter six. Arash Abizadeh, "Cooperation, Pervasive Impact, and Coercion: On the Scope (Not Site) of Distributive Justice," *Philosophy and Public Affairs* 35,4 (2007).
4. Alberto Melucci, *Challenging Codes: Collective Action in the Information Age* (Cambridge, UK: Cambridge University Press, 1996), 29–30.
5. Crossley provides an excellent account of how researchers since the 1960s have caricaturized these approaches and been overly hasty in their dismissal. See: Crossley, *Making Sense of Social Movements*.
6. Francesca Polletta and James M. Jasper, "Collective Identity and Social Movements," *Annual Review of Sociology* 27,1 (2001), 286.
7. Cyrus Ernesto Zirakzadeh, "Crossing Frontiers: Theoretical Innovations in the Study of Social Movements," *International Political Science Review* 29,5 (2008), 528.
8. Within rational choice perspectives, John D. McCarthy and Mayer N. Zald's work on social movement organizations was particularly important. Structuralists came to rely especially on Theda Skocpol's state-centred approach, while cultural perspectives used Melucci as a key touchstone.
9. Doug McAdam, Sidney Tarrow, and Charles Tilly, *Dynamics of Contention* (Cambridge: Cambridge University Press, 2001), 14.
10. Doug McAdam, Sidney Tarrow and Charles Tilly, "Toward an Integrated Perspective on Social Movements and Revolution," in *Comparative Politics: Rationality, Culture, and Structure*, ed. Mark Iving Lichbach and Alan S. Zuckerman (Cambridge: Cambridge University Press, 1997), 142.
11. Ibid., 159–60.
12. Mary Bernstein, "Nothing Ventured, Nothing Gained? Conceptualizing Social Movement 'Success' in the Lesbian and Gay Movement," *Sociological Perspectives* 46,3 (2003); Melinda D. Kane, "You've Won, Now What? The Influence of Legal Change on Gay and Lesbian Mobilization," *The Sociological Quarterly* 51 (2010); Arnold Fleischmann and Laura Moyer, "Competing Social Movements and Local Political Culture: Voting on Ballot Propositions to Ban Same-Sex Marriage in the U.S. States," *Social Science Quarterly* 90,1 (2009). On the relationship between outcomes and mobilization in a non-LGBT context, namely the anti–death penalty movement, see Devashree Gupta, "The Power of Incremental Outcomes: How Small Victories and Defeats Affect Social Movement Organizations," *Mobilization* 14,4 (2009).
13. For example: Nancy Nicol and Miriam Smith, "Legal Struggles and Political Resistance: Same-Sex Marriage in Canada and the USA," *Sexualities* 11,6 (2008), 684.
14. Indeed, the opposite appears to be the case. See: Elizabeth F. Emens, "Monogamy's Law: Compulsory Monogamy and Polyamorous Existence," *New York University Review of Law and Social Change* 29,2 (2004), 522; Diane Richardson, "Desiring Sameness? The Rise of a Neoliberal Politics of Normalisation," *Antipode* 37,3 (2005).
15. McAdam, Tarrow, and Tilly, *Dynamics of Contention*, 13, 62, 69, 102, 243; Gerald Platt, "Unifying Social Movement Theories," *Qualitative Sociology* 27,1 (2004), 107.
16. Richard Flacks, "Knowledge for What? Thoughts on the State of Social Movement Studies," in *Rethinking Social Movements: Structure, Meaning and Emotion*, ed. Jeff Goodwin and James M. Jasper (Lanham, MD: Rowman and Littlefield, 2004), 139, 151; Jeff Goodwin and James M. Jasper, "Caught in a Winding, Snarling Vine: The Structural Bias of Political Process Theory," in *Rethinking Social Movements*, 3; Zirakzadeh, "Crossing Frontiers 530, 532; Platt, "Unifying Social Movement Theories," 114.

17. McAdam, Tarrow, and Tilly, *Dynamics of Contention*, 5.
18. Mancur Olson, *The Logic of Collective Action* (Cambridge: Harvard University Press, 1965); Anthony Downs, *An Economic Theory of Democracy* (New York: Harper, 1957).
19. Pierre Bourdieu, *Pascalian Meditations*, trans. Richard Nice (Stanford: Stanford University Press, 2000), 139–40.
20. Melucci, *Challenging Codes*, 70. In fact, a constructivist approach toward identity is currently the norm among social movement researchers. See, for example, McAdam, Tarrow, and Tilly, *Dynamics of Contention*, where the authors affirm a constructivist approach to identity (55–56) and include constructivist processes such as identity shift (162) as mechanisms that help explain contentious political action.
21. Alberto Melucci, "The Process of Collective Identity," in *Social Movements and Culture*, ed. Hank Johnston and Bert Klandermans (Minneapolis: University of Minnesota Press, 1995), 44–45.
22. Tom Warner, *Never Going Back: A History of Queer Activism in Canada* (Toronto: University of Toronto Press, 2002), 222. See also: Michael Warner, *The Trouble with Normal: Sex, Politics, and the Ethics of Queer Life* (New York: The Free Press, 1999), 88–89; and Tim McCaskell, *Queer Progress: From Homophobia to Homonationalism* (Toronto: Between the Lines Press, 2017).
23. Melucci, *Challenging Codes*, 13. (Anarchist groups challenge this model, as I explain in chapter five.)
24. Indeed, as a social psychologist, Melucci's contributions are themselves implicitly and at times explicitly reliant upon social-psychological approaches. William Gamson, "The Social Psychology of Collective Action," in *Frontiers in Social Movement Theory*, ed. Aldon D. Morris and Carol McClurg Mueller (New Haven/London: Yale University Press, 1992), 72–73; Scott A. Hunt, Robert D. Benford, and David A. Snow, "Identity Fields: Framing Processes and the Social Construction of Movement Identities," in *New Social Movements: From Ideology to Identity*, ed. Enrique Laraña, Hank Johnston, and Joseph R. Gusfield (Philadelphia: Temple University Press, 1994); Sheldon Stryker, "Identity Competition: Key to Differential Social Movement Participation?," in *Self, Identity, and Social Movements*, ed. Sheldon Stryker, Timothy J. Owens, and Robert W. White (Minneapolis: University of Minnesota Press, 2003); Verta Taylor and Nancy E. Whittier, "Collective Identity in Social Movement Communities: Lesbian Feminist Mobilization," in *Frontiers in Social Movement Theory*); David A. Snow and Doug McAdam, "Identity Work Processes in the Context of Social Movements: Clarifying the Identity/Movement Nexus," in *Self, Identity, and Social Movements*; David A. Snow et al., "Frame Alignment Processes, Micromobilization, and Movement Participation," *American Sociological Review* 51,4 (1986).
25. Melucci, *Challenging Codes*, 29–30. See also: Mario Diani and Ivano Bison, "Organizations, Coalitions, and Movements," *Theory and Society* 33,3/4 (2004), 282.
26. Joshua Gamson, "Messages of Exclusion: Gender, Movements, and Symbolic Boundaries," *Gender and Society* 11,2 (1997), 179; Polletta and Jasper, "Collective Identity and Social Movements," 294.

    Marc Steinberg instrumentalizes framing processes generally, but including framing about collective identity, by including them within repertoires of contention, which are discussed in the next chapter. See: Marc Steinberg, "The Roar of the Crowd: Repertoires of Discourse and Collective Action among the Spitalfields Silk Weavers in Nineteenth-Century London," in *Repertoires and Cycles of Collective Action*, ed. Mark Traugott (Durham and London: Duke University Press, 1995).
27. Polletta and Jasper, "Collective Identity and Social Movements," 296–97.

28. Dermot Barr and John Drury, "Activist Identity as a Motivational Resource: Dynamics of (Dis)Empowerment at the G8 Direct Actions, Gleneagles, 2005," *Social Movement Studies* 8,3 (2009), 257.
29. Stryker, "Identity Competition," 26.
30. Bourdieu, *The Logic of Practice*, 42. See also: Crossley, *Making Sense of Social Movements*, 140.
31. Scott Lash, "Pierre Bourdieu: Cultural Economy and Social Change," in *Bourdieu: Critical Perspectives*, ed. Craig Calhoun, Edward LiPuma, and Moishe Postone (Chicago: University of Chicago Press, 1993), 201–202.
32. Melucci, *Challenging Codes*, 10.
33. Charles Tilly, "Getting It Together in Burgundy, 1675–1975," *Theory and Society* 4,4 (1977).
34. Charles Tilly, "Contentious Repertoires in Great Britain, 1758–1834," in *Repertoires and Cycles of Collective Action*, ed. Traugott, 26.
35. Nick Crossley, "Repertoires of Contention and Tactical Diversity in the UK Psychiatric Survivors Movement: The Question of Appropriation," *Social Movement Studies* 1,1 (2002), 48–49.
36. Tilly, "Contentious Repertoires in Great Britain," 27.
37. Iris Marion Young, "Activist Challenges to Deliberative Democracy," in *Debating Deliberative Democracy*, ed. James S. Fishkin and Peter Laslett (Malden, MA: Blackwell Publishing, 2003).
38. Graeber, "The New Anarchists," 30.
39. Tilly, "Contentious Repertoires in Great Britain," 28.
40. Crossley, "Repertoires of Contention and Tactical Diversity in the UK Psychiatric Survivors Movement," 49–50.
41. Tilly, "Contentious Repertoires in Great Britain," 27–28; Sidney Tarrow, "Cycles of Collective Action: Between Moments of Madness and the Repertoire of Contention," *Social Science History* 17,2 (1993), 302.
42. Frances Fox Piven and Richard Cloward, "Power Repertoires and Globalization," *Politics and Society* 28,3 (2000), 414.

Chapter Three: Conformity and Failure
1. Nick Crossley, "The Phenomenological Habitus and Its Construction," *Theory and Society* 30 (2001), 116.
2. In his reading of Bourdieu, Charles Taylor suggests that we only develop individual identities through relations to, and concerted actions with, other individuals who share our sense of the meaning of practices. Deference, for example, can only make sense as a social practice if there is someone who defers and someone who is deferred to. Charles Taylor, "To Follow a Rule..." in *Bourdieu: Critical Perspectives*, ed. Craig Calhoun, Edward LiPuma, and Moishe Postone (Chicago: University of Chicago Press, 1993), 48, 50.
3. Pierre Bourdieu, *Outline of a Theory of Practice*, trans. Richard Nice (Cambridge: Cambridge University Press, 1977), 3; *The Logic of Practice*, 26.

    For example, Bourdieu points to Saussurean structural linguistics as an exemplary instance of objectivist thinking. The major achievement of structuralism lies at the ontological level. Rather than positing the existence of a world comprised of independent objects with essential properties belonging only to themselves—what he and others refer to as substantialist thinking—structuralism envisions a world in which the meaning of objects can only be determined with reference to all of the other objects belonging to the same system. Although Bourdieu also broke from objectivism and structuralism, he insisted on the importance of this kind of relational thinking. *The Logic of Practice*, 4; *Distinction: A Social Critique of the Judgment of Taste*, trans. Richard Nice (Cambridge, MA: Harvard University Press, 1984), 22.

4. Bourdieu makes use of the map metaphor in *Outline of a Theory of Practice*, 35. His more detailed rejection of objectivist formalism is developed in his analysis of Kabyle marriage and kinship practices, ibid., Chapter I Section II; *The Logic of Practice*, Part II Chapter 2.
5. *Outline of a Theory of Practice*, 4–9; *The Logic of Practice*, Chapter 6.
6. Patricia Thomson, "Field," in *Pierre Bourdieu: Key Concepts* (Stocksfield: Acumen, 2008), 68–72.
7. William Schinkel, "Pierre Bourdieu's Political Turn?," *Theory, Culture & Society* 20,6 (2003), 76.
8. Bourdieu, *Pascalian Meditations*, 134–35.
9. *Distinction*, 32.
10. Bourdieu et al., *The Weight of the World*, 124–25.
11. An example of a labour of conversion would be to take economic capital and transform it into political capital by purchasing political advertising and then "profiting" from the political capital acquired by having more people support your policy position, political organization, or whatever the target of the advertising was.
12. Bourdieu, "Forms of Capital," 106.
13. *The Logic of Practice*, 53.
14. Pierre Bourdieu, *Language and Symbolic Power*, ed. John B. Thompson, trans. Gino Raymond and Matthew Adamson (Cambridge, MA: Harvard University Press, 1991), 50–51.
15. Pierre Bourdieu, *Practical Reason*, trans. Randall Johnson (Stanford: Stanford University Press, 1998), 9.
16. Angela McRobbie, "Notes on 'What Not to Wear' and Post-Feminist Symbolic Violence," in *Feminism after Bourdieu*, ed. Adkins and Skeggs.
17. Bourdieu uses the term himself, which is perhaps misleading. Maton, by contrast, argues that researchers tend to reduce habitus to social background or socialization because habitus cannot be directly observed and there appear to be few methodological resources for establishing which structures of a habitus are being triggered at a given time. See Karl Maton, "Habitus," in *Pierre Bourdieu: Key Concepts* (Stocksfield: Acumen Inc, 2008), 62.
18. Bourdieu, *Pascalian Meditations*, 140–41; emphasis original.
19. Ibid., 134. This section relies heavily on the excellent work by Nick Crossley, who argues that adaptation and habituation are an evolutionary advantage for humans and that habituation can be contrasted to the operation of animal instincts in survival. Crossley, "The Phenomenological Habitus and Its Construction," 111.
20. Crossley, "The Phenomenological Habitus and Its Construction," 102.
21. Bourdieu, *The Logic of Practice*, 73.
22. *Language and Symbolic Power*, 50–51.
23. *Pascalian Meditations*, 130.
24. Taylor, "To Follow a Rule...," 48.

25. I will engage debates about whether Bourdieu was insufficiently attentive to the role of conscious deliberation below. For now, it is worth noting that Bourdieu acknowledged that habitus does not exclude the possibility of strategic, conscious calculation, but he insisted that while both conscious calculation and habitus aim at "an estimation of chances presupposing transformation of the past effect into an expected objective" the habitus's responses are first defined by a probable "upcoming future" that excludes deliberation. Bourdieu, *The Logic of Practice*, 53.
26. Jean-François Fourny, "Bourdieu's Uneasy Psychoanalysis," *Substance* 93 (2000), 105.
27. Bourdieu, *Pascalian Meditations*, 166.
28. Ibid., 165.
29. Ibid., 166.
30. Ibid.
31. For a superlative overview of psychoanalytic descriptions of how plenitude and trauma provoke subjectivity and sociality, consult Lauren Berlant, *Desire/Love* (New York: Punctum Books, 2012), especially at 27–29.
32. See, for example, Loïc Wacquant, "Review Article: Why Men Desire Muscles," *Body and Society* 1,1 (1995).
33. Bourdieu, *Pascalian Meditations*, 166.
34. Jean-Jacques Rousseau distinguished between two types of self-love. *Amour-de-soi* is self-love that comes from natural self-interest and an inclination for self-preservation. *Amour propre* is self-love based on comparison with others. While *amour-de-soi* is individualistic, *amour propre* is deeply social.
35. Bourdieu, *Pascalian Meditations*, 11–12.
36. *Distinction*, 386, 390.
37. Ibid., 65–67.
38. *Outline of a Theory of Practice*, 79; *The Logic of Practice*, 57.
39. *Pascalian Meditations*, 210.
40. Ibid., 204; see also 144.
41. Ibid., 208.
42. *Practical Reason*, 79.
43. *Pascalian Meditations*, 143.
44. Judith Butler, "Performativity's Social Magic," in *Bourdieu: A Critical Reader*, ed. Richard Shusterman (Oxford; Molden, MA: Blackwell Publishers, 1999), 118.
45. George Steinmetz, "Bourdieu's Disavowal of Lacan: Psychoanalytic Theory and the Concepts of 'Habitus' and 'Symbolic Capital,'" *Constellations* 13,4 (2006), 446, 452.
46. Beverly Skeggs, "Context and Background: Pierre Bourdieu's Analysis of Class, Gender and Sexuality," in *Feminism after Bourdieu*, ed. Adkins and Skeggs, 27.
47. Bourdieu, *Pascalian Meditations*, 167.
48. Ibid., 168.
49. *Distinction*, 111.
50. Nietzsche, *Beyond Good and Evil*, 9.

Chapter Four: Collective Identity and Symbolic Power

1. Pierre Bourdieu, *Sociology in Question*, trans. Richard Nice (London: Sage Publications, 1993), 90.
2. The four teenagers were Seth Walsh, age 13, of Tehachapi, California; Billy Lucas, age 15, of Greensburg, Indiana; Tyler Clementi, age 18, of New Jersey; and Asher Brown,

age 13, who lived in the suburbs of Houston, Texas. Jesse McKinley, "Suicides Put Light on Pressures of Gay Teenagers," *New York Times*, www.nytimes.com, Oct. 4, 2010.
3. Dan Savage and Terry Miller, "It Gets Better: Dan and Terry," It Gets Better Project, www.itgetsbetter.org.
4. David Taffet, "Dan Savage: It's 'Never Been Worse' for LGBT Youth," dallasvoice.com, Feb. 2, 2012.
5. Jasbir Puar, "Coda: The Cost of Getting Better," *GLQ* 18,1 (2011), 151.
6. For an interesting Bourdieuian analysis of the power-laden and exclusionary nature of gay spaces in Toronto, see: Adam Isaiah Green, "Playing the (Sexual) Field: The Interactional Basis of Systems of Sexual Stratification," *Social Psychology Quarterly* 74 (2011).
7. Savage and Miller, "It Gets Better."
8. Hiram Perez, "You Can Have My Brown Body and Eat It, Too!," *Social Text* 23,3/4 (2005), 177.
9. Poverty and Employment Precarity in Southern Ontario (PEPSO), "It's More Than Poverty: Employment Precarity and Household Well-Being" (Toronto: 2013).
10. Puar, "Coda," 151.
11. Lisa Duggan, "The New Homonormativity: The Sexual Politics of Neoliberalism," in *Materializing Democracy: Toward a Revitalized Cultural Politics*, ed. Castronovo and Dana D. Nelson (Durham/London: Duke University Press, 2002). Richardson, "Desiring Sameness?," 521–23. Eng et. al call this unification "queer liberalism." David L. Eng, Judith Halberstam, and José Esteban Muñoz, "Introduction: What's Queer About Queer Studies Now?," *Social Text* 23,3/4 (2005), 10–11.
12. Importantly, this distinguishes what I'm doing from liberal and Foucauldian accounts, a distinction I elaborate further in chapter six.
13. William Gamson, "The Social Psychology of Collective Action," 57; Diani and Bison, "Organizations, Coalitions, and Movements," 282; Mary Bernstein, "Identity Politics," *Annual Review of Sociology* 31 (2005), 59.
14. Anonymous, "All Queers Read This; Why I Hate Straights," in *We Are Everywhere*, ed. M. Blasius and S. Phelan (New York: Routledge, 1997), 773.
15. Audre Lorde, *Sister Outsider* (Freedom, CA: The Crossing Press, 1984), 146, 151.
16. Bourdieu, *Pascalian Meditations*, 75.
17. As noted in the Preface, Bourdieu's use of "capital" is different from the Marxist usage. Bourdieu distances his usage from the political economic sense familiar to Marxists.
18. Jane Ward, "Producing 'Pride' in West Hollywood: A Queer Cultural Capital for Queers with Cultural Capital," *Sexualities* 6,1 (2003), 89. See also: Joshua Gamson, "The Organizational Shaping of Collective Identity: The Case of Lesbian and Gay Film Festivals in New York," *Sociological Forum* 11,2 (1996); and Amin Ghaziani, "Post-Gay Collective Identity Construction," *Social Problems* 58,1 (2011), 118.
19. Elsewhere, Ward extends her argument in a less Bourdieuian tone to "diversity skills" in major LGBT organizations in Los Angeles to demonstrate how cultural capital in the form of knowing how to deploy diversity rhetoric can actually operate to suppress forms of difference not captured by "respectable" forms of diversity. See: Jane Ward, *Respectably Queer: Diversity Culture in LGBT Activist Organizations* (Nashville: Vanderbilt University Press, 2008).

Keith Topper offers an account of how these dynamics might be reversed in: Keith Topper, "Arendt and Bourdieu between Word and Deed," *Political Theory* 39,3 (2011). He argues that AIDS activists were able to develop the specific (scientific) linguistic

capital needed to insert themselves into research and testing decisions over AIDS medication. There are, however, a number of problems with Topper's analysis. First, Topper acknowledges that speech competence is about an entire "social personality," and yet he fails to fully situate AIDS activists as part of a broader movement exerting moral pressure through political tactics. That is, he does not consider the extent to which the "seat at the table" was won through political action rather than linguistic competence. This is theoretically important insofar as it would provide a more consistent read of Bourdieu and point us toward consideration of the circulation of capital rather than purely linguistic exchanges (which are, in a sense, epiphenomena of capital, or perhaps symptoms of capital). Similarly, Topper gestures toward the exclusions that this mastery duplicated—racial, gender, class, and the possibility that lay experts were "captured" by their linguistic mastery; in each case these exclusions raise doubts about their representative potential. Normatively speaking, these aspects of the dynamics and processes of what we might call *collective social personalities* would be essential to providing an overall account. In particular, it would help to determine whether the Arendtian power generated was actually successful. He notes at the beginning, for example, a lack of funding for anti-infectives (at the expense of funding for anti-viral treatments). He does not, however, indicate whether this lack was remedied. In fact, capture and disclosure perhaps represent a central problem as much as capture vs. rapprochement. If an agent is captured, then what they are able to disclose must be problematic. If the self that one discloses has already been instrumentalized by the need to render oneself intelligible within a public space, then it is not clear that an Arendtian expression of power as the keeping open of public space has been achieved.
20. Bourdieu, "Forms of Capital," 115, n. 3.
21. *Pascalian Meditations*, 169.
22. Ibid.
23. Mustafa Emirbayer and Chad Alan Goldberg, "Pragmatism, Bourdieu, and Collective Emotions in Contentious Politics," *Theory and Society* 34,5 (2005), 472; Lory Britt and David Heise, "From Shame to Pride in Identity Politics," in *Self, Identity, and Social Movements* (Minneapolis: University of Minnesota Press, 2003), 255–59; Deborah B. Gould, "Passionate Political Processes: Bringing Emotions Back into the Study of Social Movements," in *Rethinking Social Movements*, ed. Goodwin and Jasper, 169; David M. Halperin and Valerie Traub, "Beyond Gay Pride," in *Gay Shame*, ed. David M. Halperin and Valerie Traub (Chicago: Chicago University Press, 2009).

On a slightly different register there have also been new efforts to theorize the cultural, social, and embodied manifestations of affect and emotion, as well as their political implications. See: Melissa Gregg and Gregory J. Seigworth, eds., *The Affect Theory Reader* (Durham, NC: Duke University Press, 2010); Ann Cvetkovich, "Public Feelings," *South Atlantic Quarterly* 106,3 (2007); Lauren Berlant, *Cruel Optimism* (Durham and London: Duke University Press, 2011).
24. Trans people and their allies commonly use "cisgender" to indicate people who identify as the sex/gender they were assigned at birth. Avoiding "non-trans" or equivalent expressions refuses to naturalize cisgender people and thereby mark out transgender people as deviant or "other." At the time of writing, so-called bathroom wars were raging in North Carolina, Alberta and elsewhere. In these and other jurisdictions, preventing trans people from using the bathroom that matches their gender identity has become the post-marriage battleground of choice for a number of cultural and religious conservatives.

25. Bourdieu, *Pascalian Meditations*, 185.
26. Bourdieu, *Language and Symbolic Power*, 19.
27. Gayatri Chakravorty Spivak, "Can the Subaltern Speak?," in *Marxism and the Interpretation of Culture*, ed. Cary Nelson and Lawrence Grossberg (Chicago: University of Illinois Press, 1988), 291.
28. Kristie Dotson, "Tracking Epistemic Violence, Tracking Practices of Silencing," *Hypatia* 26,2 (2011), 242.
29. Bourdieu, *Language and Symbolic Power*, 80.
30. Ibid., 81.
31. Ibid., 80.
32. Ibid., 41.
33. Jane McConkey, "Knowledge and Acknowledgement: 'Epistemic Injustice' as a Problem of Recognition," *Politics* 24,3 (2004), 198, 199.
34. Bourdieu, *Language and Symbolic Power*, 221.
35. Christine Donald, cited in Tom Warner, *Never Going Back*, 176.
36. Tom Warner, *Never Going Back*, 219–25. See also McCaskell, *Queer Progress*.
37. Michael Warner expresses such a sentiment about the movement for relationship recognition generally in *The Trouble with Normal*, 84.
38. Tom Warner, *Never Going Back*, 231.
39. John Kennedy, "Just John," *fab magazine*, July 8, 1999, 11.
40. Ibid.
41. "Nudity at the Pride Parade: The Debate in 6 Reader Comments," *Toronto Star*, March 5, 2014; Louise Brown, "Trustees to Ask City to Bar Nudity at Pride Parade," ibid. Sotiropoulos was defeated in the 2014 Toronto District School Board elections.
42. Lawler, "Rules of Engagement," 122.
43. Smith's analysis in *Lesbian and Gay Rights in Canada* has persuasively demonstrated the role of the Charter of Rights and Freedoms in bolstering what Bourdieu would describe as the symbolic value of legalist movement strategies (see especially 109–110). Smith does not account for the inertia that acquiescing to existing distributions of symbolic power fosters, as evidenced by her optimism that same-sex marriage will "radically transform" the institution of marriage (76).
44. Tom Warner, *Never Going Back*, 222. See also Michael Warner, *The Trouble with Normal*, 88–89.
45. Michael Warner, *The Trouble with Normal*, 178.
46. Ibid., 68, 79.
47. Miriam Smith, *Lesbian and Gay Rights in Canada: Social Movements and Equality-Seeking* (Toronto: Toronto University Press, 1999), 41, 76. See also: Bernstein, "Nothing Ventured, Nothing Gained?"
48. Smith, *Lesbian and Gay Rights in Canada* 142, 151.
49. Michel Foucault, *The History of Sexuality, vol. 1* (New York: Pantheon Books, 1978), 95. See also: "The Subject and Power," in *Michel Foucault: Power*, ed. James D. Faubion (New York: The New Press, 1994), 346–47.
50. Bernstein, "Identity Politics," 56–57; Jonathan Alexander, "Beyond Identity: Queer Values and Community," *Journal of Gay, Lesbian, and Bisexual Identity* 4,4 (1999), 302–303; Annamarie Jagose, *Queer Theory: An Introduction* (New York: New York University Press, 1996), 78, 83.
51. Judith Butler, *Gender Trouble; Feminism and the Subversion of Identity* (New York; London: Routledge, 1990), 136.

52. Ibid., 140.
53. Ibid., 137.
54. "Doing Justice to Someone: Sex Reassignment and Allegories of Transsexuality," *GLQ* 7,4 (2001), 622, 634. I have also noted Butler's and Skeggs's parallel critiques of Bourdieu, where each argues that there is a necessary ambivalence at the core of subject formation; see chapter two.
55. *Gender Trouble; Feminism and the Subversion of Identity*, 138; "Performativity's Social Magic," 123–24.
56. The language here may be unintentionally misleading. Butler does not intend the incorporation of norms or the "assignment" of gender roles, etc., to be understood in voluntarist terms. Here she and Bourdieu concur that processes of habituation and the performances they evoke are non-cognitive and generally preconscious.
57. Judith Butler, *Undoing Gender* (New York; London: Routledge, 2004), 8.
58. Gamson, "Messages of Exclusion." For an excellent analysis of how identification and disidentification strategies are pursued by opposing movements, see: Cindy Patton, "Tremble, Hetero Swine!," in *Fear of a Queer Planet: Queer Politics and Social Theory*, ed. Michael Warner (Minneapolis: University of Minnesota Press, 1993).
59. Through a detailed ethnographic study of a Malaysian peasant community, Scott describes, for example, "the prosaic but constant struggle between the peasantry and those who seek to extract labour, food, taxes, rents, and interest from them," with emphasis on "the ordinary weapons of relatively powerless groups: foot dragging, dissimulation, false compliance, pilfering, feigned ignorance, slander, arson, sabotage, and so forth." James C. Scott, *Weapons of the Weak: Everyday Forms of Peasant Resistance* (New Haven: Yale University Press, 1985), 29.
60. Beverley Skeggs, "Exchange, Value and Affect: Bourdieu and 'the Self,'" *Sociological Review* 52 (2004), 88.
61. McNay, "Agency and Experience," 188.
62. Ibid.

Chapter Five: Tactic and Antimony

1. Tilly, "Getting It Together in Burgundy," 493.
2. Canadian Press, "Conservatives Make No Apology for High Cost of G8-G20"; Radwanski, "A History of Violence"; Weltman, "Assessment of Planned Security Costs for the 2010 G8 and G20 Summits," ii.
3. Janet Conway, "Civil Resistance and the 'Diversity of Tactics' in the Anti-Globalization Movement: Problems of Violence, Silence, and Solidarity in Activist Politics," *Osgoode Hall Law Journal* 41,2/3 (2003).
4. Adorno, *Minima Moralia*, 43.
5. McAdam, Tarrow, and Tilly, *Dynamics of Contention*, 24.
6. Bourdieu et al., *The Weight of the World*, 189–91.
7. Lawler, "Rules of Engagement," 122.
8. Richard Day has been prominent among observers who question the usefulness of summit protests. Where Day questions state-centred "politics of demand" generally, my interest is in the antinomies produced by symbolic domination as a specific mode of power—which may or may not include the state as an actor or target of action. See: Day, *Gramsci Is Dead*, 80.
9. Barr and Drury, "Activist Identity as a Motivational Resource," 257.
10. Conway, "Civil Resistance and the 'Diversity of Tactics,'" 510.

11. Ibid., 516.
12. Although anarchists tend to emphasize respect for plural tactics, Dupuis-Déri notes that not all anarchist and anti-authoritarian organizations have demonstrated such respect themselves. Francis Dupuis-Déri, "The Black Blocs Ten Years after Seattle: Anarchism, Direct Action, and Deliberative Practices," *Journal for the Study of Radicalism* 4,2 (2010), 59.

    It is worth noting that although currently heavily associated with anarchism, as Linda Martín Alcoff argues that affinity-based direct action was in fact an invention of feminist organizers and rooted in 1960s feminist critiques. She also notes that structurelessness was deeply contested, even then. Linda Martín Alcoff, "Then and Now," *Journal of Speculative Philosophy* 26,2 (2012), 269.

    Conway, "Civil Resistance and the 'Diversity of Tactics,'" 510.
13. In Montreal, for example, a Black Bloc activist smashed the window of a Canadian Forces office and was "shoved back by a pack of marchers as she tried to blend back into the crowd." Benjamin Shingler, "To Smash or Not to Smash? In Montreal, Pacifists Tell Vandals to Tone It Down," Huffington Post (Canada), www.huffingtonpost.ca, April 30, 2012.

    Marcus Gee, "Why Some G20 Protesters Won't Condemn Violence," *Globe & Mail* [Metro Toronto], June 24, 2010, A14; Jennifer Yang and Liam Casey, "As Protesters and Police Move in, Downtown Workers Move Out," *Toronto Star*, June 23, 2010, A4; Sid Ryan, "Thousands Stood up for Humanity; Marchers Braved Hooligans, Police and Even the Weather to Push People's Agenda," *Toronto Star*, June 29, 2010, A19; Canadian Labour Congress, "Statement by Ken Georgetti, President of the Canadian Labour Congress on Vandalism Surrounding the G20 Meeting," Canadian Labour Congress, www.canadianlabour.ca, June 26, 2010.
14. Pierre Bourdieu and Loïc Wacquant, "Newliberalspeak: Notes on the New Planetary Vulgate," *Radical Philosophy* 105 (Jan./Feb. 2001), 2; Bourdieu et al., *The Weight of the World*, 182; Schinkel, "Pierre Bourdieu's Political Turn?," 79; Lisa Duggan, *The Twilight of Equality? Neoliberalism, Cultural Politics and the Attack on Democracy* (Boston: Beacon Press, 2003), ix–xxii; Jamie Peck and Adam Tickell, "Neoliberalizing Space," *Antipode* 34,3 (2002), 383.
15. Bourdieu et al., *The Weight of the World*, 182.
16. Day, *Gramsci Is Dead*, 7.
17. Duggan, *The Twilight of Equality*, xiv; Peck and Tickell, "Neoliberalizing Space," 381; Loïc Wacquant, "Pointers on Pierre Bourdieu and Democratic Politics," *Constellations* 11,1 (2004), 2.
18. Duggan, "The New Homonormativity," 179.
19. Donatella Della Porta and Olivier Filleule, "Policing Social Protest," in *The Blackwell Companion to Social Movements*, ed. David A. Snow, Sara A. Soule, and Hanspeter Kriesi (Malden, MA: Blackwell, 2004), 235.
20. Lynn Sanders, "Against Deliberation," *Political Theory* 25,3 (1997), 370.
21. John Rawls, *A Theory of Justice* (Cambridge, Mass.: Harvard University Press, 1971), 364.
22. Ibid., 365.
23. Bourdieu and Wacquant, "Newliberalspeak," 2; Roger Keil, "'Common Sense' Neoliberalism: Progressive Conservative Urbanism in Toronto, Canada," *Antipode* 34,3 (2002), 584.
24. Angus Reid, "Canadians Want Federal Government to Pick up the Tab for G20 Disruption," http://angusreidglobal.com, July 1, 2010.

25. Verta Taylor and Nella Van Dyke, "'Get up, Stand Up': Tactical Repertoires of Social Movements," in *The Blackwell Companion to Social Movements*, ed. David A. Snow, Sara A. Soule, and Hanspeter Kriesi (Malden, MA: Blackwell Publishing, 2004), 282–83.
26. Grenfell, "Postscript: Methodological Principles," 220–21.
27. Richard Lautens, "Tear Gas Fired in Rampage; Mayor Calls Violent Protesters 'Criminals,' Says They're 'Not Welcome in This City'," *Toronto Star*, June 27, 2010, A6; Canadian Civil Liberties Association, "A Breach of the Peace: A Preliminary Report of Observations During the 2010 G20 Summit" (Toronto: CCLA, 2010), 10.
28. Ryan, "Thousands Stood Up for Humanity," A19.
29. Community Solidarity Network, "Get Off the Fence," http://g20.torontomobilize.org/getoffthefence.
30. Dupuis-Déri, "The Black Bloc Ten Years after Seattle," 48.
31. Day, *Gramsci Is Dead*, 29.
32. Conway, "Civil Resistance and the 'Diversity of Tactics,'" 535.
33. Dupuis-Déri, "The Black Bloc Ten Years after Seattle," 54–55.
34. Jesse Mclean, "In Black and Running Wild: Masked Members of Anarchist Group Responsible for Much of Window-Bashing," *Toronto Star*, June 27, 2010, A7.
35. Andrew Chung, "Police Targeted Quebecers, Say Protest Organizers: 'For Us It's Not Violence,' Activist Says of Rampage," *Toronto Star*, June, 29 A6. Francoeur was similarly quoted in: Ingrid Peritz, "Protest Group Accuse Police of Profiling Quebeckers," *Globe & Mail* [Toronto], June 29, 2010, A10.
36. It is not my intention to give a full accounting of how violence had been constructed prior to the protests nor even a full account of its construction during the meetings. Although such an analysis would be useful, my focus is on the efforts of one set of actors—Black Bloc activists—and the problematic strategy of using symbolically devalued tactics in struggles to construct meaning.
37. Bourdieu, *The Logic of Practice*, 141.
38. Pierre Bourdieu, *Acts of Resistance: Against the Tyranny of the Market*, trans. Richard Nice (New York: The New Press, 1998), 98; Staf Callewaert, "Bourdieu, Critic of Foucault: The Case of Empirical Social Science against Double-Game-Philosophy," *Theory, Culture & Society* 23,6 (2006), 78.
39. Patrick McCurdy, "Breaking the Spiral of Silence: Unpacking the 'Media Debate' within Global Justice Movements. A Case Study of Dissent! And the 2005 Gleneagles G8 Summit," *Interface: A Journal for and about Social Movements* 2,2 (November 2010).
40. Della Porta and Filleule, "Policing Social Protest," 235; Frances Fox Piven and Richard Cloward, "Normalizing Collective Protest," in *Frontiers in Social Movement Theory*, ed. Aldon D. Morris and Carol McClurg (New Haven: Yale University Press, 1992), 315.
41. Ryan, "Thousands Stood Up for Humanity," A19.
42. Ibid.
43. Piven and Cloward, "Normalizing Collective Protest," 318.
44. Graeber, "The New Anarchists," 66.
45. Ibid., 68. See also: Day, *Gramsci Is Dead*,130.
46. Graeber, "The New Anarchists," 72.
47. Ibid.
48. It is worth emphasizing that although structured and relatively stable, fields are not determining precisely because agents acting within them rely on *practical reason*, which is itself based on partial perspectives, more or less accurate perceptions of one's own and other's dispositions and stocks of capital, and so on, and therefore

amenable to error. This is the crux of Bourdieu's break with structuralism and objectivist approaches and how he escapes accusations of determinism and reproductivism.
49. Bourdieu, *Practical Reason*, 80.
50. As analytic categories, "protension" and "project" have no content in terms of being either radical or conservative. If the habitus through which one responds to the immediately inscribed future is oppositional, then protensive action will be also be oppositional. However, judging whether or not action is oppositional requires some external measure. What protension captures is the immediate and prereflective nature of certain actions, rather than the specific content of actions in relation to the unfolding of fields.
51. Melucci, *Challenging Codes*, 74.

Chapter Six: Suffering and Justice
1. Nietzsche, *The Gay Science*, 130, s. 76.
2. Melucci, *Challenging Codes*, 1.
3. Classic examples of such a project are found, of course, in Plato's *Republic* and David Hume's *Principles of Justice*. A more contemporary (and liberal, but nonetheless illustrative) example is found in Abizadeh, "Cooperation, Pervasive Impact, and Coercion."
4. My thinking here is influenced by: Steven Lukes, *Power: A Radical View*, 2nd ed. (New York: Palgrave Macmillan, 2005), 30.
5. Iris Marion Young, *Justice and the Politics of Difference* (Princeton, New Jersey: Princeton University Press, 1990), 6. Similarly, Holloway grounds his project in attention to "the scream ... of sadness, a scream of horror, a scream of anger, a scream of refusal" from which theoretical reflection ought to originate. John Holloway, *Change the World without Taking Power* (London: Pluto Press, 2002), 1.
6. The foundational thinkers in the social contract tradition are Thomas Hobbes, John Locke, and John Rawls. For an introduction to theories of deliberative democracy, see: Amy Gutmann and Dennis Thompson, *Why Deliberative Democracy?* (Princeton, NJ: Princeton University Press, 2004).
7. Simone Chambers, "Theories of Political Justification," *Philosophy Compass* 5,11 (2010).
8. See: Michael Blake, "Distributive Justice, State Coercion, and Autonomy," *Philosophy and Public Affairs* 30,3 (2002); Isaiah Berlin, "Two Concepts of Liberty," in *Liberty: Incorporating Four Essays on Liberty*, ed. Henry Hardy (Oxford: Oxford University Press, 1991); Alan Buchanan, "Assessing the Communitarian Critique of Liberalism," *Ethics* 99 (1989); John Rawls, "Justice as Fairness," *Philosophical Review* 67,2 (1958); Simone Chambers, "Deliberative Democratic Theory," *Annual Review of Political Science* 6 (2003).
9. Lukes, *Power*, 16–17, 25.
10. Ibid., 27.
11. Bourdieu, *Pascalian Meditations*, 175. For an excellent illustration of how states construct and impose schemes of perception via official classifications, see: Rogers Brubaker, *Nationalism Reframed: Nationhood and the National Question in the New Europe* (New York: Cambridge University Press, 1993), ch. 2.
12. For a particularly interesting account of the arbitrary origins of the state, see: Charles Tilly, "War Making and State Making as Organized Crime," in *Bringing the State Back In*, ed. Peter Evans, Dietrich Rueschemeyer, and Theda Skocpol (Cambridge: Cambridge University Press, 1985). For Bourdieu's account of the origins of state power see: *Practical Reason*, ch. 3.
13. *Pascalian Meditations*, 176.

14. Ibid., 176–77, 178.
15. Adbusters, "#Occupywallstreet: A Shift in Revolutionary Tactics," www.adbusters.org, July 16, 2011.
16. Congressional Budget Office, "Trends in the Distribution of Household Income between 1979 and 2007 (Full Summary)," (Washington: Congress of the United States, Congressional Budget Office, 2011), 3.
17. PEPSO, "It's More Than Poverty," 6–7.
18. Armine Yalnizyan, "The Rise of Canada's Richest 1%" (Ottawa: Canadian Centre for Policy Alternatives, 2010), 3. For an overview of the material inequality motivating the Occupy Wall Street actions in the United States, see: William Tabb, "Extending Occupy Wall Street's Message and Critique," *International Critical Thought* 2,3 (2012): 266–68.
19. For a thorough discussion of the evolution and implications of neoliberalism, see: Duggan, *The Twilight of Equality?*.
20. Young, *Justice and the Politics of Difference*.
21. Desmond Cole, "The Skin I'm In: I've Been Interrogated by Police More Than 50 Times—All Because I'm Black," *Toronto Life*, April 21, 2015; Dan Taekema, "Black City Councillor Says Hamilton Police 'Carded' Him," *Toronto Star*, April 27, 2016.
22. Marilyn Frye, *The Politics of Reality* (Trumansburg, N.Y.: Crossing Press, 1983), 4; Young, *Justice and the Politics of Difference*, 41.
23. It is worth noting that Young's work on oppression came relatively early in her intellectual trajectory. Her later work focused on phenomenology, global distributive justice, and deliberative democracy. I focus on her treatment of oppression mainly as a way into the distinction between Foucauldian and Bourdieuian conceptions of power that I develop in the latter part of this section. For some of Young's important later contributions see: "Throwing Like a Girl" in *On Female Body Experience: "Throwing Like a Girl" and Other Essays in Feminist Philosophy and Social Theory* (Bloomington: Indiana University Press, 1990); "Responsibility and Global Justice: A Social Connection Model," *Social Philosophy and Policy* 23,1 (2006); "Activist Challenges to Deliberative Democracy"; *Inclusion and Democracy*.
24. *Justice and the Politics of Difference*, 37.
25. Ibid., 3, 15–22, 34–42, 53–58, 61, 163, 184. See also "Activist Challenges to Deliberative Democracy," 109–11, 116.
26. *Justice and the Politics of Difference*, 59.
27. Ibid., 32.
28. Foucault, *The History of Sexuality, vol. 1*, 93–95.
29. Bourdieu, *Pascalian Meditations*, 141. For the importance of silent, ordinary injunctions see also: *Language and Symbolic Power*, 50–51; *The Logic of Practice*, 69.
30. While I am interested in drawing out the distinctions between Bourdieu and Foucault on power, they also held significantly different epistemological positions. These divisions are particularly apparent in terms of the relationship of sociology to philosophy and the relativism at the core of Foucault's treatment of the history of knowledge. For an excellent overview see: Callewaert, "Bourdieu, Critic of Foucault."
31. For example, Cronin rejects Foucault's vision, arguing that the mechanisms of control available in institutions—above all surveillance and discipline enacted directly on the body—are either unavailable outside those settings or insufficient for explaining phenomena of power such as racism and class conflict. Ciarin Cronin,

"Bourdieu and Foucault on Power and Modernity," *Philosophy and Social Criticism* 22,6 (1996): 59–63.
32. Foucault, *The History of Sexuality, vol. 1*, 110–11.
33. Cronin, "Bourdieu and Foucault on Power and Modernity," 61.
34. Young, *Justice and the Politics of Difference*, 41.
35. Ibid., 31.
36. Bourdieu et al., *The Weight of the World*, 4.
37. Bourdieu, *Pascalian Meditations*, 169.
38. *Distinction*, 22.
39. *Language and Symbolic Power*, 166. Bourdieu's approach can be distinguished here from other constructivist approaches. For example, while Berger and Luckmann argue that intersubjective interaction produces a reliable, shared or common sense from "the normal, self-evident routines of everyday life," Bourdieu insists on both the imposed nature of this common sense (that is, its origins in relations of power) and the lack of commonality that derives from the differential social backgrounds from which agents encounter one another. Peter L. Berger and Thomas Luckmann, *The Social Construction of Reality: A Treatise in the Sociology of Knowledge* (Garden City, New York: Anchor Books, 1967), 23. Bourdieu, *Pascalian Meditations*, 57; *Language and Symbolic Power*, 44.
40. *The Logic of Practice*, 73.
41. *Pascalian Meditations*, 184.
42. Ibid., 169.
43. Ibid., 169, 184.
44. Andrew Sayer, "Class, Moral Worth and Recognition," in *(Mis)Recognition, Social Inequality and Social Justice*, ed. Terry Lovell (Abingdon, UK; New York: Routledge, 2007), 90.
45. Ibid., 94.
46. Steph Lawler, "Disgusted Subjects: The Making of Middle-Class Identities," *Sociological Review* 53,3 (2005), 438. Considerable work has been done on the sexuality, class, and disgust. See: Green, "Playing the (Sexual) Field"; McRobbie, "Notes on 'What Not to Wear' and Post-feminist Symbolic Violence"; Liz Frost and Paul Hoggett, "Human Agency and Social Suffering," *Critical Social Policy* 28,4 (2008); Diane Reay, "Gendering Bourdieu's Concept of Capitals? Emotional Capital, Women and Social Class," *The Sociological Review* 52, Issue Supplement s2 (2005); "Beyond Consciousness? The Psychic Landscape of Social Class," *Sociology* 39,5 (2005).
47. Wendy Brown, *States of Injury* (Princeton: Princeton University Press, 1995), 69–71.
48. Although central to debates within many movements, such exclusions and replications have been particularly contested through queer and liberationist critiques of gay and lesbian "rights" and "equality" discourses. See: Richardson, "Desiring Sameness?" See also: Joshua Gamson, "Must Identity Movements Self-Destruct?: A Queer Dilemma," in *Queer Theory/Sociology*, ed. Steven Seidman (Oxford; Cambridge MA: Blackwell, 1996), 400.
49. Melucci, *Challenging Codes*, 1.
50. Foucault, "The Subject and Power," 341.
51. Ibid., 342.
52. Lois McNay, *Foucault: A Critical Introduction* (Cambridge: Polity Press, 1994), 149–53, 157.
53. Bourdieu suggests, in this regard, that it is equally true that agents take advantage of the opportunities of a field to satisfy their drives and desires and that fields make use

of agents by forcing them (through sublimation and reward) to adapt to the structure of demands and opportunities the field presents. *Pascalian Meditations*, 165.

54. Ibid., 126.

Chapter Seven: New Stakes and New Strategies

1. Bourdieu, *Acts of Resistance*, 9.
2. Bourdieu, *The Logic of Practice*, 25.
3. Bourdieu, *Pascalian Meditations*, 123.
4. Ibid., 67–68.
5. Bourdieu's analysis of opinion polling suggests that possession of technical competence in terms of political communication is insufficient. Technical competence depends on social authority and entitlement: "'Technical' competence depends fundamentally on social competence and on the corresponding sense of being entitled and required by status to exercise this specific capacity, and therefore to possess it." That is, to understand political participation, one cannot look at an individual's capacity alone, but also at their sense of entitlement to be concerned with politics, their sense of being authorized to speak about them, and so on. Such senses have demonstrably classed and gendered distributions. *Distinction*, 409.
6. Peter Hall, "The Role of Interests, Institutions, and Ideas in the Comparative Political Economy of Industrialized Nations," in *Comparative Politics: Rationality, Culture, and Structure*, ed. Mark Iving Lichbach and Alan S. Zuckerman (Cambridge, UK; New York, NY: Cambridge University Press, 1997), 174–75.
7. Bourdieu, *Language and Symbolic Power*, 172.
8. One could, of course, argue that political struggles are not about the state but about control of "social resources," but in keeping with Bourdieu's own view, my interest is not in developing a typology of fields and determining once and for all what counts as "inside" any given field or "outside" of it. Rather, I am trying to illustrate the kinds of questions that an analysis of fields must answer in order to see who is acting, how, for what stakes, and what implications practical strategies have for normative and political analysis.
9. Bourdieu, *Language and Symbolic Power*, 173–74.
10. Holloway, *Change the World without Taking Power*, 63–64.
11. Dupuis-Déri, "The Black Blocs Ten Years after Seattle," 60.
12. Obviously this potential is relative. Bourdieu does not take the scientific field to be a fully universal social space, only one that offers insights into how dispositions might be channeled toward universality.
13. Nick Crossley, "On Systematically Distorted Communication: Bourdieu and the Socio-Analysis of Publics," *Sociological Review* 52 (2004), 91.
14. Incidentally, in pointing to the accumulation of capital and the relative agreement over the norms of scientific practice as central to the field, Bourdieu distinguishes his conception of scientific progress from that of Thomas Kuhn. Bourdieu suggested that Kuhn's scientific "revolutions" were not as revolutionary as he thought and that he undervalued important continuities in terms of scientific tradition, community, and the sociological relation of scientific practice to the outside social world. Bridget Fowler, "Autonomy, Reciprocity and Science in the Thought of Pierre Bourdieu," *Theory, Culture & Society* 23,6 (2006), 104–105.
15. *Pascalian Meditations*, 126.

16. Wendy Brown, "Women's Studies Unbound: Revolution, Mourning, Politics," *Parallax* 9,2 (2003), 6.
17. For a discussion of the difficulties of externally establishing "objective" interests, see: Lukes, *Power*, 144–51.
18. Bourdieu, *Pascalian Meditations*, 126.
19. Lash, "Pierre Bourdieu," 198.
20. Bourdieu, *Distinction*, 32.
21. *Language and Symbolic Power*, 172.
22. Charles Camic, "Bourdieu's Cleft Sociology of Science," *Minerva* 49,3 (2011), 284.
23. Wacquant, "Pointers on Pierre Bourdieu and Democratic Politics," 12.
24. For resources on deliberative democracy, see: Chambers, "Theories of Political Justification" and "Deliberative Democratic Theory"; Amy Gutmann and Dennis Thompson, *Why Deliberative Democracy?* (Princeton, NJ: Princeton University Press, 2004); Young, *Inclusion and Democracy*; Amy Gutmann and Dennis Thompson, "Deliberative Democracy Beyond Process," in *Debating Deliberative Democracy*, ed. James S. Fishkin and Peter Laslett (Oxford: Blackwell Publishing, 2003).
25. Piven and Cloward, "Power Repertoires and Globalization."
26. Smith, *Lesbian and Gay Rights in Canada*, 41.
27. Crossley, "From Reproduction to Transformation," 51.
28. Barr and Drury, "Activist Identity as a Motivational Resource."
29. At this point I want to reiterate my previously indicated concerns about representative politics. There is certainly a risk of reading collective action as a panacea, when in fact collective actors themselves can be rife with exclusionary practices. This is as true of progressive movements as any other, and even anarchist and other radical groups produce exclusions based on gender and class, as Kennelly has demonstrated. Jacqueline Kennelly, *Citizen Youth: Culture, Activism and Agency in a Neoliberal Era* (New York: Palgrave Macmillan, 2011).
30. Della Porta and Filleule, "Policing Social Protest," 235.
31. Fourny, "Bourdieu's Uneasy Psychoanalysis," 111.

Chapter Eight: Resistance and Democracy

1. Lawler, "Rules of Engagement," 112–13.
2. Matthew Adams, "Hybridizing Habitus and Reflexivity: Towards an Understanding of Contemporary Identity?," *Sociology* 40,3 (2006), 522–25.
3. Chambers, "Deliberative Democratic Theory," 308.
4. Gutmann and Thompson, *Why Deliberative Democracy?*, 7.
5. Ibid.
6. Sanders, "Against Deliberation"; Young, "Activist Challenges to Deliberative Democracy."
7. Laurie Adkin, "The Rise and Fall of New Social Movement Theory?," in *Critical Political Studies: Debates and Dialogues from the Left*, ed. Abigail Bakan and Eleanor MacDonald (Montreal: McGill-Queen's University Press, 2002), 294; Adrian Little, "Community and Radical Democracy," *Journal of Political Ideologies* 7,3 (2002), 374.
8. Chantal Mouffe, "Deliberative Democracy or Agonistic Pluralism," *Social Research* 66,3 (1999), 755.
9. BlackLivesMatter TO (@BLM_TO), Twitter post, July 3, 2016, 5 p.m.
10. Pride Toronto, Pride Toronto's Statement Regarding Police Participation in the Parade," May 7, 2017.

11. Shanifa Nasser, "Black Lives Matter NYC 'Inspired' by Toronto Chapter's Call for Removal of Uniformed Police," CBC News, www.cbc.ca., June 26, 2017.
12. John Campbell, "Motion to Amend ED21.5 Major Cultural Organizations Allocations," ed. Toronto City Council (Toronto: City Council, 2017). In 2010, when QuAIA participated in the parade, the grant was $250,000. By 2016, when BLM TO participated, the annual grant had grown to $260,000.
13. Although inclusivity is listed as a core value on the Pride Toronto website, it has not been the primary theme of recent Pride festivals in Toronto. Indeed, in the last seven years, only the 2016 theme refers to inclusivity. Other themes include: + (2017); You CAN sit with us (2016); Come Out and Play (2015); World Pride (2014); SuperQueer! (2013); Celebrate and Demonstrate (2012); and Dream Big (2011).

Index

Abizadeh, Arash, 188n3
abstractions, 5
accountability, 175
action: adaptation, 50; agency and, 15; anarchists' use of, 119; contentious (*see* contentious repertoires); differentiation, 150; fields and, 104, 149, 198n50; judgements, 104; justice and, 15, 126; knowledge and, 104; meaning and cause, 114; morality substitution, 145; political goods and, 160–1; power, 148–9; vs. security, 145; suffering and, 146; symbolic, 105; violence and, 112. *See also* agency; civil disobedience; collective action
activists (general), 6, 21–2. *See also* protests; social movement tensions; social movement theory
Acts of Resistance (Bourdieu), 152
Adams, Matthew, 173
adaptation: ability to, 102; action, 50, 63–4; children, 51; definition, 45; discourse, 84; domination and habitus, 147; effort, 49–50; overview, 47; social acting, 143; suffering and, 134
Adbusters, 132
Adorno, Theodor, 7, 8, 19, 25, 101, 160
adversarial relations, 175
affinity groups, 105–6, 118–19, 120, 121, 161, 197n12
agency: action mistaken for, 15; Bourdieu social phenomenology and, 127, 140; through conformity, 102; corporeal schema, 53; desire vs. actual, 95; discourse and, 93; distant actions, 41; fields and, 127, 201n53; habitus and, 50; individuals and social structures, 11; rational choice theory, 27; reflexivity, 58; as strategic, 130; subjectivism and, 40; symbolic interactionism, 30. *See also* action
agreements, 124
AIDS, 76, 193n19
Alcoff, Linda Martín, 197n12
allodoxia, 82, 95–6, 176
alterglobalization: action and agency, 15; conclusion of analysis, 127–8; G20 protest Toronto, 3, 100, 103–4, 109, 110, 116–17 (*see also* Black Bloc; People First; tactical selection); history of, 100; immediate reduction of suffering, ix; moral justifications, 100; name of, 186n9; representation monopolization, 160; security, 145; strategies/goals, 15; usefulness of, 196n8. *See also* tactical selection
alt-right movement, 183
anarchism, 106–7, 111–12, 118–19, 159, 160–1, 197n12, 203n29. *See also* affinity groups; Black Bloc
anticipation, 81, 84, 119–20, 155
anti-globalization. *See* alterglobalization
applause/booing, 181–2
arbitrary vs. natural, 80–1
autonomy, 129, 135, 160, 165–6. *See also* anarchism

Beyond Good and Evil (Friedrich Nietzsche), 21
The Bijou, 88–9
Black Bloc: Get Off the Fence action, 110–11, 113–15; new language of

protest, 118–19; overview, 111–13; People First and, 101; state power, 104; support, 106, 109, 113, 116, 122–3, 197n13. *See also* affinity groups; anarchism; disruption

Black Lives Matter–Toronto (BLM TO), 4, 69–70, 75, 176–82

body knowledge, 142–3

book summary, 153–5, 173–4

Bourdieu social phenomenology (general): aesthetic universalism, 78; allodoxia, 82; background to theory, 10, 11–12, 186n13; civil disobedience, 112; class, 45, 62, 95, 167; common sense, 201n39; communicative rationality, 162, 165; critiques of, 58–63; discourse, 84; *doxa*, 81, 82, 117, 130, 144–5; emotions, 143; euphemization, 66; exposure, 47; Foucault and, 92, 136–40, 148–9, 169, 200n30; interest, 11; legitimacy, 131; negation, 12; normative political theory and, 13–14; objectivism, 59, 72, 147, 164, 168, 190n3, 198n48; objectivism/subjectivism, 10–11, 13, 40–2, 51–2, 62–3, 114, 155, 156 (*see also* subjectivism); overview, 11–13, 26; political capacities and, 151, 158–60, 163–4; poverty vs. incidental suffering, 140; rational choice theory, 27; realist ideals, 152; vs. Scott, 95; social space and physical space, 42; strategic thinking, 72, 74; subjectivism, 47, 137 (*see also* objectivism/subjectivism); symbolic fields, 76; violence (general), 2. *See also* social movement theory

Bourdieu social phenomenology: capital: agency, 127, 140; of BLM TO, 180; collective identity and, 31, 75; collectivization, 167–8; conversion of, 191n11; cultural, 35, 44, 71, 80, 150, 193n19 (*see also* Bourdieu social phenomenology: habitus); definition, viii, 79; distinction, 43; distribution (*see* distribution of capital); fields and, 59–60, 79, 166; gaining, 79, 157–8; goals and, 120; habitus and fields linkage, 79; LGBT/Q community, 90, 168; overview, 44–5; political, 157–61, 166; practical reason, 139; project/protension and, 121; psychic energy, 53; social, 44, 166; strategies/goals and, 55, 59–60; success and, 104; suffering and, 8, 63, 173; symbolic capital and agency, 140; symbolic capital and Black Bloc, 113; symbolic capital and innovation, 36; symbolic capital and LGBT/Q community, 90; symbolic capital and People First, 116–17; symbolic capital and symbolic power, 105; symbolic capital in conflict, 176; symbolic capital overview, 80, 82; symbolic power and, 32, 105. *See also* distribution of capital

Bourdieu social phenomenology: fields: action, 104, 149, 198n50; agency, 127, 201n53; agents and, 56; as arbitrary, 80–1; capital and, 59–60, 79, 166; certainty of, 120, 121; competence in, 162–3, 202n5; domination (symbolic violence) and, 44, 113; habitus and, 43–4, 54–5, 58, 59, 104, 119–20, 146–7, 156–7, 162, 164; ideal, 168–9; justice and, 146–7; morality, 156; overview, 11, 21, 42–4; placement in, 158–9; political, 157–61, 163, 166, 167; of power, 44; practical reason, 139, 198n48; rules, 80, 81; scientific, 162–3, 166–7, 169, 202n12, 202n14; strategies/goals, 13; symbolic fields, 76; symbolic power and, 101, 105, 183. *See also* classifications

Bourdieu social phenomenology: habitus: adaptation, 47, 49–51, 54, 56, 63–4, 147; agency, 127; ambivalence of formation, 60; anticipation, 56–7; capital, 150; changing consciousness and, 112–13; classifications, 149; conformity, 94–5; conscious calculation, 192n25, 196n56; correction, 49–51, 54, 56; definition, 45–6; discourse, 85; distribution of capital, 147; emotions, 142; exposure, 47; failure of, 58–65; fields and, 43–4, 54–5, 58, 59, 104, 119–20, 146–7, 156–7, 162, 164; freedom and, 131; injuries as forming, 134; judgements, 172; justice, 146–7; knowledge, 48–9; LGBT/Q community and, 61–2; makeover shows, 46–7; mimesis, 49–51, 54; overview, 11,

13, 45–6, 71; phenomenology, 51–2; practical reason, 139; recognition, 141; rethinking, 12; rules, 45–7; skills, 150; symbolic power and, 81, 183; systems of meaning, 141–2; trajectory, 56–7; triggering of, 191n17; unease and, 143; universality, 156, 157
breaching limits. *See* limits
Brown, Wendy, 145
Butler, Judith, 59, 92–3, 196n56

Campbell, John, 179–80
Canadian Charter of Rights and Freedom ands, 23, 130, 195n43
capital. *See* Bourdieu social phenomenology: capital
capitalism, 4, 7, 18, 160. *See also* neoliberalism
Caribana, 179
causal process theory/mechanisms, 24–5, 26
censorship, 182–3
Chantelois, Mathieu, 176–7
children, 51–2, 54–5
Christopher Street West Pride Celebration, 80
cisgender, 193n24
civil disobedience, 35, 107–8, 112, 145. *See also* Black Bloc; disruption
class, 80, 95, 159, 167, 196n56
classifications: conformity, 142; difference, 46; distortions, 136; habitus, 149; neoliberalism, 108, 113; new language of protest, 118; overview, 149; recognition, 64; trajectory, 57; values, 143
Coalition for Lesbian and Gay Rights in Ontario (CLGRO), 87
coercion, 129–31
collective action: combatting power, vii; as exclusionary, 203n29; importance of, 32; political system entry, 168; social movement theory, 10, 20–1; strategies/goals as objective, 72. *See also* action
collective identity: capital, 72, 81–2; as conceptual, 73; disgust, 144; dominant epistemes and, 76–7, 83; as durable, 99; failure and, 94, 96; grievances/opportunities, 36; justice, 76, 164; LGBT/Q community, 28, 74–6, 78, 90, 91, 144; normalization, 90; overview, 27–31, 71; perceiving duration of movement, 121–2; political action, 189n20; practical reason and, 72; processes, 85; purpose of, 72; strategies/goals, 73; suffering and, 73; symbolic power, 72; unequal negotiations, 91
collectivization (general), 32–3, 70–1, 154, 166, 167–8
Collins, Patricia Hill, 83, 84
common sense, 36, 106–7, 201n39
communication, 107, 109–10, 175
communicative rationality, 162, 165
conflict: avoidance, 107; vs. communication, 107, 109–10, 115; mobilization and, 165; protest as response to, 22, 34; radical/reformist, 5–6, 87–94, 154–5, 174 (*see also* alterglobalization; LGBT/Q community; tactical selection); revaluing, 170, 176; in social movement definition, 20, 21; strategies/goals, 103. *See also* tactical selection
conformity: agency, 102; appeal of, 54; classifications, 142; commitment and, 125; depoliticization, 80; distortions, 169–70; domination (symbolic violence), 169–70; failure and, 15, 63–4; habitus, 94–5; as inherent, ix; LGBT/Q community, 74; logical, 142, 144–5; marginalization and, 55, 58, 91, 95; morality of, 102; recognition and, 55; social movement tensions, 15–16; strategies/goals and, 59; symbolic capital, 90; symbolic power, 144, 164. *See also* renunciations
consensus, 33, 72, 85, 108–9, 165, 175
contentious politics, 25, 26
contentious repertoires, 31–7
contradictions, 95, 101–2
corporeal schema, 48, 53
correction, 49–51
counter-publics, 91
credibility, 86
critical theory: capitalism and, 18; distortions, 125–6; experience, 127; individuals and collectives, 126–7; justice, 108; negation, 9–10, 12, 30, 125–6;

reflexivity losers, 173, 174; roots of, 7; Samuel's use of, 153; social movement theory and, 19; suffering and, 7–9, 134; symbolic power, 144. See also normative political theory
"Critical Thought as a Solvent of *Doxa*" (Wacquant), 18
Cronin, Ciarin, 200n31
Crossley, Nick, 12, 32, 38, 162

Day, Richard, 106, 196n8
deliberative democratic theory, 175
delegation of leaders, 86, 159–61
democracy, 163–70, 175–6, 180–1, 182–3
demonstrations. See protests
depoliticization, 80
desire/possibility, 67–9, 173–4
devaluation, 28, 70, 78–9, 90
difference: classifications, 46; democracy, 175; LGBT/Q community, 77–8, 90, 193n19; marginalization and, 70, 77; politics of difference, 150; principle of difference, 141; sensitivity to, 54; suffering and, 28, 70, 77–8; suppression of, 193n19
direct action. See Black Bloc; civil disobedience
discourse, 74–5, 78, 83–6, 92–3, 138–9, 148
disruption: vs. communication, 107, 109–10, 115; as against efficiency, 116; importance of, 168; politics of, 111–15; vs. security, 145. See also Black Bloc; civil disobedience
distortions: by Black Bloc, 104; classifications, 136; collective identity, 99; conformity, 169–70; critical theory, 125–6; discourse, 85; habitus and fields linkage, 147; of justice, 95; negotiation of meanings, 85–6; power, 8, 31, 95; of success, 102; suffering and, 147; symbolic power, 99; tactical selection, 96, 102; uneven distribution of capital, 72
distribution of capital: collective identity and, 81–2; conforming to succeed, 102; delegation of leaders, 86; distortions, 72; domination and, 45; It Gets Better project, 69; justice and, 133, 147;

LGBT/Q community, 69; political capital, 157; political goods, 5, 116, 158, 159, 160; power, 166; skills, 79–80; smoothing gaps, 63; universality and, 165. See also Bourdieu social phenomenology: capital
Diverlus, Rodney, 178
diversity of tactics. See tactical selection
domination (symbolic violence): allodoxia, 82, 95–6, 176; Bourdieu conceptual tools and, 26; collective identity and, 31, 122; collusion in, 83, 85, 88, 95, 122, 145, 164; communicative rationality, 165; complexity of, 10; components of, 140; conformity, 169–70; definition, 83, 135; discourse, 85–6; distributions of capital and, 45, 83; ethics and effectiveness, 102; failure and, 60, 62; fields and, 44, 113; hidden, 9–10, 13; judgements, 81–2; objectivism, 164; oppression, 136, 140; replicated, 15, 148, 161, 174; shared conceptions of justice and, 108; social movement tensions and, 6, 69, 156; variations and, 62. See also marginalization; violence
Dotson, Kristie, 83
double inclination, 59, 60
doxa, 81, 82, 117, 130, 144–5
Dupuis-Déri, Francis, 161, 197n12
Dynamics of Contention (McAdam et al.), 24–5, 189n20

economic theory, 27
efficacy, 103, 109, 115–18
embodied judgement, 40
emotions, viii–ix, 47, 81, 112, 140, 142–4
employment, 132
epistemes, 76–7, 90, 95, 122–3
equality, 77, 78–9, 90, 144, 179–80
experience, 144–7, 160
exploitation. See suffering

fab magazine, 88–9
failure: as beneficial, 63; commitment and, 125; conformity and, 15, 63–4; of dominant actors, 60, 62; of habitus, 58–65; as inherent, ix; LGBT/Q

community, 144; due to liberal pluralism, 117–18; marginalization and, 94; norms and, 93; as other agents' success, 93–4; political antinomies, 101; strategies/goals and, 60. *See also* risks
fascism, 7
feminist theory, 95, 197n12
fields. *See* Bourdieu social phenomenology: fields
Foucault, Michel, 91–2, 135, 136–40, 148–9, 150, 169, 200n30, 200n31
Francoeur, Mathieu, 112
Frankfurt School, 7
Free Trade Area of the Americas (FTAA), 103
Frye, Marilyn, 134

G20 summit. *See under* protests
The Gay Science (Nietzsche), 124
gender, 92–3, 194n24
Gender Trouble (Butler), 92
"Getting It Together in Burgundy, 1675–1975" (Tilly), 98
goals/strategies. *See* strategies/goals
Graeber, David, 118

habit, 38
habitus. *See* Bourdieu social phenomenology: habitus
Hegel, Georg Wilhelm Friedrich, 14
heteronormativity, 4. *See also* normalization
History of Sexuality (Foucault), 149
Holloway, John, 160
Holocaust, 7
homogeneity, 92, 140, 169
homonormativity, 69, 70, 144. *See also* normalization
homophobia, 4, 29, 67–8, 73, 179. *See also* LGBT/Q community
hope, 153–4, 173
Hume, David, 131
Husserl, Edmund, 57, 119, 120

identity. *See* collective identity; individual identity. *See also* sexual identity
ignorance, 83–4
inclination, 59, 60

income disparity, 132–3. *See also* equality; poverty
individual identity, 190n2
It Gets Better project, 67–9, 73

judgments, 40, 81–2, 104, 172
justice: action and, 15; collective identity, 76; conception of, 147, 151; definition, 135; distortions of, 95; distribution and, 133, 147; externally derived, 164; fields and, 146–7; habitus and, 146–7; liberal politics views on, 129–30, 131; politics and suffering, 144–5; power and, 13; reconceiving, 8; relevancy, 187n3; shared conceptions of, 108; sites of, 76, 126, 127, 131, 146–7, 155–6, 164; social interactions and, 4; suffering and, 16, 126, 144–5

Kennedy, John, 88–9
knowledge, 41, 48–50, 104, 142–3
Kuhn, Thomas, 202n14

Lawler, Steph, 143–4, 172
laws and autonomy, 129
leaders, 86, 159–61
legitimacy, 129–31, 164–5, 175
Lesbian and Gay Rights in Canada (Smith), 194n43
LGBT/Q community: acronym of, 185n4; Canadian Charter of Rights and Freedom, 23, 130, 195n43; capital, 168; collective identity, 28, 74–5, 78, 90, 91, 144; collectivization, 70–1; conclusion of analysis, 127–8; conformity, 74; devaluing resistance, 70, 90; difference, 77–8, 90, 193n19; failure, 74, 144; gender, 92, 194n24; habitus and, 61–2; heteronormativity, 4; homonormativity, 69, 70, 144; justice concepts, 164; lesbians' repression in, 87; lobbying organizations, 28–9; mainstream interests, 14–15, 67–70, 77, 80, 87–91, 144, 164; police and, 4, 88–9, 176–80; poverty, 68–9; progress, 69; public sexuality, 88–9; racialized people, 69; racism in, 74–5, 178–9; radical interests, 77, 80, 87–94, 144, 164; rights-based

strategy, vii, 23–4, 88–90, 91, 130; security, 145; sexual identity, 52–3; statistical research, 23; strategies/goals, vii, 23–4, 87, 94; suffering, 14; suicide, 67; survival of, ix. *See also* homophobia; Pride Toronto; queer theory
liberal politics, 107–9, 128–9, 135, 182. *See also* homonormativity; pluralism
limits, 20
linguistic exchange. *See* discourse
Lorde, Audre, 74
Lukes, Steven, 129–30

marginalization: capital and, 173; conformity and, 55, 58, 91, 95; delegation of leaders, 161; desire/possibility, 67–9; difference and, 70, 77
Marx, Karl, 7, 14
mass media, 104, 112, 114
mastery, 53–4. *See also* professionalism
McAdam, Doug, 22, 24–5, 26, 189n20
Melucci, Alberto, 20–1, 27–8, 125, 147–8, 188n8, 189n24
Merleau-Ponty, Maurice, 48, 53
metaphysical thinking, 13–15, 39, 153
Miller, Terry, 67–8
mimesis, 49–51, 142
Minima Moralia (Adorno), 19
morality, 100, 102, 145, 156. *See also* metaphysical thinking

negation, 9–10, 12, 30, 99, 102, 125–6
neoliberalism, 70, 76, 80, 104, 106–9, 108, 117–18. *See also* capitalism
Nietzsche, Friedrich, vii, 16, 124, 145
normalization: ability to meet norms, 143; Bourdieu scientific field and, 169; vs. Bourdieu social phenomenology, 149; discourse and, 148; practical reason, 137–40; of protests, 115; queer theory, 4; radical/reformist LGBT/Q, 87–94; violations, 144
normative political theory: Bourdieu social phenomenology and, 13; definition, 4, 186n8; deliberative democratic theory, 175; distribution of capital, 153; epistemic violence, 94; injuries, 134; introduction, 4–6; metaphysical thinking and, 13, 14–15; repertoires of contention, 36; social movement theory and, 6, 10; variations and, 62; Young and, 150. *See also* critical theory
normative social theory, 164

objectivism, 72, 147, 164, 168, 190n3, 198n48
objectivism/subjectivism, 10–11, 13, 40–2, 51–2, 62–3, 114, 155, 156. *See also* subjectivism
Occupy movement, 100
oppression, 136, 140, 150
optimism. *See* metaphysical thinking
order, 13–14

paradoxes. *See* desire/possibility; radical/reformist conflict; truth/falsity
Pascalian Meditations (Bourdieu), 50–1
People First, 101, 104, 106, 109, 110, 115–17, 122–3
Perez, Hiram, 68
"The Phenomenological Habitus and Its Construction" (Crossley), 38
phenomenology (general), 51–2, 61. *See also various Bourdieu social phenomenology*
pluralism, 115–18, 157. *See also* liberal politics
police: The Bijou, 88–9; G20 protest (Toronto 2010), 3, 100, 103–4, 116; Pride Toronto, 4, 176–80; racial profiling, 134
political antinomies, 101–2, 111
political goods, 116, 158, 159, 160
political process theory, 22–4
political science, 186n8
political theory (general), 4–5, 126, 128–9, 186n8
poverty, 68–9, 76, 140. *See also* income disparity
power: action, 148–9; challenging vs. reworking, 149; consolidation of, 161; disciplinary, 136–8; distortions, 8, 31, 95; distribution, 166; fields of, 44; Foucault ideas of, 91–2; hierarchy of, 150; imbalances, vii; justice and, 13; liberal conceptions of, 135; queer theory and, 53; as relational, 135–6, 139;

renunciations and, 61; suffering and, 7; as supple, vii; third dimension of, 130; unrecognized, viii; visibility of, 103–4, 148; world as obvious, 53–4, 82. *See also* symbolic power

practical reason, 13, 60, 72, 74, 137–40, 139, 198n48. *See also* reason

prediction, 109

prefigurative politics, 119, 156

prereflection, 57

Pride Toronto, 3–4, 176–82, 204n12, 204n13

principle of difference, 141

privilege, 53–4, 82

professionalism, 80, 82, 87, 193n19. *See also* mastery

project/protension, 57–8, 119–21, 198n50

property destruction, 111–14. *See also* Black Bloc; civil disobedience; disruption

protests: efficacy, 103, 109, 115–18; ethics, 105–6, 107–9, 118, 122–3; G20 (Toronto 2010), 3, 100, 103–4, 109, 110, 116–17 (*see also* Black Bloc; People First; tactical selection); Occupy movement, 100, 131–2; pluralism and, 115–18; Pride Toronto, 4, 176–81; as responsive to social system, 22; Tahrir Square, 132; transforming language of, 118–19; vetting signs, 3–4. *See also* activists; disruption; tactical selection

psychic capital, 53

psychoanalysis, 51–2, 54, 61

queer theory, 52–3, 60–2, 70, 90–1

queers. *See* LGBT/Q community

Queers Against Israeli Apartheid (QuAIA), 3–4, 69–70

racial profiling, 134

racialized people, 68, 69, 74–5, 134, 181. *See also* Black Lives Matter–Toronto (BLM TO)

racism: Black women experiencing, 74, 84; discourse, 78; LGBT/Q community, 74–5, 178–9; police, 2, 134, 182; as violence, 2. *See also* Black Lives Matter–Toronto (BLM TO)

radical democratic theory, 175

radical/reformist conflict, 5–6, 87–94, 154–5, 174. *See also* alterglobalization; LGBT/Q community; tactical selection

rational choice theory, 27, 59

Rawls, John, 107–8

reason, 5, 162–3. *See also* practical reason

recognition, 54–5, 61, 64–5, 80, 82, 108, 140–1

reflexivity, 30–1, 58, 173, 174

reflexivity losers, 173

renunciations, 56, 61

repertoires of contention, 31–7

representation, 122, 159–61. *See also* delegation of leaders

resistance (general), research on, 95

resources. *See* Bourdieu social phenomenology: capital

ressentiment, 145

risks, 6, 64. *See also* failure

Rousseau, Jean-Jacques, 54, 192n34

rules: action and, 33; choice, 11; domination and, 15, 174; fields and, 80, 81; habitus and, 45–7; homogeneity, 169; political goods, 158; respecting, 98; structure and, 139; submission to, 102; as symbolic capital, 80; symbolic power, 82

Rules of Engagement (Lawler), 172

Ryan, Sid, 106, 116

safe spaces, 182

same-sex marriage, 9, 23–4, 70, 73, 87

Saussure, Ferdinand de, 141, 190n3

Savage, Dan, 67–9, 73

scholars vs. activists, 6

science, 162–3, 166, 202n12

Scott, James, 95, 196n56

security, 145

self, 92–3, 149

self-love, 54, 61, 64, 65, 192n34

sexual identity, 52–3

Shan, Neethan, 180

Skeggs, Beverley, 60–1

skills, 79–80, 143, 150, 193n19

Skocpol, Theda, 188n8

Smith, Miriam, 23, 194n43

social change (general), 39

social investment, 54
social movement agenda, 22
social movement tensions: collective identity and, 28; collectivity, 10; conformity and failure, 15–16; divergent tactics, 101, 108–9; domination, 6, 69; freedom and success, 15; justice in, 155–6; paradoxes, 8–9; with police, 34; simplification and value, 154
social movement theory: Bourdieu and, 25–7, 65; collective action, 10; collective identity, 29–30; contextualization of, 20–1; critical theory and, 19; early research, 21–2, 27; failure of, 115; metaphysical thinking and, 39; modern research, 23–4, 95; normative political theory and, 6, 10; prophetic function, 147–8, 180; rational choice theory, 27; repertoires of contention, 31–7; resistance research, 95; resisting casual mechanisms, 25; sensitivity of, 27; truth/falsity, 36. *See also various Bourdieu social phenomenology*
sociology, 186n8
Sociology in Question (Bourdieu), 66
solidarity, 20
Sotiropoulos, Sam, 89
speaking conditions, 83–5
Spivak, Gayatri Chakravorty, 83
Steinberg, Marc, 189n26
strategic thinking, 72, 74
strategies/goals: alterglobalization, 15; anticipation, 57; capital and, 55, 59–60; challenging power, 149; collective action, 72; collective identity, 73; as conflicting, 103; conformity and, 59; correct, 35–6; debates over, 6–7; discourse selection, 138–9; diverse visions, 74; evaluation, 6–7; failure and, 60; fields and, 13; irrationality and, 81–2; LGBT/Q community, vii, 23–4, 87, 88–90, 91, 94, 130; as obvious, 72, 88–9; priorities, 73; success and, 102. *See also* tactical selection
structuralism, 40–1, 50, 190n3, 198n48
subjectivism, 47, 49, 50, 93–4, 137. *See also* objectivism/subjectivism
success, 101, 102, 104, 174

suffering: action and, 146; adaptation and, 134; as beneficial, 9, 134; capital and, 8, 63, 131, 173; collective identity and, 73; critical theory, 7–9, 9, 134; difference and, 28, 70, 77–8; distortions and, 147; distribution of, 8; dominant epistemes and, 76; failure causing, 93; fetishization of, 145; immediate reduction of, ix, 6, 14, 77–8, 88; incidental, 133–5, 136, 140; justice and, 16, 126, 144–5; LGBT/Q community, 14; as mediated, 147–8; metaphysical thinking and, 14; paradoxes and, 9; politics and justice, 144–5; power and, 7, 8; relevant forms of, 129–31; vs. survival, 95; symbolic power and, 133
suicide, 73
symbolic capital. *See under* Bourdieu social phenomenology: capital
symbolic democracy, 163–70, 175–6, 180–1, 182–3
symbolic interactionism, 30
symbolic markets, 115, 117
symbolic order, 140–1
symbolic power: Bourdieu analysis (general), 13, 25, 54; capital and, 32, 105; collective identity, 72, 86; conformity/failure, 144, 164; critical theory, 144; disciplinary power and, 136–8; distinction, 42–3; distortions, 96, 99; distribution of, 99, 127–8, 133; fields and, 80–1, 101, 105, 183; habitus and, 81, 105, 183; justice and, 71–2; overview, 13, 82; political capacities and, 151; recognition, 90; suffering, 133; universality, 151. *See also* power
symbolic struggle, 55
symbolic violence. *See* domination

tactical selection: autonomy, 118, 120; Black Bloc, 104, 110–11, 112–15; Black Bloc support, 106, 109, 113, 122–3, 197n13; conflict vs. communication, 107; definition, 99; distortions, 96; divergent tactics, 100–1, 105–6, 119, 122; for large crowds, 115–17; liberal ethics, 108–9; People First and state power, 104; prefigurative, 119, 156;

property destruction, 111–14; visions and, 35–6. *See also* strategies/goals
Tarrow, Sidney, 22, 24–5, 26, 189n20
Taylor, Charles, 190n2
Tilly, Charles, 22, 24–5, 26, 31–2, 33, 35, 98, 189n20
Topper, Keith, 193n19
trauma, 51–2, 54
truth/falsity, 8–9, 19, 124

universality, 156–7, 161–2, 165, 168, 176, 202n12

value, 141, 142, 158
vandalism. *See* civil disobedience; property destruction
vetting protest signs, 3–4
violence: definition of, 111, 112–13; epistemic, 77, 83, 85, 94, 122–3; "inert," 2; of normalization, 4. *See also* domination (symbolic violence)

Wacquant, Loïc, 9, 18
Ward, Jane, 80, 193n19
Warner, Michael, 91
Warner, Tom, 87
The Weight of the World (Bourdieu), 2

Young, Iris Marion, 34, 128, 134, 135–7, 139, 150, 200n23